On Reading the Will

On Reading the Will

Law and Desire
in Literature
and Music

Jeremy Tambling

sussex
ACADEMIC
PRESS
Brighton • Portland • Toronto

2 4 6 8 10 9 7 5 3 1

First published in 2012 by
SUSSEX ACADEMIC PRESS
PO Box 139
Eastbourne BN24 9BP

and in the United States of America by
SUSSEX ACADEMIC PRESS
920 NE 58th Ave   Suite 300
Portland, Oregon 97213-3786

and in Canada by
SUSSEX ACADEMIC PRESS (CANADA)
8000 Bathurst Street, Unit 1, PO Box 30010, Vaughan, Ontario L4J 0C6

British Library Cataloguing in Publication Data
A CIP catalogue record for this book is available from the British Library.

Library of Congress Cataloging-in-Publication Data
Tambling, Jeremy.
On reading the will : law and desire in literature and music / Jeremy
   Tambling.
p. cm.
Includes bibliographical references (p.   ) and index.
ISBN 978-1-84519-499-4 (h/b : alk. paper)
   1. Literature—History and criticism—Theory, etc. 2. Will in
literature. 3. Philosophy of mind in literature. I. Title.
PN441.T36 2012
809'.93353—dc23

                                                            2011028431

Typeset and designed by Sussex Academic Press, Brighton & Eastbourne.
Printed by TJ International, Padstow, Cornwall.
This book is printed on acid-free paper.

CONTENTS

PREFACE AND ACKNOWLEDGEMENTS

It is always intriguing to trace how a book came together as a project. In this case I can remember two early incentives: one, F.R. Leavis at York on texts which he considered *voulu*, created out of a will to write rather than from a spontaneous drive; the vocabulary deriving from D.H. Lawrence. The second, reading Michael Black's *Poetic Drama as Mirror of the Will*, around the end of the 1970s, which got me from Mallarmé's interest in Wagner, to Wagner, where I have stayed, and with Nietzsche and the end of *The Genealogy of Morals*: 'man would rather will nothingness than not will at all'. In the 1980s, with a sense of the power of the death-drive, I wanted to write about a tendency in opera to be 'half in love with easeful death'; its effect was felt in my *Opera, Ideology and Film*, in 1987, where I discuss Thomas Mann's *The Magic Mountain*, which describes Hans Castorp's 'favourite records', those operatic pieces of the nineteenth century pairing love and militarism and the desire for death. Early drafts of material which became this book began when I was working in Hong Kong, and writing *Dante in Purgatory: States of Affect* (Brepols, 2010), on Dante's writing of affectual, or emotional states as historically created, giving the sense that a history of the emotions must be written. I moved some material on affect and the infected will out of that book, and started thinking how the will has been represented in literary texts. No Dante is here; but writing on the will has involved many exclusions.

I would like to thank those who have helped with comments on drafts of this book, including the publisher's reader, or who have discussed it with me. P.N. Furbank read an early draft and supplied some lovely quotations. Chris Terry read everything with enthusiasm, and gave good encouragement. Roger Holdsworth, as always, has helped invaluably with the Shakespeare material: the will in Shakespeare is a very comprehensive subject, and one of the few words the Harvard Concordance of

Shakespeare does not bother to list because it is so frequent. Chapter 4 was first published in *Essays in Criticism* 59.3 (2009), and I am grateful to the editors for permission to reprint, and to the late Stephen Wall, whose help to me over twenty years in encouraging and publishing my work there I am pleased to acknowledge. This was the last article of mine which he was able to accept for the journal. Bob Jones, whose work on George Eliot I have appreciated, read the chapter on Eliot.

Jonathan Hall's intellectual commitments have always been stimulating for me, and I am grateful for his reading of the Introduction. I re-met Ackbar Abbas in his house, and enjoyed a good conversation with him on the subject, and it is not his fault that I did not write about *The Master Builder*, which he suggested. Antony Tatlow gave helpful comments on Nietzsche, which means that all my significant intellectual interlocutors from Hong Kong Comparative Literature have left their mark, and been present in the book, just as, also from Hong Kong, I am grateful to Giorgio Biancorosso, who read the material on Verdi, to Daniel Chua, and to David Clarke, who has been encouraging throughout. Stuart Christie gave me the quotation from Lionel Trilling about the relaxed will in Forster. Those students who studied for doctoral work with me there, especially Louis Lo and Ian Fong and Isaac Hui, have been invaluable in terms of intellectual stimulus. Chapter 2 was given a sharp reading by David Carnegie when we were visiting fellows at St Catherine's College, Oxford during the autumn term of 2009. I am grateful to the invitation and to the College, and its Master, Professor Roger Ainsworth. Peter Franklin, to whom I owed the invitation, helped with comments on Mahler and Delius, as did Bryan Magee with Schopenhauer. Nicholas Powell, himself a lawyer, has given me helpful comments on the subject of testamentary wills, and especially on Turner. In Manchester, Lucia Nigri read chapter 2, and I am aware of help and friendship from Jeremy Gregory. With Peter Cave I mused on why only three out of ten people in the UK make wills. Adrian Armstrong advised on Villon. My colleagues in English and American studies listened to the seminar where I read the material on Lacan. Excellent and thoughtful PhD students, some very sharp intellects, such as James Smith, and Joel Swann and Paul Fung, who have kept a weekly reading group on theory going since the beginning of 2007, have taught me much: so have Alfie Bown and Ben Moore, coming a little later, and also Jonathan Welsh and Iain Bailey. They have been, at all times, intellectually stimulating. And I am sensitive to how much I have learned from *all* my students, and thank them all. Many thanks to Will Simpson for help with the editing. My family – Pauline, Kirsten and Felix – have always been interested in what I am writing on, and wonderfully helpful, while suffering from long gaps when I was mentally not there, because of the writing. I thank them especially.

Last, the dedication. The book is for my brother William; first, with his name, it could be for no-one else, second, because at a late stage of this book he persuaded me to travel with him over the First World War battlefields. Seeing Ypres and Passchendaele and the Somme, and the evidence of all those Hans Castorps mowed down in a war which claimed nearly ten million lives, recalled one of the primary projects of the book – going back to the 1980s, to try to describe that will to nothingness which, armed with technological superiority, has allowed, and willed, such continued annihilation.

INTRODUCTION
Reading the Will

Nature, that framed us of four elements
Warring within our breasts for regiment,
Doth teach us all to have aspiring minds.
Our souls, whose faculties can comprehend
The wondrous architecture of the world,
And measure every wandering planet's course,
Still climbing after knowledge infinite,
And always moving as the restless spheres,
Wills us to wear ourselves and never rest,
Until we reach the ripest fruit of all,
That perfect bliss and sole felicity,
The sweet fruition of an earthly crown.
(MARLOWE, *Tamburlaine the Great*, 1)[1]

Many historians contend that the French failed at Borodino because Napoleon had a cold in the head, and that if it had not been for this cold the orders he gave before and during the battle would have been still more full of genius, and Russia would have been annihilated and the face of the world would have been changed. To historians who believe that Russia was shaped by the will of one man – Peter the Great – and that France was transformed from a republic into an empire, and French armies marched into Russia at the will of one man – Napoleon – the argument that Russia remained a power because Napoleon had a bad cold on the 26th of August may seem logical and convincing.
(TOLSTOY, *War and Peace*)[2]

We can no longer conceal from ourselves *what* this willing directed by the ascetic ideal actually expresses in its entirety: this hatred of the human, and even more of the animal, of the material, this revulsion from the senses, from reason itself, this fear of happiness and beauty,

1

this yearning to pass beyond all appearance, change, becoming, death, desire, beyond yearning itself. All this represents – may we be bold enough to grasp this – a *will to nothingness*, an aversion to life, a rebellion against the most fundamental pre-conditions of life, but which is and remains none the less a *will*! . . . And to say once more in conclusion what I said at the beginning: man would rather will *nothingness* than *not* will at all . . . ['Lieber will noch der Mensch *das Nichts* wollen, als *nicht* wollen']

(NIETZSCHE, *The Genealogy of Morals*)[3]

I DEFINITIONS

'Will' is a name, and a synonym for an aspiring mind, for a restlessness like that in the universe itself, which is wholly affirmative, though it makes Tamburlaine 'wear' himself out. It is a figure for personal aspiration, with the force of destiny, either in Tamburlaine, Peter the Great or Napoleon, whom Tolstoy sees as a megalomaniac thinking that his own will decides everything.

'Will' names an affect, or an appetite, which began to be thought of as a property of the self with the Stoics and in the Christianity of Augustine (c.354–430); it responds to the will of God, for Christians must say, 'Thy will be done' (Matthew, 6.10) whether thinking about God's rule, or confronting what they cannot understand – St Paul's apparently irrational desire to go to Rome: 'The will of the Lord be done' (Acts, 21.14). Since Augustine, the will is sometimes supplemented with the word 'free' – free will, though unnecessarily, since, definitionally, if a person has a will, it must be free, however many constraints may be on it from the outside. Judith Shklar quotes from Rousseau's *Emile*: 'I have always the power to will, but not always the strength to do what I will. When I yield to temptation I surrender myself to the action of external objects'. And 'Man is not one; I will and I will not, I feel myself at once a slave and a free man'.[4] Rather than speak of 'free will', I see the will as split, conflictual with itself.[5]

The will is wilfulness, making it perverse, as this Introduction argues. In *Hamlet*, the fear of something after death 'puzzles the will', a synonym for which is 'resolution' – 'the native hue of resolution'. Hamlet wishes that his 'too too' sullied flesh would 'melt, / Thaw and resolve itself into a dew' (1.2.129–30): three verbs of action suggesting that the meaning

2

of the final one, 'resolve', must be 'dissolve', as *OED* confirms. Resolution and dissolution are the same: the will sets on, creating determination, and liquefies unified purpose. Hamlet reflects on his will's inability to secure resolution, by revenging:

> I do not know
> Why yet I live to say 'This thing's to do',
> Since I have cause, and will, and strength, and means,
> To do it. (4.4. 33–36)

The combination of these qualities – cause, will, strength, means – may be the hindrance to action, implying that the will, rather than supplementing resolution, removes something. Considering the will as an appetite, which includes it within the sexual, Hobbes is sceptical about it being rational, able to complete itself, as with a last will and testament:

> In deliberation, the last appetite, as also the last fear, is called *will*, viz. the last appetite, will to do, or will to omit. It is all one therefore to say *will* and last *will*: for though a man express his present inclination and appetite concerning the disposal of his goods, by words or writings, yet shall it not be counted his will, because he hath still liberty to dispose of them otherways: but when death taketh away that liberty, then it is his will.

After this comment on what defines a 'last will', and how it should never be believed that any will is the last, as opposed to being the latest, Hobbes continues that '*appetite*, *fear*, *hope*, and the rest of the passions are not called *voluntary*; for they proceed *not from, but are the will*; and the will is not voluntary, for a man can no more say that he will will, than he will will will will, and so make an infinite repetition of the word [*will*]; which is absurd, and insignificant'. Hence:

> Forasmuch as *will to do* is *appetite*, and *will to omit*, *fear*; the *cause* of *appetite* and *fear* is the *cause* also of our *will*: but the propounding of the benefits and of harms, that is to say, of reward and punishment, is the cause of our appetite, and of our fears, and therefore of our wills.[6]

Hobbes's sense of the will anticipates a Utilitarian reading of it; we

3

would have no appetite, or fear, if not for self-interest, so an instinctual self-interest is classifiable as a will. Enlightenment thought moved away from the self-interested private will to the 'General Will', which Rousseau's *Social Contract* called 'the will against inequality' – as opposed to the 'particular will', which makes people seek privileges, forming groups interested in preserving inequality. Rousseau's Legislator would have to keep particular wills in check, and submit to the General Will, expressed in law, as an equalising protection against the individual will. Rousseau took from Montesquieu the belief that 'only by the protection of the laws [can] the equality of nature be recovered in society'.[7] A republic could not be built on the model of the family, nor on natural affection, which is part of the particular will, but on equality, ensuring public happiness. Hegel's response to that is vivid, seeing the will as the demand for absolute freedom, where 'the world is for [the will] simply its own will'. He opposes Rousseau's General Will; the French Revolution demonstrated how *any* demand to express the will could only be seen as factional, unjust, not a general will: *any* demand to express the will could only meet a corresponding Terror, negating that 'absolutely free self'. The tension in Hegel is between the demand of the will, which he accepts, and a corresponding Terror, another will, which it produces.[8]

A will is a legal document, a 'last will and testament': willing after death. Will-making associates with Roman law; the Roman citizen, with his individualistic attitude to property rights, would have had no sympathy for the attacks sometimes made on will-making, such as calling it 'the expression of the will of a man who no longer has any will, respecting property which is no longer his property; . . . the act of a man no longer accountable for his deeds to mankind . . . an absurdity', adding that 'an absurdity should not have the force of law'.[9] People write testaments to dispose of their property in ways that are pleasing to them, resisting unavoidable or distasteful appropriation of property they consider uniquely theirs, and one idea behind will-making is the desire to preserve a 'symbolic existence'.[10] A 'testament' is Latin for a will, being a formal declaration, usually in writing, of what the person wishes to happen to the personal property (as opposed to land) that death is taking him away from. A last will and testament applied to real, and to personal property: the terms are of the late medieval period. A will, properly speaking, settles lands, or real property, but the distinction was not always marked, even in the early modern period.

4

A literary tradition makes texts into wills: Villon called his satire his 'Testament', written in 1461, 'en l'an de mon trentiesme aage' (ln. 1). When the text, as the last will and testament, is read out, you will find out just what the now dead author thought of you.[11] Henryson's *Testament of Cresseid* (c.1490) ends with Cresseid giving her body to the ground, her possessions to the leper folk so that she can be buried, her ring to Troylus and her spirit to Diane (lns. 575–91).[12] Thomas Nashe's play *Summmer's Last Will and Testament* (1592) brings on the ghost of Will Summers, Henry VIII's Fool, who died in 1560, to act as Prologue to Summer coming on and yielding his throne to Autumn and making winter, also his heir, his executor.[13] Another example is John Donne's mock testament, 'The Will', one of the *Songs and Sonets*. Perhaps all writing partakes of writing the will, since, for Derrida, 'all graphemes are of a testamentary essence'.[14] The history of how writers want their works to be left, attempting to exert posthumous control over their personal and literary reputations, and the history of will-making, go together.[15]

The testamentary will, where the subject desires to assert his authority, and yet by writing it, shows a willingness to surrender it, is paradigmatic of how the personal will holds on and exerts itself, and yet wills its own destruction. For Hannah Arendt, willing has to do with the future:

> Our Last Will and Testament, providing for the only future of which we can be reasonably certain, namely our own death, shows that the Will's need to will is no less strong than Reason's need to think; in both instances the mind transcends its own natural limitations, either by asking unanswerable questions or by projecting itself into a future which, for the willing subject, will never be.[16]

If willing is forward-thinking, that is because the will cannot will backwards, because time does not run backwards. The will must be always directed towards the future, towards a future project. That does not mean that it does not intend, or wish, to will backwards. The impossibility of doing this causes resentment and the desire to destroy the past. Hence writing a will is complex: it suggests wanting to assert an identity now, or, it has the sense that the end of identity in death must be overcome. Or it may be an act of revenge, wishing to undo something in the past, or revenge something done in the past.

5

This response to the past makes the will perverse. As *ressentiment*, an embittered feeling, it is analysed throughout Nietzsche's essays comprising *On the Genealogy of Morals* (1888), till, in the third and final one, 'What is the Meaning of Ascetic Ideals', it reaches the conclusion already quoted. That essay began saying that the 'ascetic ideal' means so many things to people because of:

> a fundamental truth about human will, its *horror vacui: it must have a goal* – and it would even will *nothingness* rather than not will at all. (*GM*, 3.1.77)

Nietzsche imagines a reader who cannot comprehend this, which gives him the opportunity to commence the analysis of 'ascetic ideals'; toconclude with the words which are this book's *leitmotif*: 'man would sooner have the void for his purpose than be void of purpose'.[17] The power of willing is so great that rather than cease, if it can find nothing else to work on, it will destroy, taking everything with it in a death-drive, continuing, even though it has nothing to work on, in imperious mode. To read this means reading Schopenhauer (1788–1860), writer of the ascetic ideal.

II SCHOPENHAUER

While Hegel called the will the expression of the self and the demand for freedom, Schopenhauer wants to negate it. Georg Simmel (1858–1918) argues that philosophers prior to Schopenhauer 'conceived of man as a rational being', but *The World as Will and Representation* (*Die Welt als Wille und Vorstellung*) (1819) made the will determinative of being and consciousness. Simmel summarises Schopenhauer: 'I do not will by virtue of values and goals that are posited by reason, but I have goals because I will continuously and ceaselessly from the depth of my essence'.[18] The basis of identity, or of knowledge, becomes unknowable. Shakespeare's 'will' is the appetite challenging rationality, though it can lead to cold-blooded, rational defrauding of the other. Schopenhauer's 'appetite' is part of a self-conflictual rationality. It argues that 'science':

> can never reach a final goal, or give an entirely satisfactory explanation. It never aims at the inmost nature of the world; it can never get

beyond the representation . . . it really tells us nothing more than the relation of one representation to another. (7.28)[19]

So 'the world is my representation' (1.3): not that 'representation' represents, or imitates a Platonic reality that we cannot know, but that there is nothing else but presentation; we have no knowledge of 'the inmost nature of the world'. Schopenhauer's Kant is a 'transcendental idealist' for whom, beyond systems of representation, there is the 'thing in itself' the unknowable world. So 'if I remove the thinking subject, the whole corporeal world must at once vanish: it is nothing save an appearance in the sensibility of our subject and a mode of its representations'.[20] The thing in itself, outside representation, causality, time and space, is the will, which is embodied; its every act being a 'manifest act of the body' (1.18.101). The body is an object of representation, but 'we find in [the body] nothing but the will' (19.105). Every part is the will: the digestive system is 'objectified hunger', 'the genitals are objectified sexual impulse' (20.108). Section 22 says that up till now, the concept of will has been subsumed under the concept of force, but this must be reversed: every force in nature should be thought of as will (111). But what motivates this will, which is the 'thing-in-itself', cannot be said; it is 'completely groundless' (23.113). The will individuates itself when it appears, and is seen in all forms, including vegetation – 'what appears for the representation as plant, as mere vegetation, as blindly urging force, will be taken by us, according to its inner nature, to be will, and it will be recognised by us as that very thing which constitutes the basis of our own phenomenon [i.e. appearance in nature], as it expresses itself in our actions, and also in the whole existence of our body itself' (23.117). Blindly urging, it cannot leave room for free will, which is an illusion existent in how someone is taken up by the will; if free will presupposes the intellect's power, Schopenhauer presupposes the will's active power:

> Spinoza (*Epist.* 62) says that if a stone projected through the air had consciousness, it would imagine it was flying of its own will. I add merely that the stone would be right. The impulse is for it what the motive is for me. (24.126)

It seems impossible to speak of free will: acts of willing take place within the world as will: even gravitation is an inclination or desire (24.127).

Yet 'the higher Idea or objectification of will' can only appear by subduing lower ideas, lower manifestations (objectifications) of it. The will, then, is not single:

> Everywhere in nature we see contest, struggle, and the fluctuation of victory, and later on we shall recognise in this more distinctly that variance with itself essential to the will. . . . This universal conflict is to be seen most clearly in the animal kingdom . . . the will-to-live generally feasts on itself, and is in different forms its own nourishment, till finally the human race, because it subdues all the others, regards nature as manufactured for its own use. (27.146–47)

This confirms Hobbes' *homo homini lupus* – man is a wolf to man (27.147). The will moves from being 'blind impulse' (27.149) at the lowest stages of being, or of objectification, towards becoming the human intellect, where 'the will must live on itself, since nothing exists besides it, and it is a hungry will. Hence arise pursuit, hunting, anxiety, and suffering' (28.154). Anxiety comes from the will's sadism towards itself. Its split nature is reinforced with the will-to-live, which is sexual; in the sexual act 'is expressed the most decided *affirmation of the will to live*' (60.328). 'The affirmation of the will to live' with 'its centre in the act of generation (vol. 2, 45.571), is a chapter-title in the supplementary volume 2, succeeding 'The Metaphysics of Sexual Love' (2.45), on the differences between believing in love, and sexuality as a mode of continuing the species. In man, 'it is clothed in so much knowledge and moreover, is veiled by the capacity for dissimulation that its true nature only comes to light almost by chance and in isolated cases' (28.156). Here, guilt appears, derived 'not in willing, but in willing with knowledge', making the will an 'endless striving', marked by absence of aim and limits (29.164), and self-divided: tragedy showing its antagonism with itself (51.253).

The third Book considers forms of representation as ways of escape from this 'endless becoming, endless flux' (29.164). And something in the will, its 'self-knowledge' (35.184), divides it against itself, so that it destroys itself. Art, as a form of knowledge, gives knowledge of the will (36.184). Willing springs 'from lack, from deficiency, and thus from suffering' and its subject 'is constantly lying on the revolving wheel of Ixion, is always drawing water in the sieve of the Danaids, and is the eternally thirsting Tantalus' (38.196). Discussion of art-forms culminates with tragedy, which shows the highest degree in which art can represent the frustrated will, and fully exhibiting its 'antagonism . . . with itself'. This happens first as the result of 'chance and error' which intrudes from without, second:

> through the self-mortifying efforts of will on the part of individuals, through the wickedness and perversity of most. It is one and the same will, living and appearing in them all, whose phenomena fight with one another and tear one another to pieces', requiring the hero of tragedy to give up, not merely life, but 'the whole of the will-to-live itself. (51.253)

Schopenhauer makes guilt essential to tragedy: the hero atones for 'original sin, in other words, the guilt of existence itself' (51.254). Being human – not a plant or animal – means being held by a knowledge inside the will and dividing it. Schopenhauer quotes Calderón's *Life is a Dream*: 'man's greatest offence / Is that he has been born', and glosses this, saying that with tragic catastrophe, we are convinced that 'life is a bad dream from which we have to awake' (referencing Calderón). So tragedy lifts the self above the will, in 'the dawning of the knowledge that the world and life can afford us no true satisfaction, and are therefore not worth our attachment to them. In this the tragic spirit consists; accordingly it leads to resignation' (2.51.433–34). So the will gives knowledge of itself: i.e. that nothing is worth it. Though it seems blind, as it appears in objectified forms in art, it has self-knowledge:

> The will, considered purely in itself, is devoid of knowledge, and is only a blind, irresistible urge [. . .] through the addition of the world as representation . . . the will attains knowledge of its own willing, and what it wills, namely that this is nothing but this world, life, precisely as it exists. We have therefore called the phenomenal world the mirror, the objectivity, of the will, and what the will wills is always life . . . (54.275)

But not just life; through knowledge of the will, there dawns another knowledge, which makes for a giving up on the will. So, for Peter Szondi, Schopenhauer's 'description of tragedy interprets the tragic as the self-destruction and self-negation of the will . . . the will not only turns against itself [in reaching self-knowledge] but also brings about this knowledge through the tragic action whose sole hero is the will, the will that destroys itself'.[21]

The will produces boredom, so that an hour cannot be got through without diversion. Anyone would refuse to endure it again, would 'prefer to choose complete non-existence' (59.324): Schopenhauer agrees with Hamlet's 'To be or not to be' soliloquy; but, like Hamlet, thinks suicide not worth it; death is not annihilation; beyond death there is not nothing. Chapter 59, evoking Dante's Hell, shows how any scene after life is only a repetition of what has already been seen on earth: Dante's poetic material derives from 'this actual world of ours'. To look for help from any god is futile: only the 'will-power' of the self serves (326), and Schopenhauer concludes calling optimism 'not only an absurd but also a really *wicked*, way of thinking, a bitter mockery of the unspeakable sufferings of mankind' (326).

Inseparable from the will, part of it, going beyond maintaining the individual body, is 'the sexual impulse', which shows life going beyond individual life, with a blind purpose within it. The idea of guilt reappears, for sexuality affirms the body, and bodily knowledge; disallows the transcending of the body, as in the desire for salvation. Hence the shame the Christian feels, because of 'the dogma of the Christian teaching that we all share the sin of Adam (which is obviously only the satisfaction of sexual passion) and through it are guilty of suffering and death' (60.328). Proserpine tasting the pomegranate in the lower world is a parallel: she must not return to the upper world; the power of the sexual will means she fails to fast in the lower world. A third quotation, from Clement of Alexandria, on those who have castrated themselves for the kingdom of heaven, confirms that only complete world-abstention denies the will; but that impossibility affirms 'the sexual impulse as the decided and strongest affirmation of life' (329), and, in this sexual manifestation, 'not troubled by death, because death exists as something already included in and belonging to life' (330). Hence:

> ... the will performs the great tragedy and comedy at its own expense, and is also its own spectator. The world is precisely as it is, because the will, whose phenomenon is the world, is such a will as it is, because it wills in such a way. (331)

Section 60 adds to the sexual impulse the ego's power. The will is present in each individual; all that he is, is the will; others appear to him 'only in his representation [. . .] he is conscious of them always only as his representation, and so merely indirectly, and as something dependent on his own inner being and existence' (60.332). This is Kantean idealism, whose solipsism is egoism, the expression of the individual's will: 'hence his own inner being and its preservation come before all others taken together' (332). Such will-power demonstrates itself in the display of self-conceit and vanity and explains 'world-devastating wars' (333).

Sections 62 and 63 discuss justice, seeking which is futile. To escape from wickedness by causing another person's suffering, which necessarily happens in the quest for justice, means forgetting that both modes of being are part of the same will. The person seeking justice is 'the boatman . . . in his small boat, trusting his frail craft in a stormy sea that is boundless in every direction, rising and falling with the howling mountainous waves'. Drawing the analogy:

> in the midst of a world full of suffering and misery the individual man calmly sits, supported by and trusting the *principium individuationis*, or the way in which the individual knows things as phenomenon. (63.352–53)[22]

The attempt to maintain the sense of being an individual leads to a vain pursuit of individual justice. But that can produce nothing but conflict, which in struggling to maintain individuality means that the difference between the person who 'inflicts suffering and he who must endure it is only phenomenon, and does not concern the thing-in-itself which is the will that lives in both'. Hence 'in the fierceness and intensity of its desire [the will] buries its teeth in its own flesh'. 'Tormentor and tormented are one'. Beings caught up in the will are self-divided, ambivalent, striving against others where that struggle is really internal to themselves because they consider themselves individual, a state which means accepting the torments of the will.

The last section turns to will-denial, and asceticism, the state of mind where, having seen the world's suffering, 'the will now turns away from life; it shudders at the pleasures in which it recognises the affirmation of life' (68.379).[23] There is no apathy in this shuddering, which is bodily, and involuntary.[24] The superego the will becomes, feels affect; the male ascetic has a 'body, healthy and strong' which:

11

expresses the sexual desire through the genitals, but he denies the will, and gives the lie to the body; he desires no sexual satisfaction on any condition. Voluntary and complete chastity is the first step in asceticism or the denial of the will-to-live. (68.380)

Chastity is insufficient: the body must first feel sexual desire, the genitals expressing the will, as Augustine or Shakespeare show. Until the will is asserted, no 'voluntary' chastity can take place. The will taboos and is tabooed:

> For as the body is the will itself only in the form of objectivity . . . that whole will-to-live exists potentially so long as the body lives, and is always striving to reach actuality, and to burn afresh with all its intensity. (68.391)

> . . . the genitals, for example, as the visibility of the sexual impulse, are there and in health; but yet in the innermost consciousness no sexual satisfaction is desired. The whole body is the visible expression of the will-to-live, yet the motives corresponding to this will no longer act; indeed, the dissolution of the body, the end of the individual, and thus the greatest expression of the natural will, is welcomed and desired. (70.403)

The superego, the force of law, demands the maximum expression of desire before it can work. With will silenced, a man 'looks back calmly and with a smile on the phantasmagoria of this world which was once able to move and agonise even his mind' (70.390). Serenity knows:

> that evil and wickedness, suffering and hatred, the tormented and the tormentor . . . are themselves one, phenomenon of the one will-to-live that objectifies its conflict with itself by means of the *principium individuationis*. They have learned to know both sides in full measure, the wickedness and the evil; and since they ultimately see the identity of the two, they reject them both at the same time; they deny the will-to-live. (394)

The antitheses identify activity and passivity, sadism and masochism, as inherent in the will. But suicide is rejected as asserting not denial but that 'the suicide wills life and is dissatisfied merely with the conditions on which it has come to him' (69.398).

Nietzsche interprets this as a 'sensuality' that cannot be cancelled out, 'only transfigured . . . no longer present to consciousness as a sexual impulse' (*GM*, 3.8.91). This pre-Freudian insight reinforces a Schopenhauerian point, that the silenced will has been silenced by the will, which is therefore still present. Hence the bad faith. Nietzsche's critique of Schopenhauer sees in him an 'ascetic ideal' wanting pessimism, life-refusal, and the negation of the body, treating life 'as a wrong track on which one must retrace one's steps', as a desire 'not to master some isolated aspect of life but rather life itself' (*GM*, 3.11.96, 97). Suffering can be justified, because then mankind is offered a meaning. For man 'does *not* repudiate suffering as such; he *desires* it; he even seeks it out, provided that he has been shown a *meaning* for it, a *reason* for suffering' (*GM*, 3.28.136). Suffering must be given a logical form, must not be seen as irrational. 'For every suffering man instinctively seeks a cause for his suffering, more precisely, a doer, more definitely, a *guilty* doer . . . on whom he can upon any pretext discharge his feelings . . . '. The form of suffering is '"I am suffering: someone must be to blame"' and the response of the Schopenhauerian ascetic priest, as he is called, is: '"someone must be to blame: but you are yourself this someone, you alone are to blame – *you alone are to blame for yourself*"' (*GM*, 3.15.105–6). Told that its suffering has to do with its guilt, the will works on, torturing itself. Told that someone else is to blame, it can plan, or, out of *ressentiment*, take revenge. Nietzsche speaks of 'the will to truth', as the search for a sure foundation, such as identifying God with truth, to give meaning to life, and to suffering identified with life (*GM*, 3.24), such a will to truth contains its own nihilism, as rejecting life's heterogeneity.

Nietzsche's *Twilight of the Idols* (*Götzen-Dämmerung*, 1888) supplements why the will goes on willing. The categories of the will, the spirit and the ego are the three fictions that the self must believe in. There is a 'fetishism of language' involved in believing in the doer and the deed, the will as the cause, and the 'I' as being, as having substance.[25] If the will must will, that is because it is the fetish which supports belief in a unique, and free, identity. Its willing guarantees the existence of the self, as the will to truth guarantees that the self has a meaning.

But considering the dominance of the will here, even where it thinks it has overcome the will, requires considering it psychoanalytically. The next section looks at St Paul, and Jacques Lacan on Paul, while discusssing Schopenhauer's master, Kant. The analysis, reinforc-

13

ing a sense of the will's perversity as a structure, impacts on all that
follows.

III ST PAUL WITH LACAN

7. What shall we say then? Is the law sin? God forbid. Nay, I had
    not known sin but by the law: for I had not known lust except
    the law had said, Thou shalt not covet.
8. But sin, taking occasion by the commandment, wrought in me
    all manner of concupisence. For without the law, sin was dead.
9. For I was alive without the law once: but when the command-
    ment came, sin revived and I died.
10. And the commandment which was ordained to life, I found to
    be unto death.
11. For sin, taking occasion by the commandment, deceived me,
    and by it slew me.
12. Wherefore the law is holy, and the commandment holy, and
    just, and good.
13. Was then that which is good made death unto me? God forbid.
    But sin, that it might appear sin, working in me by that which
    is good, that sin by the commandment might become exceed-
    ingly sinful.
14. For we know that the law is spiritual, but I am carnal, sold under
    sin.
15. For that which I do I allow not: for what I would, that do I not;
    but what I hate, that do I.
16. If then I do that which I would not, I consent unto the law that
    it is good.
17. Now then it is no more I that do it, but sin that dwelleth in me.
18. For I know that in me, (that is, in my flesh), dwelleth no good
    thing; for to will is present with me, but how to perform that
    which is good I find not.
19. For the good that I would I do not, but the evil which I would
    not, that I do.
20. Now if I do that I would not, it is no more I that do it, but sin
    that dwelleth in me.
21. I find then a law, that when I would do good, evil is present
    with me.

22. For I delight in the law of God after the inward man:
23. But I see another law in my members, warring against the law of my mind, and bringing me into captivity to the law of sin which is in my members.
24. O wretched man that I am! who shall deliver me from the body of this death?
25. I thank God through Jesus Christ our Lord. So then with my mind I serve the law of God, but with the flesh the law of sin. (Romans, 7.7–25)

Saint Paul argues that Christians have, definitionally, been delivered from the Law of Moses; including the Ten Commandments (Exodus, 20.1–17). Though he checks the thought that the Law was sinful, and that this was why Christians needed to be delivered from it, nonetheless the idea gives him difficulty. In the first part of the passage (7–13), the prohibition of the law brings out desire. Outside, or without the law, sin was dead; but as soon as the commandment came, sin, as a disposition to do wrong, sprang to life, 'and I died'. The commandment, which should have led to life, proved to be a death-sentence. He concludes by affirming the law to be holy, just and good. Paul, as an ex-Pharisee, could never have had a time in his life when he was outside the law; commentators have divided over the question who the 'I' is that speaks, but he is not primarily speaking autobiographically.

The commandment 'Thou shalt not covet' (Exodus, 20.17) is the tenth of the ten. 'Covet', in Greek ('I would not have known *epithymia* if the law had not said *ouk epithymeseis*'), translates as 'desire' – 'You shall not desire'.[26] Other commandments interdict specific actions: this tenth awakens desire. Sin produced in him all kinds of desire. The tension is between Law and Desire. In v.9, he says 'I died', and v.11 adds: sin 'slew me'. He thought that he could keep the commandments, which were ordained towards life (e.g. Leviticus, 18.5).[27]

How did sin kill him? It found an opportunity in the commandment: he says it deceived him. But what kind of excuse is that? What else would sin do? The language is that of Eve saying that the serpent deceived her by saying that she would not die if she partook of the tree of the knowledge of good and evil (Genesis, 3.11). But Eve chose to believe a lie; it is hard to see how she was deceived. Nor did the excuse avail her anything. But the idea of being deceived by the serpent prompts the question: if the serpent could so trick her, by quoting the commandment (Genesis, 3.2), why did God test her? If Sin could so use the commandment, there seems something strange in the relationship between Law and sin. The commandment seems at fault, and affirming the holiness of the law in v.12 seems forced compared to v.7's plainer statement, that only through the law did he know sin. Also strained is the orthodoxy in v.13: that the commandment had the effect, if not the function, of showing how exceeding sinful Paul was. There may be a displacement in saying that sin deceived him. The law seemed to promise life (Exodus, 19.1–8), and did not.

The next section (14–25) follows, in the present tense. Paul says he is carnal, sold under sin, a realisation given by the law. The price paid in consenting to the idea that the law is good is that he does what he does not will. To prove that the law is indeed holy, just and good, as opposed to acknowledging that it is oppressive, he must say 'I do not understand my own actions', another translation of 'For that which I do I allow not'.[28] He concludes that what countermands his will is sin (v.17). In contrast to the law, 'I know that in me . . . dwelleth no good thing'. The law has created a will to serve but since he is dominated by the flesh, 'to will is present with me but how to perform that which is good I find not'. This division is not on the lines of the soul and the body, as Alain Badiou points out.[29] It is the will as divided on the lines of the law: the law incites a will towards the 'good'; the 'will' therefore gains its strength from the law. But that will to do something good, product of both the law and the will, induces another doing which of necessity is characterised as 'evil' (v.19).

There are two laws: the law of God, the law of my mind, and the other, the law of sin, which is in his members, 'the law of sin and death' (8.2). There are not two wills, only the will to do the good, which is frustrated by sin, which does what the 'I' does not will (19, 20). The principle learned from, or imposed by, the law is: 'when I would do good, evil is present with me'. Hence the law of God is seen in ambivalent terms: I delight in it inwardly, objectively, but it works as another law in the body's members, opposing 'the law of my mind', i.e. the will and inclination, subjecting Paul to 'the law of sin which is in my members'. The law is the 'law of God' (22) and the 'law of sin'. As James Dunn says in his commentary, 'under the power of sin the law is experienced as very different from the law of God' (395). The language half-acknowledges that the law of God is also 'the law of sin and death' (8.2), that it has made Paul more and more associated with sin. It cannot be two things at once; it has to be concluded that the law of God is the law of sin and death. While the first section (7–13) is factual statement, the second (14–25) is a horrified sense of the self. Hating his every action of desire, he cannot quite say that the problem resides in the law which wills him to do things. The law creates in him the will as identity: it constructs a will aligned with the law. The deception Paul does not attribute to the law is this: it summons forth a will that commits itself, that wills in a way that internalises the law, and then undermines that will. The will is the expression of the law, its instrument, but finds itself undone by the power of sin, but since, as Saint Paul says, 'the strength of sin is the law' (1 Corinthians, 15.56), that is also the law at work, and law, will and sin are to be identified with each other.

Paul's words are commented on by Jacques Lacan, in Seminar VII, *The Ethics of Psychoanalysis*, lectures delivered through 1959–60, and indirectly through 'Kant with Sade', intended for a Preface to Sade's *Philosophy in the Bedroom*, but published in *Critique* in 1963. *The Ethics of Psychoanalysis* argues that there is no system of ethics – Aristotelian, Kantian, Benthamite – which can survive the findings of psychoanalysis. So what can we say about how we should live? Perhaps one conclusion is that no one can speak for anyone else. Lacan's thesis is that:

> the moral law, the moral command, the presence of the moral agency [i.e. the will] in our activity, insofar as it is structured by the symbolic, is that through which the real is actualised – the real as such, the weight of the real.[30]

Lacan speaks of three modes of existence. The first is the *imaginary*, where the subject makes a narcissistic identification of itself with itself, and which, because it is prior to insertion into the language of patriarchy, is associated with the mother. The second is the *symbolic*, as the order of language into which the subject is inserted under the power of the father. The third is the *real*, that which escapes the symbolic and all symbolisation. Life within the symbolic order does not show the presence of the real, but when it appears, in all its unassimilable force, it has the power of trauma.

In this Seminar VII, 'the real' relates to something else, which Lacan calls *das Ding*, the Thing, saying that Freud introduced this term at the beginning, in the *Project for a Scientific Discovery* (1895). Freud discusses the 'fellow human-being', the *Nebensmensch*, who is remembered not for

17

any specific feature, but for something which Freud calls 'a thing'. If the *Nebensmensch* is the other, then the 'thing' in him is the other of the other. There is in the *Nebensmensch* something strange, unaccountable, haunting, beyond what conscious memory can recall: that is the first sense of 'the Thing'.[31] The Thing in Lacan is the 'lost object', a phrase derived from Freud on Negation [*Die Verneinung*], (1925) where the subject is a repressed image; but this image has an ambiguous relationship with reality, being both inside (intimate) the subject and outside, 'extimate' (Lacan, 139). Freud writes in 'Negation':

> Experience has shown the subject that it is not only important whether a thing (an object of satisfaction for him) possesses the 'good' attribute and so deserves to be taken into his ego, but also whether it is there in the external world, so that he can get hold of it whenever he needs to. [. . .] [A]ll presentations originate from perceptions, and are repetitions of them. Thus originally the mere existence of a presentation was a guarantee of the reality of what was presented. The antithesis between subjective and objective does not exist from the first. It only comes into being from the fact that thinking possesses the capacity to bring before the mind once more something that has once been perceived, by reproducing it as a presentation without the external object having to be there. The first and immediate object, therefore, of reality-testing, is not to *find* an object in real perception which corresponds to the one presented, but to *refind* such an object, to convince oneself that it is still there.[32]

According to Lacan, the object, or thing, exists as a repressed image in the mind, but, as lost, it has a hold on the subject. Repressed images substitute for the sense of something which has been lost. For Lacan, the 'thing' evades perception: 'something sifts, sieves, in such a way that reality is only perceived by man, in his natural spontaneous state at least, as radically selected' (Lacan, 47). As 'the absolute Other of the subject', it is found only as something missed (52), and what it is, is never stated by Freud (58). For Lacan it is characterised by 'its absence, its strangeness' (63).

But then Lacan gets into the Ten Commandments, and relates them to the incest-taboo, noting that the Commandments never prohibit incest with the mother. They cannot, because Lacan argues that the Commandments are the embodiment of speech, and all speech is founded on the prior exclusion of incest (67–69). Hence, 'the Sovereign Good', the object of Aristotelian ethics, 'which is *das Ding*, which is the mother, is also the object of incest, is a forbidden good, and . . . there is no other good'. And this is 'the foundation of the moral law as turned on its head by Freud' (70); so that the desire for the mother as the lost object is the absolutely interdicted basis of the moral law, which is based on repression, not on something rationally worked through.

Lacan's next chapter, 'On the Moral Law', makes *das Ding* the 'extimate', that which is 'at the centre only in the sense that it is excluded', 'something strange to me though it is at the heart of me' (71). It is the source of all the 'good'. This term leads into discussion of Kant's *Critique of Practical Reason* as the text on ethics which commands the will into being – but not for anything pleasurable, or giving a sense of well-being. So, in 'Kant with Sade', since 'No phenomenon can lay claim to a constant relationship with pleasure', 'no law of feeling good can . . . be enunciated that would define the subject who puts it into practice as "will"'.[33] Instead, 'we make ourselves hear commandments inside of ourselves, the imperative nature of which is presented as categorical, in other words, unconditional' (KS, 646). This follows Kant saying that:

> There is something so special in the boundless esteem for the pure moral law stripped of all advantage – as this law is presented to us, for compliance, by practical reason, whose voice makes even the boldest offender tremble and compels him to hide from his own sight [or 'from the law's sight' – its gaze] . . . [34]

The power of the voice operates: this being also the voice of the moral law heard inside the subject, who almost literally hears voices, making him virtually schizophrenic. The subject must respond with fear to some other in himself. The Kantian moral law has also the power of the gaze; it looks and the offender must hide from that sight (the gaze of the law and of the self being the same thing). What is commanded is the will. Equally, what commands is the will.

The good commanded 'appears only by excluding everything the subject may suffer from, due to his interest in an object, whether drive or feeling – what Kant designates, for that reason, as "pathological"' (KS, 646). The will, following the categorical imperative, with which it is identified, must be formed by excluding personal feeling. So, Lacan's Seminar defines how Kant sees the basis of moral action: 'Act in such a

19

way that the maxim of your action may be accepted as a universal maxim' (Lacan, 76). But 'if a rational being is to think of his maxims as practical universal laws, then he can think of them only as principles that contain the determining basis of the will not by their matter but merely by their form' (Kant, 27, 40). The moral character of willing is determined not by the content of what is willed, but only formally; there is nothing save an abstraction, the moral law, to be adhered to.[35] 'Kant with Sade' notes this:

> We encounter anew here what led Kant to express his regret that no intuition offers up a phenomenal object in the experience of the moral law.
>
> I agree that this object slips away throughout the *Critique*. But it can be surmised in the trace left by the implacable suite [pursuit] Kant provides to demonstrate its slipping away, from the which the work derives an eroticism . . . (KS, 647)

There is no articulation of an object to be pursued in this demand for the ethical. But that, for Lacan, arouses an eroticism since the demand is always motivated by an object which, for the subject, is absent. In Kant, what is missing is always the unknowable *Ding an sich*, the thing in itself, the very thing, which Schopenhauer identified with the will (vol. 1, 110).

Lacan then turns to Sade's *Philosophy in the Bedroom*, to set this against the emptiness of Kant's formal law. The principle to act that the maxim of your will could hold as a principle of a universal legislation', is reversible.[36] If my will is to do evil, that becomes as much a guiding principle as the principle of doing good. The fundamental imperatives of the moral law allow as much for the Sadeian view 'let us take as the universal maxim of our conduct the right to enjoy any person whatsoever as the instrument of our pleasure' (Lacan, 79). The instruction's coldness removes from Sade's maxim any category of sentiment. Lacan draws Kant closer to Sade in one detail, quoting Kant on pain:

> the moral law as the determining principle of will, by reason of the fact that it sets itself against our inclinations must produce a feeling that one could call pain. (80)[37]

We return to Kant's unconscious eroticism. And it is 'the other's pain as well as the pain of the subject himself, for on occasions they are simply one and the same thing' (80).

Lacan discusses the Ten Commandments, for example the second, prohibiting making of images or representations. This he relates to 'the elimination of the function of the imaginary' (81) – so to the absence of the mother. Iconoclasm may suggest an attack on the maternal. He focuses on the tenth commandment, which stumbled Paul: 'Thou shalt not covet thy neighbour's house, thou shalt not covet thy neighbour's wife, neither his man servant, nor his maid servant, neither his ox, nor his ass, nor anything that belongs to thy neighbour' (82). The word 'thing' has been smuggled in; for Lacan, that indicates 'the Thing' as other; the law against coveting awakens desire for the other. Since the category of the 'neighbour' recalls, partly, the *Nebensmench*, and includes all others, it evokes the thought of the father, and of incest; coveting seems to bring in its wake both incest and the taboo. The commandment is distant from 'the Thing', which cannot be articulated, cannot come into the symbolic order, but Lacan collapses this distinction by adapting Paul:

> Is the Law the Thing? Certainly not. Yet I can only know of the Thing by means of the Law. In effect, I would not have had the idea to covet it if the Law hadn't said, 'Thou shalt not covet it'. But the Thing finds a way by producing in me all kinds of covetousness thanks to the commandment, for without the Law, the Thing is dead. But even without the Law, I was once alive. But when the commandment appeared, the Thing flared up, returned once again, I met my death. And for me, the commandment that was supposed to lead to life turned out to lead to death, for the Thing found a way and thanks to the commandment seduced me; through it I came to desire death. (83)

For Lacan, 'the dialectical relationship between desire and the Law causes our desire to flare up only in relation to the Law, through which it becomes the desire for death' (83–84). Sin means for Lacan 'lack and non-participation in the Thing'; the law makes it take on 'an excessive, hyperbolic character' (84).

The Law names the Thing, so that it stands apart from desire, and constitutes it, and is itself beyond the law. Desire becomes a series of metonymic displacements, 'all kinds of covetousness', as named in the tenth commandment, all substituting for the obscure 'Thing'. The result is the desire for death as beyond 'the pleasure principle', or any Utilitarian principle; introducing 'an erotics that is above morality' (84). Defining desire as willing death contrasts with Paul's idea: that his will, created by the law, desired the good. It suggests that the law, as it works in his members, works death. On the logic by which Paul virtually says that the law is sin, Lacan calls the law the Thing.[38]

Desire being desire for death compares with what Lacan says when closing the later Seminar XI (1964), where he affirms that it is not tenable to say that desire has to do with love:

> Experience shows us that Kant is more true, and I have proved that his theory of consciousness, when he writes of practical reason, is sustained only by giving a specification of the moral law which looked at more closely, is simply desire in its pure state, that very desire that culminates in the sacrifice, strictly speaking, of everything that is the object of love in one's human tenderness – I would say, not only in the rejection of the pathological object, but also in its sacrifice and murder. That is why I wrote *Kant avec Sade*.[39]

Kant's prescription of a moral imperative is a form of sadism which, rejecting all feelings as 'pathological', is murderous, because subjection to the law demands the sacrifice of the object. Such sacrificing, it seems, is pleasurable.

'Kant with Sade' shows Sade illuminating Kant. If we follow how Lacan virtually unites law and desire, his point should be recalled: 'we make ourselves hear commandments inside of ourselves' (KS, 646). There seems to be an act of will here. The subject hearing the categorical imperative is split, between a self imposed upon, and a self imposing a law. Lacan notes about Sade, that the maxim proposed is:

> 'I have the right to enjoy your body', anyone can say to me, 'and I will exercise this right without any limit to the capriciousness of the exactions I may wish to satiate with your body.' (KS, 648)

But the maxim includes the law in its 'anyone': as a voice it makes 'me' an object; or both subject and object. Lacan expands the point: the moral commandment 'commissions us as Other':

The bipolarity upon which the moral law is founded is nothing but the split in the subject brought about by any and every intervention of the signifier. . . In coming out of the Other's mouth, Sade's maxim is more honest than Kant's appeal to the voice within, since it unmasks the split in the subject that is usually covered up. (KS, 650)

The point, familiar from Benveniste's linguistics, is that the 'I' who speaks and the 'I' who appears in the sentence that 'I' speak are not the same. Lacan refers to these two as 'the enunciating subject' [*sujet de l'énonciation*] and the subject of the statement [*sujet de l'énoncé*]. Hence, reverting to Lacan's point about pain (Lacan, 80), the splitting of the subject into one who commands and one who is commanded, means that the self both gives out, and receives, pain. As with Paul, the category of the will is that which divides the subject, structures it as ambivalent, active and passive. Such a sense of the doubleness within the subject appears in 'Kant with Sade', where desire is unconsciously blocked:

In psychoanalysis, displeasure is understood to provide a pretext for repressing desire, displeasure arising, as it does, along the pathway of desire's satisfaction, but displeasure is also understood to provide the form this very satisfaction takes in the return of the repressed.

Similarly, pleasure redoubles its aversion when it recognises the law, by supporting the desire to comply with it that constitutes defence. (KS, 663)

The first paragraph suggests that when desire is embarked upon, there is also the presence of displeasure, whose satisfaction outweighs the pleasure. Displeasure appears in terms of 'the return of the repressed' as a symptom, a problem, but this problematic symptom – such as an hysterical symptom – is a source of satisfaction: it is the pleasure which has been denied in terms of the pathway of desire's satisfaction. The second paragraph supplements that: pleasures appear as displeasure when pleasure recognises the law which it puts in the way. The desire for pleasure becomes the desire to satisfy the law. Pleasure, confronted with the law, intensifies its repressive tendencies, because these are themselves productive of pleasure. So desires appear as displeasurable, and that repression appears as desire. Lacan takes the point from Freud's essay on 'Repression' [*Verdrängung*] (1915) which begins: 'one of the vicissitudes an instinctual impulse may undergo is to meet with resist-

23

ances which seek to make it inoperative'.[40] Freud argues that since 'satis-faction of an instinct is always pleasurable', 'we should have to assume certain peculiar circumstances, some sort of process by which the pleasure of satisfaction is changed into unpleasure' (146). And repres-sion produces a 'substitutive formation' which entails the forming of symptoms (154). Such substitutes for the earlier desire are themselves ambiguously satisfying. John Rajchman says that Freud was 'fascinated by this desire', that these 'hysterics' – obviously this term is problem-atic – defied their doctors to 'cure' them by locating something problematic in the body, and struggled with the 'curious intransigence' of his patients: 'why does Irma persist in refusing the 'solution' to her troubled passion, as sure as the chemical formula of a drug?' For Rajchman, the discovery that there was no desire for a 'normative' cure was central to Freud: psychoanalysis discovered the impossibility of driving out an irrational symptom by appealing to rationality, or the patient's ultimate good.[41] The point suggests Lacan on 'displeasure' being the form that satisfaction takes in the return of the repressed.

So psychoanalysis argues against Paul saying that the law awakens dormant desire. Rather, desire is inseparable from the law from the start; when desire is awakened, it also desires its own repression: it craves the law. Hence the sadism, which is also masochism; when I wish to do a thing, I also wish to bring in the category of 'displeasure'. Sade remains within the Pauline logic that does not see the truly perverse nature of desire; Sade 'stopped at the point where desire and the law become bound up with each other' (KS, 667). He 'remained tied to the law in order to take the opportunity, mentioned by Saint Paul, to become inordinately sinful'.

This reflects an earlier statement in the Seminar, discussing a Kantian example: 'the individual who is placed in the situation of being executed on his way out [this is the threat he has received] if he wants to spend time with the lady whom he desires unlawfully' (Lacan, 188). Kant thinks no man would spend that time with the woman on the condition of being executed on his way out. Lacan replies that 'one only has to make a conceptual shift and move the night spent with the lady from the cate-gory of pleasure to that of *jouissance* [sexual pleasure, outside language], given that *jouissance* implies precisely the acceptance of death' for Kant's example to be ruined.[42]

It is enough for *jouissance* to be a form of evil, for the whole thing to

24

change its character completely, and for the meaning of the moral law itself to be completely changed. Anyone can see that if the moral law is, in effect, capable of playing some role here, it is precisely as a support for the *jouissance* involved, it is so that the sin becomes what Saint Paul calls inordinately sinful. (Seminar, 189)

The law invites a rephrasing of the experience, commanding *jouissance* in a *volonté de jouissance*. Alenka Zupančič summarises:

> For Kant it is unimaginable that someone would *want* his own destruction – this would be diabolical. Lacan's answer is not that this is nevertheless imaginable, and that even such extreme cases exist, but that there is nothing extreme in it at all: on a certain level every subject, average as he may be, wills his destruction, *whether he wills it or not*.[43]

These two wills, law and desire, remain separate for Sade, making desire reactive, excited towards the attempt to transgress a given law. Lacan says that these cannot be maintained as separate, which is the conclusion Paul could not draw, and says about Sade that 'there is precious little here – in fact, nothing – by way of a treatise that is truly on desire' (KS, 667). The potentiality of desire, that it requires and accepts death, and is inherently beyond the pleasure principle, is less explored by Sade, than that a pregiven law demands transgression. We have returned to Nietzsche: 'man would rather will *nothingness* than *not* will at all'. The will desires pleasure, but also craves the repression of that will, and so brings in the law. But the law is also the will; as with the will of the sovereign. And, in Kant's example the will craves its own death, rather than to not will. The law wills desire, desire wills the law.

Psychoanalytically, Paul seems sadistic and masochistic. As sadistic, he passes judgements on himself – 'I know that in me, that is in my flesh, dwelleth no good thing'. He speaks of the law in him which wars against the law of his mind, bringing him into captivity to the law of sin which is in his members. As masochistic, he praises the law, and delights in it 'after the inward man' however much, or *because* however much, it condemns him. The rhetoric becomes strained in proportion to this sense of guilt. He cannot allow a desire which was destructive, and which imposed its own law, nor admit that the law is an agent of destruction to him. If he did, he could not claim that his will was towards the law, as opposed to death and the real of 'no good thing'. He could not allow his own *jouissance* towards the law of sin in his members.

Instead of this desire driving towards death, where the law assigns it, Lacan asks for 'sublimation', which recognises the tendency within desire towards death and towards nothing. Sublimation 'creates a certain number of forms, amongst which art is not alone', which includes artistic forms. Sublimation means 'raising an object . . . to the dignity of the Thing' (112). We can paraphrase: '"sublimation" means nothing else than the possibility of coming into contact with the Thing without losing oneself as a subject'.[44] For Lacan, art allows coming to terms with the indescribable and unnameable 'thing'; recognising the obscenity, the real within desire. So he discusses Heidegger on 'The Thing', alluding to Heidegger talking about a vase as that which 'creates the void' (120). So 'primitive architecture can be defined as something organised around emptiness' (135). Architecture points not to inhabitable space, but to something *unheimlich*, indecipherable, an emptiness speaking of what is lost. It gives a space to that emptiness. Rajchman comments that this sublimation indicates:

> not just why a particular painting is beautiful, but why painting is. In painting we would love what remains "invisible" in the visions it offers us; in architecture what is "uninhabitable" in the habitations it makes for us; in literature what is "unsayable' in what it says to us. (Rajchman, 75)

If the will wills the void, art's compensatory tendency is to show the void, but in such a way that to see that, and to live within it suspends the will to truth, for it allows, or requires resting in 'illusion' or 'artifice' (136). Lacan thinks of Lascaux as art around emptiness. Temple-architecture, he says, is 'a construction around emptiness that designates the place of the Thing . . . [as] the figuration of emptiness on the walls of this emptiness itself' (Lacan, 140). Emptiness and the *in*visible, is within the picture. To relate to this nothing through art is for the spectator to 'lay down his gaze there as one lays down one's weapons. This is the pacifying, Apollonian effect of painting' (Seminar XI 101). The identity as the will, guarding itself as armour, is appeased; it loses its defiance, its need for self-protection. We shall return to this in chapter 7, with *The Birth of Tragedy*.

IV ON READING THE WILL

vorrei, e non vorrei
(ZERLINA, *Don Giovanni*)

It will appear, from 'Kant with Sade', that no unitary value can be ascribed to 'the will'. This book treats it as a perverse desire, illuminating it through different textual examples. I am less concerned with the question whether there 'is' a will, than in what has been said of it, and what readings of texts consideration of it enables. The examples, literary, philosophical and musical, recognise that arguments about the will are textual; they do not exist as ahistorical propositions about the mind/body relationship, and whether a will associates with that dualism. And in a text 'the will' may be only a place-holder for something urgent which escapes representation.[45]

The three parts of the book are not the history of a unified topic: 'the will'. PART ONE, 'The Will and Identity', marks the emergence of a subjectivity which defines itself as single, in specular, self-reflective terms. The 'will' becomes an issue for the entire personality, and I trace it through to Shakespeare. Nonetheless by then, the concept has been reinvented, because it goes back to at least Augustine, and his reading of St Paul. And the question is, how, in considering a 'history of the subject' we can think of Augustine speaking of himself in the *Confessions* as a discrete subject. Does his wilfulness point to the will marking off an *individual*? I supplement that question with a brief comment on one medieval text, William Langland's *Piers Plowman*. Is the 'Will' in Langland, which names a faculty which has the power of distinguishing individuality, and which also names the subject who writes, as significant as the 'Will' in Shakespeare? But that, of course, assumes that the name 'Will' in the Sonnets (see chapter 4) makes the autobiographical self the subject. Chapter 1 continues with Shakespeare's *Troilus and Cressida*, not so much analysing the play, but finding in it definitions of the will, in relation to affect, the affections, and appetite.

Chapter 2 examines the comedies, beginning with Portia, in *The Merchant of Venice*, who, faced with the will of a dead father, does not circumvent this, but uses it, in an exercise of her own will, which both strengthens patriarchy and the bonds that associate Bassanio with her, not Antonio. That use of the will finds ultimate expression with Iago's will, manipulating Othello's: Iago embodies what the chapter concentrates on discussing: how the will, especially in Malvolio, and Malevole in Marston's *The Malcontent*, characteristically means 'ill-will', malevolence, and takes in the malcontented, and discontented, and the melancholic. If the will is ill-will, there is a topic here which is to be further discussed by Nietzsche, as it is in chapter 8.

Chapter 3, on *Measure for Measure*, returns to Romans 7 and considers that play's relationship to both will and law; on the basis that the law is an appetite, and has a will, and that this will brings on sexual desire. Chapter 4 looks at the craft of seduction as this is articulated through *Venus and Adonis*, *The Rape of Lucrece*, the Sonnets, and *A Lover's Complaint*. Here, the will takes its most fleshly force, since seduction is in the realm of the man's will, and the woman's will, so that the will establishes, and overrrides sexual difference. Whereas in *The Rape of Lucrece*, the man rapes the woman, in *Venus and Adonis* a woman attempts seduction of a man, and in the last group of Sonnets (127–54), her will becomes supreme, making the man 'nothing', only 'your what you will'. Pursuit of the will, especially in those Sonnets with a word-play on the (proper) noun 'Will', is pursuit of *das Ding*, which makes all sexual difference – expressed in the terms 'something' and 'nothing' – elusive, making everything of the sexual substitute for something which is nothing.

PART TWO, 'The Posthumous Life of the Will', engages with writers for whom the testamentary will and the personal will overlap: I study the lawyer and the law, and the testamentary will through Trollope, and Dickens (ch. 5), and George Eliot (ch. 6). Trollope's theme is always law and lawyers and an inheritance which must be rightfully secured beyond the death of the testator; his plots, showing him on the side of the will-maker and enforcer, draw out the near-impossibility of doing this. Dickens is absorbed by the force of the testamentary will, which creates a legal fiction entangling those who becomes partners to the suit. In *Bleak House*, they come under the power of Chancery, which supplements the contested will, and has its own power of ruin. But my principal interest is with *Little Dorrit*, where the will as volitional, as sexual and personal, is inseparable from the will as testamentary, and partial, and invidious, inciting to *ressentiment*. Comments on George Eliot run through *The Mill on the Floss*, *Felix Holt*, *Middlemarch*, and, outstandingly, *Daniel Deronda*. Here, lawyers become powerful, expressing a destiny threatening tragedy, while wills and contested inheritances represent the power of 'the dead hand', which is equivalent, in its ruinous effect, to the 'murderous will' of Grandcourt, and Gwendolen Harleth.

28

PART THREE, 'The Will to Truth', stays with the nineteenth century, in a European perspective, as it continues discussion of Schopenhauer, this time specifically on music, as, for him, a will whose power is heard and felt. Chapter 7 shows how the will is evoked through two operas – *Tristan und Isolde*, and *La forza del destino* – from composers who may be taken as giving the hegemonic view of the will within operatic discourse. The will must be refused, but. operatic music, in the aria, or the orchestra, or when both sound together, means the expression of the will *and* its refusal, or transcension. In Wagner, as a sexual power, the will must be renounced, but, ambivalently, as Nietzsche and Freud and Adorno comment. Verdi's opera is read in terms of the unconscious compulsion to repeat which works, as an uncanny will, drive, or destiny. Discussion here gives me most opportunity to discuss Freud's develop-ment of Schopenhauerian thought, through 'The Uncanny' and 'Beyond the Pleasure Principle', essays of 1919.

Chapter 8 examines Nietzsche, first through 'will to power', of which he speaks so affirmatively; this involves consideration of Heidegger's reading of Nietzsche, which I use for considering *Thus Spoke Zarathustra*. I discuss the opposite of the 'will to power': that is, the will's 'ill will' towards time and its 'it was': for Nietzsche the spirit of revenge. Revenge, and its 'spirit', a topic which has been pursued through many texts explored here, is reactive, filled with *ressentiment*, and the will requires the thought of eternal return, to unthink the idea of identity, if this equates with belief in the power of the personal will in all its vengefulness. The chapter concludes by considering Mahler's setting of 'O Mensch', from *Thus Spoke Zarathustra*, in the Third Symphony. It compares it with Delius's setting, in *The Mass of Life*, seeing how some music, post-Nietzsche, contests the will.

Chapter 9, the conclusion, moves from Nietzsche to D.H. Lawrence, in *Women in Love* and to Heidegger on 'the will to will', which is part of his discussion of technology as a wilful power which controls, and enframes. This prompts, in Foucault, the idea of the 'will to knowl-edge' (*la volonté de savoir* – the French title of *The History of Sexuality*), the umbrella title of a series of historical investigations carried out in the 1970s, whose object was to form 'a morphology' of that will.[46] I close with the relationship between the will to truth (Nietzsche) and the will to knowledge (Foucault), asking how there can be resistance to the will, and what that means, and the political and strategic value of such resistance.

PART ONE

THE WILL AND IDENTITY

1

THE WILL
Three Instances

I AUGUSTINE

Can there be a history of the will? While there is no discrete entity which we can call 'the will' – we are all the time dealing in concepts which have been historically produced – there are interlocking issues which show that the term can be probed through looking at its changing uses in discourse. This chapter concerns three uses, beginning with Augustine (354–430), and continuing with *Piers Plowman* in the fourteenth century, before reaching Shakespeare's *Troilus and Cressida*. In that play, the will has no single meaning, but rather absorbs everything affectual, as well as everything that might be thought of as other to the will: wit, or any process of cognition. Yet at the same time, it becomes that which creates subjectivity, or a sense of self, which was a sense already implicit in Augustine's *Confessions*.

Aristotle had considered *boulesis*, wanting, or willing, but concluded that rational choice (*proairesis*) would apply, in the sphere of the possible. Willing did not oppose reason: Aristotle thought that Socrates believed that someone could only do wrong out of ignorance. Aristotle was interested in *akrasia*, lack of control (*kratos*, power), and so recognised a tension between knowing something and willing it.[1] Yet the Greeks did not have a word for the will; choice was rational.[2] But, as the concept of evil seems to be Stoic and Christian, so that performing a deed now shows – because of the deed's nature – the quality of the person, so the idea of the will seems to be Roman, with *libera voluntas* appearing first in Lucretius (*De rerum naturam*, 2.251–93). Christianity contains the idea of the will as that which can be overridden: Christ can pray 'not my will [*thelema*] but thine be done' (Luke, 22.42).[3] But by the time of

33

Augustine, the will, both double and split, is central; as in *De libero arbitrio voluntatis* ('On the Free Choice of the Will).[4]

In the *Confessions* (397) Augustine accepted the view, against the Manichees, who wished to limit the unitary power of God by positing a race of darkness in opposition to God, that 'we do evil because we choose to do so of our own free will':

> I knew that I had a will . . . when I chose to do something or not to do it, I was quite certain that it was my own self and not some other person, who made this act of will, so that I was on the point of understanding that herein lay the cause of my sin. If I did anything against my will, it seemed to me to be something which happened to me rather than something which I did, and I looked upon it not as a fault, but a punishment.[5]

Though Augustine proposes the will as the mind-set which determines actions, there is still an 'I' outside the will, who dictates to it, and is not identical to it; something beyond the will decides on an action, different from the will, and says 'I will', or says 'I have no will'. This I who speaks is different from the 'I' inside the sentence 'I will'. The point is familiar from Benveniste's linguistics.[6] Grammar opens up a split in the subject, a lack of the unitary. The will of which the 'I' speaks names that which may be other in himself, which cannot be brought under control. Book 8 of the *Confessions* has been called 'the book of *voluntas*'.[7] Here he undertakes a re-reading of St Paul, and thinking of the will as divided. He cannot imitate the Christian hero Victorinus, whose life was narrated by Simplicianus – who had baptized Ambrose in 374, when he became Bishop of Milan (8.2). Augustine writes:

> I was held fast, not in fetters clamped upon me by another, but by my own will, which had the strength of iron chains. The enemy held my will in his power and from it he had made a chain and shackled me. For my will was perverse and lust had grown from it, and when I gave in to lust habit was born, and when I did not resist the habit it became a necessity. These were the links which together formed what I have called my chain, and it held me fast in the duress of servitude. But the new will which had come to life in me and made me wish to serve you freely and enjoy you, my God . . . was not yet strong enough to overcome the old, hardened as it was by the passage of time.

So these two wills within me, one old, one new, one the servant of the flesh, the other of the spirit, were in conflict and between them they tore my soul apart. From my own experience I now understood what I had read, that *the impulses of nature and the impulses of the spirit are at war with one another*. (*Confessions*, 8.5.164)

This passage thinks of two wills, one of the flesh, one of the spirit; the Pauline quotation running: 'for the flesh lusteth against the Spirit, and the Spirit against the flesh, and these are contrary the one to the other, so that ye cannot do the things that ye would' (Galatians, 5.17). Augustine aligns his 'true self' with his new will, which cannot, however, defeat his old will; unlike Paul, he seems to think of two wills at work in the inward parts; because the first will has been corrupted by sin. A cento of quotations leads to Romans 7.22.24–25:

It was in vain that *inwardly I applauded your disposition* when that other *disposition in my lower self raised war against the disposition of my conscience and handed me over as a captive to that disposition towards sin, which my lower self contained*. For the rule of sin is the force of habit, by which the mind is swept along and held fast even against its will, yet deservedly, because it fell into the habit of its own accord. *Pitiable creature that I was, who was to set me free from a nature thus doomed to death? Nothing else than the grace of God, through Jesus Christ our Lord*. (8.5.165)

The force of habit, engendered by the old will, drags down the unwilling mind. Yet that will is at fault, in assenting to the practices of the old habits ('I become prey to my habits which hold me fast' – 10.40, 249). Discussion of the will resumes, in this eighth book, four chapters later, when meditating on the idea of the mind giving an order and the body responding, or the mind ordering, yet the mind not responding:

[The mind] gives the order only in so far as it wills, and in so far as it does not will the order is not carried out. For the will commands that an act of will should be made, and it gives this command to itself, not to some other will. The reason, then, why the command is not obeyed is that it is not given with the full will. For if the will were full, it would not command itself to be full, since it would be so already. It is therefore no strange phenomenon partly to will to do something and partly to will not to do it. It is a disease of the mind, which does not wholly rise to the heights where it is lifted up by the truth, because it is weighed down by habit. So there are two wills in us, because neither by itself is the whole will, and each possesses what the other lacks. (8.9.172)

Augustine has changed the model: there are not two complete wills but there is an internal split within the will, whose orders to itself are not carried out. The 'I' speaks about these from a position of surveillance. The split will does not correspond to a split between the flesh and the spirit, but is part of the reasoning process of the self, and comprises its affectual state.

De Civitate Dei Book 15 returns to the flesh/spirit antithesis, and speaks about 'emotional disturbances of the mind' (desire, fear, joy, grief) which originate with the body, equated with the flesh. Augustine says that the sinful soul has made the flesh corruptible, then, further, that sin happens by an act of will.[8] It is not that the body is sinful; that is the Manichean view which makes duality basic to the spiritual universe, and which Augustine rejects. Nor does he accept the neo-Platonic sense, expressed in Plotinus (following the Stoics) that freedom means getting away from the necessity of choice which comes from how the passions impose themselves, and that it ends in a passionless state (compare 14.8). Instead, the question for Augustine is the nature of the will in relation to the affects. *De Civitate Dei*, 14.6, makes the will an affect, having power over other affects:

> The important factor in those affects is the character of a man's will. If the will is wrongly directed, the affects will be wrong; if the will is right, the affects will be not only blameless, but praiseworthy. The will is engaged in all of them; in fact they are all essentially acts of will. For what is desire or joy but an act of will in agreement with what we wish for? And what is fear or grief but an act of will in disagreement with what we reject? We use the term desire when this agreement takes the form of the pursuit of what we wish for, while joy describes our satisfaction in the attainment. In the same way, when we disagree with something we do not wish to happen, such an act of will is fear; but when we disagree with something which happens against our will, that act of will is grief. (14.6.555–56)

The passage continues that anyone who is evil is so from a 'perversion of nature', by which Augustine means a perverse will.[9] The will, then, is the source of the evil; as an affect it directs other affects. The punishment for the will, however, is lust, which does not accept the bidding of the will; sexual arousal refuses to be a servant to the will (14.16.577); so that if 'the will' names the sexual organs, here the will is divided against the will, a state which Rochester describes in his poem 'The Fall', and contrasts with the created state of Adam and Eve, and their sexual existence: 'Enjoyment waited on desire / Each member did their wills obey'.[10]

II 'FIAT VOLUNTAS DEI': *PIERS PLOWMAN*[11]

The thirteenth-century rediscovery of Aristotle in the West posed a contrast between those Augustinians, who considered the will, however split, as decisive in actions, and the new Aristotelians, including Thomas Aquinas, who gave precedence to reason over will as controlling action. For Augustine, *incontinentia* was lack of chastity, as the use of *continentia* in 'Give me chastity and continence, but not yet' suggests *Confessions* 8.7.169; now it translated *akrasia* as akin to an intellectual failure.[12] Tensions were high: Tempier's Augustinian condemnations of the Aristotelianism of the West on 10 December 1270, which took in Averroes and parts of Aquinas, included rejection of the idea that the will, because it is passive, cannot alter a decision made by the intellect. This was the view that the will is moved of necessity by the object that is desired; it chooses under compulsion. The will was much more an active agent for an Augustinian theologian, who would have felt that 'Aristotle's ethical theory was to some extent incompatible with the Christian doctrines of freedom, sin, and moral responsibility' (Saarinen, 147–48). In the fourteenth century, the Franciscan Duns Scotus (c.1266–1308) placed the will above the intellect, in direct contrast to Aquinas, and so did all Franciscans. For Duns Scotus, 'the will commanding the intellect is the superior cause of its action. The intellect, however, if it is the cause of volition, is a subservient cause to the will' and 'the total cause of willing in the will is the will'.[13]

In *The Crisis of Will in Piers Plowman*, John Bowers looks at William Langland's allegorical poem *Piers Plowman* (c.1360–80).[14] Langland's work is existent in several versions, A, B, C and Z, but little about these texts is certain here, even which version comes first, or which last, and it is hardly possible, even, to use one version without needing to evoke another: I use the C version, but refer to B. Bowers argues that the name 'Will' should be taken both autobiographically, and allegorically, as the power of *Voluntas*. This for him means that the poem engages with the debates in the fourteenth century about the affective and cognitive powers of the Will, and as a quality in the Dreamer.

The view accords with that of Janet Coleman, whose work on the *Pelagiani moderni*, the philosophers of the fourteenth century, such as the Franciscan William of Ockham (d.1349) and the Dominican Robert Holcot (d. 1349), in contrast to the Augustinian Thomas Bradwardine (c.1290–1349), stresses their voluntarism, their belief that acts of the will were the only ones which could be judged virtuous or vicious, and hence the importance of reason guiding the will.[15] (All three, we may note incidentally, probably died of the Plague, alongside so many others.) Bradwardine's opponents were, for him, modern Pelagians, recalling Augustine's disagreements with Pelagius, because like him they minimised the role of grace, and elevated human will above Divine Will, which decides.[16] Here the Dreamer, who narrates, and who goes through visions which relate to the politics and religious life of the fourteenth century, is called Will, which on Bowers' reading unites the allegorical and a suggestion of the autobiographical, though perhaps 'unites' may not do justice to the non-single nature of whoever, or whatever it is, is called Will.[17]

In the Prologue, and the subsequent 22 books ('Passus') into which the poem is divided, the dreamer passes through eight dream-states, and becomes more and more the subject of the poem himself, as it increases in introspection. The poem becomes increasingly a question of how he can save his soul, which is the question he asks at the beginning (C.1.80). A lovely lady of learning, Holy churche, comes down from the Castle of Truth and 'calde me by name / And sayde, "Wille, slepestou?"' (C.1, 4, 5). In the A and B versions, she calls him 'sone'; but the C version gives a new attention to the name and so perhaps to its allegorical significance; and since she asks if he has been sleeping, perhaps the point is that he suffers from lack of will-power, like those on earth that 'wilneth no better' (C.1.8). This is the Passus where salvation is said to be for the person:

Who is trewe of his tonge and of his two handes
And dothe the werkes therwith and wilneth no man ylle. (C.1.84, 85)

– the man whose will has no ill-will. The poem develops into an account of a pilgrimage, which is led by Piers the Plowman. Before he goes on pilgrimage, he writes his 'biqueste" (C.8.94–111), an act which seems to have been a common practice before making such journeys. In a way the writing of the will, with the surrender this implies, is the first action that has to be taken in the saving of the soul. Such a surrender finds a complement in the voluntary poverty which is assumed by Will, and which seems to be enjoined in the poem.[18]

Will is so named more than once. In Passus 6, the figure of Repentance 'rehersede his teme [a text for a sermon]/ And made Wille to wepe water with his eyes' (6.1–2). This precedes the confession made by the Seven Deadly Sins, one after another, ending with Sloth. In Passus 10, the third of the eight visions begins, with the Dreamer walking out and sleeping. In dreaming:

> A muche man, as me thoghte ylike to myselue,
> Cam and calde me be my kynde name.
> 'What art thow?' quod y, 'that thow my name knowest?
> 'That wost thou, Wille,' quod he, 'and no wyht bettere.'
>
> (10.68–71)

This can be paraphrased: a tall man comes by, like himself, as if he is a mirror-image of him, and calls him by his own name, or his natural name. The 'natural name' could suggest the will (*voluntas*) as the name of one of the powers of the soul, alongside Reason (*ratio*).[19] When the Dreamer asks him who he is, that he should know his name, the tall man says that he knows already, no-one better, and then says that he is Thought, a personification of one part, or faculty, of the Dreamer.

That the dreamer may think of himself as tall ('muche') is also evidenced from an autobiographical section unique to the C text, 5.1–103, though noticeably, there is no specific mention of the name 'Will' there. In that passage, the 'I' of the poem justifies his apparent sloth to an audience of Conscience and Reason, by saying:

> Y am to wayke to worche with sykel or with sythe
> And to long lef me, lowe to stoupe. (C.5.23–24)
> [I am too weak to work with sickle or scythe, and too tall, believe me, to stoop low.][20]

39

He says that he lives both as a wandering mendicant, and by praying for the souls of the living and dead:

> The lomes that y labore with and lyflode deserue
> Is *pater-noster* and my prymer, *placebo* and *dirige*,
> And my sauter som tyme and my seuene psalmes.
> This y segge for here soulses of suche as me helpeth . . . (C.5.45–48)
> [The tools that I labour with and deserve my livelihood by are the
> *pater-noster* [Our Father] and my primer [a basic private prayer-book],
> *placebo* [Vespers for the dead] and *dirige* [two sets of offices, for Matins
> and Lauds], and my Psalter sometimes, and my seven Psalms [the
> Penitential Psalms]. This I say for the souls of such as help me.]

Insofar as he lives by the money left in wills to set up prayers for the dead, to see them through Purgatory, he has indeed the character of the Will, even if he is not so named.

In Passus 10, already referred to, the function of Thought is to lead Will to see Wit: in the B text, Thought says 'Here is Wil wolde wit if Wit koude teche' (B.15.127). Wit is presented here as the force of reason which goes beyond Thought, and Will wants to, desires to, wills to know ('wit') if Wit would teach him. Indeed, 'Wit' is an alternative reading for Reason in C.5.6.[21]

To what extent Will possesses will-power is in question, since, according to Bowers, this Dreamer seems prone to *acedia*, sloth, the affectual state which comes about from a failure of the will; from a loss of will-power. So 'Sleuthe' follows the language of the 'I' when he says 'Y may nat wel stande ne stoupe ne withouten a stoel knele' (C.6.3, perhaps evoking C.5.24), and quotes the proverbial line 'Heu michi, quod sterilem duxi vitam iuunenilem' (C.7.55) – 'Ah me, what a useless life I led in my youth – words which Holy churche quotes to the Dreamer about himself' (C. 1.140). *Acedia*, though in a non-abstract sense, has a powerful part to play in the poem, and 'accidie' appears in 6.417 to describe the sloth that Gluttony falls into when he is full. The danger within *acedia* is of 'Wanhope' – Despair. So the character 'False' (Favel = deceit) assembles people together:

> Glotonye a gyueth hem and grete othes togederes,
> Al day to drynke at diuerse tauernes
> And there to iangele and to iape and iuge here emcristene

And fastyng-dayes to frete before noone and drynke
With spiserye, speke ydelnesse, in vayne speke and spene
And sue forth such felawschipe till they ben falle in slewthe
And awake with wanhope and no wille to amende
For a leueth be lost when he his lyf leteth. (C.2. 96–104)
[He gives them gluttony, and great oaths together, to drink all day
at different taverns, and there to laugh and trick and judge their
fellow-Christians, and on fast-days to eat before noon, and drink with
spices, to speak idleness, and in vain speak and spend, and follow such
fellowship until they have fallen into sloth, and wake with despair
and no will to amend, believing they are lost when they let go of life.]

The 'cure' for the lack of will in Will is the power of reason, or of wit,
and the text makes the cure for sloth more important than, for
instance, the power of lechery, which Bowers (83–84) finds to be
played down by the poem; implying, then, that the sexual nature of the
Will is less evident in this text than in either Augustine, or in
Shakespeare's sense of being named Will. Though Will fails – so that
there is a lack in his name – *acedia* does not have the rich sense it has
of melancholia, or of a sense of subjectivity in ruins; it is more physical than that. However, the sense of a growing madness in the poem,
in the character of Will himself and what he praises, is noteworthy,
and seems to go beyond Wit.[22]

The point intersects with the reading given by Nicolette Zeeman, in
Piers Plowman and the Medieval Discourse of Desire. This is optimistic about
the power of the will, quoting approvingly Holcot's idea of 'doing what
is in you', as a remedy for the way the will has been wounded.[23] She reads
desire as synonymous with the will, as being that which the poem
supports, so 'what interests Langland is how one desire turns into
another, how you might use one desire to inculcate another one'.[24] This
gives power both to the will and the ability of the subject to shape desire,
but if it is essential that the 'will' is rightly ordered, then the increasing
place given to folly and to madness, which isolates the figure of Will,
and makes the poem move further and further away, in narrative terms,
from any resolution – leaving everything in a state of desire – also works
in contradiction to that. It makes the poem non-unified as a structure,
optimistic, but also with a negative sense that there is nothing but
desire. Zeeman accepts the existence of a 'medieval dyad of cognition
and volition/affect' (67), which opposes will and wit to each other. Like

Bowers, she notes the importance of Free Will in the poem; in C, the personification *Anima* from the B text is replaced by *Liberium Arbitrium* (C.16.157).[25] But that reading of the Will, which makes the human perfectible, is contested by another, more Augustinian, reading which the poem also acknowledges. Zeeman cites the Augustine of *Confessions* 8.5, which I have already quoted, and sees that Augustine uses the word *voluntas* for 'all kinds of desire, both spiritual and carnal, reinforcing the possibility of confusing distinct models of reason and will'.[26] Perhaps the problem is that 'the will' may be a catachresis, covering whatever there is of desire, where, if we follow Freud, even the distinction between the carnal and spiritual involves a repression. Perhaps the distinction between will and reason, so important for thinking after 1270, cannot be maintained; the rational being also a will.

At times, it may be that the will is the 'the hidden inner life of the whole soul' (Zeeman, 92), and at that point, it seems right to identify it with 'desire'. But the text's engagement with issues of salvation, which are worked through intellectually, and with an interest in right naming, which associate with the allegorical mode, seem to sever it from 'desire' as appetite. Except that this has been sublimated into intellectual curiosity. Zeeman makes sharp use of Lacan in *The Ethics of Psychoanalysis*, on how 'illicit desire can underpin, be screened by, turn into the sublime' (32), and she quotes Lacan on how sublimation 'raises an object to the dignity of the "Thing"' (quoting *Ethics of Psychoanalysis* 112). 'Lacan notes too that this logic continues to work in more "advanced" ethical and "mystical" contexts, where guilt is felt even more intensely, but has, as a result, an even more sanctifying effect' (Zeeman, 32–33). I demur in not wanting to assimilating the sublime with Lacanian sublimation, which has to do with recognising the obscene form of desire, which is even present in the Law, but less so in *Piers Plowman*. Perhaps that is what Zeeman means when she finds the text less 'visceral' than others; it suggests that this text of the will (a) concentrates on a lack of will, rather than on its overplus, (b) that it sublimates much of its interest into an intellectual curiosity, directed towards reason as an other of the will, and (c) that its elements of folly, and of directionlessness, are fascinating ways in which desire expresses itself; subjectivity appearing in the very moment of desire as longing, and in the subject losing an ordered place which would guarantee identity.

III *TROILUS AND CRESSIDA*

TROILUS: This is the monstruosity in love, lady, that the will is infinite, and the execution confined; that the desire is boundless, and the act a slave to limit.

CRESSIDA: They say all lovers swear more performance than they are able, and yet reserve an ability that they never perform.

$$(3.2.79-85)^{27}$$

Troilus and Cressida was called 'the history of Troilus and Cressida' in the Stationers' Register of 1609 while the first Quarto called it a comedy and the Folio a tragedy. However we designate it, it was probably written and performed at the end of 1601. It is the only Shakespeare play where the heroine proves untrue – in contrast to Portia, or Rosalind, or Viola, or Desdemona, the women of chapter 2 – and it is nearly the only play with an actual cuckold, Menelaus, as opposed to figures whose jealousy make them think they have been cuckolded: for example, Bassanio and Gratiano, at the end of *The Merchant of Venice*, or Othello.[28]

In the quotation above, Troilus, about to sleep with Cressida, thinks of the will as to be paralleled with desire. The will is infinite, the desire boundless; just so, he parallels the execution and the act. He idealises will and desire, marking a contrast between the will and the sexual, as though the first was an ideal form which cannot be matched, either in sexual terms, or in everyday actions. Cressida's reply, which de-idealises, negates the power of either the will, or the desire, by saying that it is a matter of rhetoric, swearing over the limit. Yet lovers reserve an ability they never exhibit: the will, or desire, is never acted out in terms of performance (her word picks up from Troilus' 'act'); there is always more than appears; there is a reserve in their 'ability' (which may be a synonym for will, or desire). Both lovers are thinking of the limits of sexual performance, but neither mean that exclusively. Cressida, in particular, draws attention to a limitation which the will imposes on itself so that it never gives itself completely. She has already said of herself in relation to Troilus, 'Yet hold I off' (1.2.291). The swearing of lovers goes over the limit, but their reserve puts them under the limit. The will, or desire, is boundless in one way but in another way, it does not extend that far, being a slave to 'limit'. And, as Cressida implies, lovers lack the will to do that they say they have.

But the idealising/non-idealising dichotomy between Troilus and

Cressida will not hold, for the will is sexual in character, as when Hector argues that the Trojans should return Helen to the Greeks. His brother Troilus urges that she should be kept, in spite of the reasons that can be offered to let her go, and he will not hear of reason:

> Manhood and honour
> Should have hare hearts, would they but fat their thoughts
> With this crammed reason. Reason and respect
> Make livers pale and lustihood deject.
> HECTOR: Brother, she is not worth what she doth cost
> The holding.
> TROILUS: What's aught but as 'tis valued?
> HECTOR: But value dwells not in particular will.
> It holds his estimate and dignity
> As well wherein 'tis precious of itself
> As in the prizer. 'Tis mad [Folio: made] idolatry
> To make the service greater than the god;
> And the will dotes that is attributive [Folio: inclinable]
> To what infectiously itself affects
> Without some image of th'affected merit.
> TROILUS: I take today a wife, and my election
> Is led on in the conduct of my will;
> My will enkindled by mine eyes and ears,
> Two traded pilots 'twixt the dangerous shores
> Of will and judgement. How may I avoid –
> Although my will distaste what it elected –
> The wife I chose? There can be no evasion
> To blench from this and stand firm by honour.
> (*Troilus and Cressida*, 2.2.47–67)

What unites Troilus' perception of the will being limited by act and what Hector says of it is evident. In both speeches, the will is unrelated to reality; over-capacious and idealising for Troilus, for Hector, doting, in taking no regard of how much is within the person doted upon. Troilus' speeches with Hector reject reason, in the name of 'honour': the Trojans', and his. Reason is like an over-fatty meat, which can only make fat the thoughts, and put the person out of condition, and out of courage: because it is 'crammed', that suggests people are force-fed with it. Hector tries puncturing his rhetoric with a comment on Helen as not

44

worth what she costs, to which Troilus responds in subjective mode: nothing is worth anything except as someone chooses to value it. Hector replies that *anything* has an inherent value, that value lies not in 'particular will'. In contrast to an assessment reached by what he would have to call the general will, Hector speaks of the will, as meaning the individual desire which has decided it 'affects' something, in contrast to that reason which has a sense of the objective worth of what has been valued. Hector calls it idolatry when the object is worshipped more than it is worth. The will is foolish (it dotes) which attributes value to such an object which has been made a fetish (a word which *OED* cites first from 1613); it has infected itself into liking (affecting) something when it lacks some image of the merit which it likes.

The will as infected, and as infecting the affect contrasts with Troilus' sense of what reason does to the person who fats his thoughts with it; both brothers use images of being put out of condition. Yet while Hector sounds like the voice of material reason, ironically, at the end of the scene he wants to keep the war going; he is actually arguing with Troilus against his own convictions, illustrating his own wilfulness.

The will that dotes is 'attributive' (Quarto) or 'inclinable' to what it affects or infects itself with. Alice Walker's annotation says that if the will is attributive, it is prepared to pay tribute to something, staying in 'service' to it (ln. 58); if is inclinable, it is prepared to bow down to something. Palmer takes the Quarto's 'attributive' as meaning 'bestowing or ascribing the qualities which are admired' on the beloved. Muir follows this, accepting also 'inclinable', as meaning 'prejudiced', though an 'inclination' may be an euphemism for the will. Bevington follows the Folio 'inclinable', paraphrasing: 'the will is besotted that attaches itself in a mutually contagious way to the object it desires without any appearance of demonstrable merit in that object'. He adds that 'infectiously', first cited here (*OED*), means 'both "so as to infect" and "as if infected"'. The language implies a circular reciprocity. '"Attributive" . . . suggests that the will is besotted when it attributes to the desired object certain qualities which it then morbidly admires and wishes to have' (361). The will's affect has been infected, or it allows its affect to infect itself: an infection and an affection are the same, as the will and the affect seem to be the same, while 'affects' as a verb also suggests 'pretends', as in describing someone as 'affected', i.e. insincere, striking a pose.

Troilus replies with an example which uses 'will' three times, and which is ironical here: a man must maintain his wife even if later he rebels against his choice (no wonder the Greeks must try to retrieve Menelaus' wife). He begins with the will – wilfulness, not reason – making an election of the choice of wife, and then confirming the sense that the will is inferior to reason by saying that it is enflamed by his eyes and ears, his senses, which he calls 'two traded pilots between the dangerous shores / Of will and judgement'. 'Will' and 'reason' are now opposed, like opposite river-banks. Whereas 'will' was idealised by being associated with 'election', now eyes and ears are 'traded pilots', going between them, like a pander. Significantly, the agents of the senses are these 'traded pilots'; they are already on the side of the will, which has been sexually infected, enkindled, as with Troilus' words when anticipating Cressida: 'I am giddy, expectation whirls me round' (3.3.16). Eyes and ears must subvert reason, or to keep it quiet, for the will has already committed itself. Hector thought of the will as doting when it had no image of the beloved person; Troilus attempts to countermand this idea by making eyes and ears agents of sense, not judgement. The self-delusion appeared in Demetrius in *A Midsummer Night's Dream*, when, under the influence of 'love in idleness' he reverts to his love for Helena:

> The will of man is by his reason swayed,
> And reason says you are the worthier maid. (*MND*, 2.2.121–22)

It seems wrong that anyone should think the will is under the control of reason, though that is Aquinas' view, but it is not reason which is telling Demetrius he loves Helena.

It becomes more strange that Troilus should then think of the will distasting, rejecting, but in a physical way, what it chose, in the spirit of what Ulysses says: 'the present eye praises the present object' (3.3.174), because for Troilus the will cannot change its mind, being bound to 'honour', which means little more than self-estimation. Helen, the 'wife' who is no wife amongst the Trojans, may not be worth anything, may be 'distasted', but 'honour' comes in to prop up the will. Indeed, 'honour', as paired with 'manhood', and opposed to 'reason and respect', seems to be synonymous with the self-idealising will, hence the praise of 'honour and renown' (2.2.200).

Later, but before saying that he also wants to keep Helen, Hector sums up the cause for the war, starting with the idea of Nature 'craving', but then saying that Nature's craving (an expression suggesting its powerful appetite, or will) is actually also to be called a 'law', which should be opposite to 'appetite':

> Nature craves
> All dues be render'd to their owners: now
> What nearer debt in all humanity
> Than wife is to the husband? If this law
> Of nature be corrupted through affection,
> And that great minds, of partial indulgence
> To their benumbed wills, resist the same,
> There is a law in each well-ordered nation
> To curb those raging appetites that are
> Most disobedient and refractory. (2.2.174–81)

What Nature craves seems to be corrupted through affection – through the expression of the will as an appetite. That brings out a further ambiguity: should the emphasis be put on the *law* of nature, or on the law of *nature*? The first implies order; the second no order at all, only what Ulysses calls 'appetite, a universal wolf' (1.3.121). The second brings out the point that nature 'craves': perhaps marriage is institutionalised craving. So the craving, which shows itself as the law of nature, is corrupted by further 'affection', the word going back to the complex of associations in the statement 'the will dotes that is attributive / To what it infectiously itself affects' and in calling the merit that is loved 'th'affected merit'. The 'merit' may be a synecdoche for the person, or whatever in the person is desired, but 'affected' also suggests that the merit has been infected, poisoned. As with an 'affect', it is impossible to say whether the quality sought is in the person desired, or working in the person who desires. 'Affection' means love, liking, feeling, and infection.

But marriage is not the law of nature, but of societies, well-ordered nations. Bevington annotates 'affection' as 'appetite', another word used by Hector. While similar, 'raging appetites' seems stronger than 'affection'. Hector's words may be paraphrased: that the law can be broken through 'affection', meaning desire, or affect, and an exaggerated and affected disposition (perhaps towards the 'affected merit'), and great minds may resist the law of nature either because they have indulged a paralysed will, or because their will, insentient ('benumbed', a word only here in Shakespeare, and meaning not listening to anything else) gives partial (prejudiced) indulgence to resistance to the law of nature. 'Indulgence', Bevington says, implies 'remission of the punishment which is still due to sin after sacramental absolution', in other words, either the mind, or the will, says that there is no penalty to be paid if the law is resisted. It becomes apparent that the 'affection' and the 'will' may exist in apposition to each other, or may be identified with each other. Hector's argument assumes that there is a primary natural allegiance to marriage, and that appetites should naturally be subservient to marriage as a law of nature. But if the power of law as a natural principle in each person may be corrupted through affection, that would be because, as Cressida says, when separated from Troilus, it refuses to 'be moderate':

> The grief is fine, full, perfect that I taste,
> And violenteth in a sense as strong
> As that which causeth it. How can I moderate it?
> If I could temporize with my affection,
> Or brew it to a weak and colder palate,
> The like allayment could I give my grief. (4.4.3–8)

Cressida sees her grief in terms of 'taste', and it 'violenteth'. That is a neologism which is annotated as 'rages', but which implies the violence of vomiting; certainly her reaction is as violent as the cause of her grief. She cannot dilute her 'affection', ('propensity' or 'bent' – Palmer), to suit a colder 'palate' (a synonym of 'affection'), but the speech is full of her will, as the repeated 'I' suggests; the affection being its forceful expression.

Troilus responds to Hector by saying that it is 'glory' which is 'affected' by the Trojans (2.3.196). Glory – honour – is desired, willed, an appetite; and as 'affected' it is also a show, an affectation. Hector's speech assumes that law as a social phenomenon can 'curb' raging appetites which are 'most disobedient and refractory'. In chapter 2, the word 'curb' will be discussed more fully, in relation to Portia's language in *The Merchant of Venice* 5.1. For now, to move from a law of nature to a law of nations only increases division within the self; affection resists the first, but the law may only make things worse, bringing about 'raging appetites' which are 'most disobedient', actively so, as opposed to being controlled by 'benumbed wills'.

But the law is, in any case, itself an appetite, as appears in Ulysses' speech to the Greeks, following Agamemnon's comments on the trials that Jove sends to find 'persistive constancy', something missing throughout this play; 'distinction' works to separate the grain and the chaff (1.3.20, 27). Ulysses says that the reason Troy has not yet fallen is because of the failure to maintain 'order', or 'degree', resulting in the loss of justice:

> Then everything includes itself in power,
> Power into will, will into appetite;
> And appetite, an universal wolf,
> So doubly seconded with will and power,
> Must make perforce a universal prey,
> And last eat up himself. (1.3.119–24)

'Power' means the rule of the strongest, being the property of those who can assert their will, while 'will' expresses itself as appetite or desire. This, aided by will and power, consumes everything before devouring itself. Not only does power become the will which becomes the appetite, creating a powerful wilful appetite, but appetite, brought in by pre-existing will and law finds itself seconded by them, given legitimacy by a will reinforced by power. Power has become will, which means law. And appetite now has, as seconded by will and power, the force of law.[29]

Nestor notes Hector's fighting skills, 'Dexterity so obeying appetite / That what he wills he does' (5.5.27–28), which virtually equates will and appetite, suggesting that Hector's will is supplemented by his doing (his dexterity). This increase of power, enabling act, contrasts with Troilus' speech, quoted at the beginning, on the disparity between will/execution, desire/action, or Paris feeling that he has not as ample power to oppose the Greeks as he has will (2.2.141). But behind Ulysses' abstractions is resentment about a transfer of 'power', which for him means that the rest of the Grecian army, who are led by Achilles and Patroclus, respect neither degree, nor the commanders' dignity. Thersites, the bastard malcontent, satirises the state of affairs in the Grecian camp. Malcontented, marked by ill-will, he speaks nine prose soliloquies out of the play's fourteen.[30] He complains of being ordered by Ajax, saying 'I serve here voluntary'. Achilles replies: 'Your last service was suff'rance – 'twas not voluntary, no man is beaten voluntary: Ajax was here the voluntary, and you as under an impress' (2.1.96-99). Nonetheless, this figure of discontent is the 'privileged' fool (2.3.60), and he amuses Achilles and Patroclus, who take him over from Ajax. Legitimate power, for Ulysses, has slipped away from the Grecian leaders to others. Hence, Ulysses' next speech is not abstract, but angry, the expression of a man who feels that will-power belongs where it should not, hence the resentment, directed at Achilles' satire of the generals, which shows that a loss of respect is infectious, so much so that even Ajax – the Greeks' stooge – has become 'self-willed' (1.3.188).

Ulysses' anger is that the power of the will belongs with the people, not the commanders; he is self-interestedly angry about the absence of law, and 'degree'. Nestor agrees, saying that Ulysses has discovered 'the fever whereof all our power is sick' (1.3.139). The 'fever' is the power of the will; Achilles, the most anarchic and vicious person in the play shows it most: Ulysses says that Achilles makes himself his own law, he:

> carries on the stream of his dispose
> Without observance or respect of any,
> In will peculiar and in self-admission. (2.3.165–67)

The cause for the power of appetite, for Ulysses, is envy.[31] The appetite which is a universal wolf is envious in the way that it produces the breakdown of order: 'every step / Exampled by the first pace that is sick / Of his superior, grows to an envious fever / Of pale and bloodless emulation' (1.3.131–34). Envy and emulation are identified; the will emerges from envy, and produces it, as Thersites is a 'core of envy', a 'box of envy' (5.1.4, 24), not to be identified with. He gives himself away when he says 'the vengeance on the whole camp – or rather the Neapolitan bone-ache, for that methinks is the curse depending on those that war for a placket. I have said my prayers, and devil Envy say "Amen"' (2.3.18–22). His envy takes the form of thinking that there is nothing else but warring over a 'placket'; it is not so much Helen who is fought over, but the opportunity she gives for 'honour and renown', for the opportunity of displaying some mark of difference, which, of course, collapses within the play. 'Emulation', which implies competition, ambition and rivalry, appears in this play the most times of any in Shakespeare, while the word 'emulous', is virtually confined to this play.[32] Emulation dictates the competitive relationship between the Greeks and the Trojans, and cuts out 'degree', so that 'the enterprise is sick' (1.3.101–3). This is Ulysses' political conservatism, and not to be trusted, but emulation marks out everything, including the homosexuality within the play. While Thersites calls Achilles and Patroclus lovers (5.1.13–16), there is a competitive homoeroticism apparent in Achilles' desire to see Hector, 'I have a woman's longing, /An appetite that I am sick withal' (3.3.236–37). Achilles' eroticism, which constructs him as feminine – indeed, like a pregnant woman – is also inseparable in him from envy, since Hector is his rival. The sexual longing is synonymous with the will; in Achilles' speech, appetite is self-divisive in wanting both to eat (as cannibalistic) and to be 'sick'. It tastes and distastes at the same time: it rejects the other, and rejects the part of the self that also desires. As emulative, it is self-hating; it anticipates something in Iago. 'Affection' and 'appetite' and the will are synonymous with the sexual drive, itself inseparable from envy, or emulation. There is an ambivalence within desire: Achilles is passive, as a woman towards Hector, but uses his Myrmidons to kill him when Hector is passive, because unarmed.[33] 'An appetite that I am sick withal' indicates that the will is already plural, and able to comment on its obsession.[34]

Troilus warns Cressida against being tempted sexually by the Greeks. She asks, 'Do you think I will?' He responds:

> No,
> But something may be done that we will not;
> And sometimes we are devils to ourselves,
> When we will tempt the frailty of our powers,
> Presuming on their changeful potency. (4.4.91–95)

'No' followed by 'but' points to self-division, which makes 'no' mean 'yes'. There is another echo here of St Paul: 'the good that I would I do not: but the evil which I would not, that I do' (Romans 7.19). Troilus takes Cressida's word 'will' which was part of a future tense (I will be tempted), and makes it emphatic. 'Do you think I will' versus the sense he gives it: 'we do not will' makes Cressida's speech ambiguous: 'do you think I will to allow myself to be tempted?' Troilus shows that something outside the will makes things to be done, which argues for the will's weakness; and then there are devils within the self which tempt the will. 'The frailty of our powers' is then the equivalent to the will, and means that there is a will, or wills, equivalent to the 'devil' inside the self which presumes on the will's changeful potency; either that its potency is sometimes impotent, or that it has the power to change.

Constancy is not to be expected. Hence Cressida follows Troilus' speech with 'My lord, will you be true?' (4.4.99). She has suddenly realised the force of her own earlier question; she is no longer sure about the power of her will.

The psychoanalytic insight about ambivalence appears in this play in terms of the point that time is split in this play: it is both the time of war, and a time of truce: two contradictory moments. But the times of truce and war are not separate; they run together, so that the love is expressed as hatred and the hatred as love: tasting equals distasting. The talk of the will cannot disguise the point that there is an absence of will, as Troilus fears 'that I shall lose distinction in my joys' (3.2.25). Perhaps by 'distinction' he means 'recognition'; his unique self will not be noticed. Certainly, the fear of loss of 'distinction' – the second of two times this word appears in the play – is the opposite of 'the conduct of my will: / My will enkindled by mine eyes and ears'. Loss of 'distinction' is part of a state which allows Troilus to surrender Cressida, and blame that onto Time:

> Injurious Time, now with a robber's haste
> Crams his rich thievery up, he knows not how;
> As many farewells as there be stars in heaven,
> With distinct breath and consign'd kisses to them,
> He fumbles up into a loose adieu,
> And scants us with a single famish'd kiss,
> Distasted with the salt of broken tears. (4.4.41–47)

The union and separation of the lovers, which happens in one night, hastening a process which would happen anyway, is seen as the effect of Time as a robber; the food-image which begins with the word 'crams', makes the bag, into which the thievery is put, Time's own mouth. The 'many farewells' which he 'fumbles up' into a 'loose adieu' are made indiscriminate, non-differentiated, while 'loose' suggests sexual looseness. Time allows only one single kiss which becomes distasteful at that moment. In Ulysses's speech, already heard, 'Time hath, my lord, a wallet at his back / Wherein he puts alms for oblivion' (3.3.145–46). Time – pronounced 'envious and calumniating' – is personified as a beggar, consuming every thing, like the universal envious wolf, but not richer for it. Its consumption is expressed as 'oblivion', Time eating itself; hence Cressida says, 'when time is old and hath forgot itself . . .

And blind oblivion swallow'd cities up' (3.2.183, 185), and Agamemnon tells Hector that 'what's past and what's to come is strewed with husks / And formless ruin of oblivion' (4.5.165–66). This is indeed loss of distinction, of honour, of those things that the will asserts.

When Troilus sees Cressida with Diomedes, he believes what his heart says, so that he must contradict, or invert, 'th'attest of eyes and ears, / As if those organs had deceptious functions, / Created only to calumniate' (5.2.121–23). Eyes and ears are envious, and as 'traded pilots' they both betray (as traitors) and they trade (as panders, as merchants: Troilus later says that 'crown'd kings' have been turned to 'merchants' (2.2.84)). 'Traitor' and 'trader' have the same etymology. Troilus' speech registers the failure of distinction. Cressida is one 'thing inseparate'; yet she is not that unique thing, but divided:

> O madness of discourse,
> That cause sets up with and against itself!
> Bifold authority! where reason can revolt
> Without perdition, and loss assume all reason
> Without revolt. This is, and is not, Cressid.
> Within my soul there doth conduce a fight
> Of this strange nature, that a thing inseparate
> Divides more wider than the sky and earth;
> And yet the spacious breadth of this division
> Admits no orifex for a point as subtle
> As Ariachne's broken woof to enter.
> [. . .]
> The bonds of heaven are slipp'd, dissolved, and loos'd,
> And with another knot, five-finger tied,
> The fractions of her faith, orts of her love,
> The fragments, scraps, the bits and greay relics
> Of her o'er-eaten faith are given to Diomed. (5.2.141–51, 155–59)

Troilus' speech makes himself as the split subject, between heart/eyes and ears; and Cressida as a figure that 'is and is not'; something and nothing together, and yet while divided, allowing for no point of entry, as a 'placket' would. She is a thing divided more widely than sky and earth, and yet in another way, these things are not divided, since they meet at the fictional, always moving horizon. In another way the thing she is not divided at all; there is no space ('orifex') within her which can be entered. As L.C. Knights says, 'It was a deep non-logical apprehension. . . . that prompted Shakespeare to run together, in [the word] "Ariachne", the subtle filament of the spider and the clew given to Theseus. We ourselves are in this labyrinth or web'.[35] The vaginal labyrinth cannot be entered, but in another way, there is no position outside the labyrinth, and the idea of the web only associates with the female's ability to create that which has the power to entrap, being, however, virtually nothing in its thickness. And the male will which would enter is the broken woof. The 'thing inseparate', one and two, complete yet empty, holds its psychoanalytic sense as *das Ding*. An allusiveness in being is caught in 'this is, and is not, Cressid' (5.2.145), which centres for Troilus the sense of the woman as something and nothing, female and male, as the will which is both female and male; real and unsubstantial at the same time. Honourable and disgraced at the same moment means that the parts which Troilus cannot reconcile – like the Greek and Trojan forces – are different parts of a will dividing the self, making it self-emulous, in an attempt to create distinction; but having the sense that the woman is both the ideal and that which the male must abject violently; that if Diomed gets her love, he is only a mirror of Troilus, who must fight him to attempt to distinguish himself from him; perhaps there is nothing else than Cressida as a fragment which the consuming will tastes and distastes *at the same time*; time being as double as identity and the will, and what is desired and repudiated at once.

The last seven scenes are on the battlefield, fighting for distinction, and end with Troilus 'like a frustrated Malvolio, swearing his revenge'.[36] He ends with the loss of all idealism; his will is the will's ill-will against Time. But the conclusion is Pandarus' epilogue, reflecting on his imminent death as the 'agent' (5.10.36). He speaks to 'traitors and bawds', and then calls them 'traders in the flesh'; recalling the 'traded pilots' who were in the service of the will. His last words are an imagined motto, to hang up in a brothel. He has a gift: 'some two months hence my will shall here be made . . . Till then I'll sweat and seek about for eases / And at that time bequeath you my diseases' (5.10.53, 56–57). The Neapolitan bone-ache is indeed the will, and what it bequeathes. Some commentators have speculated that the 'will' means another play; but whatever testamentary gift is implied in the speech, it cannot be given now, because the prostitutes in the jurisdiction of the Bishop of Winchester might hiss him; he fears their reaction, as already diseased.

The expression of the will as a revenge, the act of a Malvolio is deferred; but an 'ill-will' must become the general infection which is spread abroad as an inheritance in the form of sexual disease which symbolises it.

2

'I'LL BE REVENGED ON THE WHOLE PACK OF YOU'
Shakespeare and Marston

O me, the word 'choose'! I may neither choose who I would nor refuse who I dislike, so is the will of a living daughter curbed by the will of a dead father. Is it not hard, Nerissa, that I cannot choose one, nor refuse none?

(*The Merchant of Venice*, 1.2.19–21)[1]

I THE DAUGHTER'S DISCONTENT

Portia's discontent, and her complaint to Nerissa at the beginning of *The Merchant of Venice*, are expressions of her own will, which is also her resourcefulness. Her complaint focuses on the power of patriarchy, as established all the more when the father is dead, and it gives the three principal meanings of 'will' that are at the heart of this book. One is the will as desire, as firm choice, wilfulness. In which case the word 'choose', which, with its cognates, appears some 48 times in the play, far more than any other by Shakespeare, is a synonym for the will. Or it may be sexual longing, perhaps wilfulness, which makes choice arbitrary. The other meaning is a testament, that which wills, and asserts itself beyond the grave.[2] To these meanings, I add those which have accumulated from the reading of *Troilus and Cressida*.

These two meanings always interact with each other, but the will of the father in this play may also imply his willing, his command, or patriarchy. *The Merchant of Venice* is later than *A Midsummer Night's Dream*, which play begins with Egeus denouncing Hermia, his daughter, for her

56

choice of Lysander, and demanding the law on her, which translates into Theseus' command: 'either prepare to die / For disobedience to your father's will / Or else to wed Demetrius . . . (1.1.86–88). But in this comedy, after the wonders in the wood, Theseus says to Egeus, 'I will overbear your will' (4.1.176). To the will of the father in his lifetime, *The Merchant of Venice* adds his testamentary will. In Portia's perception, one will hurts another; for the will is dual, both inciting and curbing, inciting by curbing.[3]

Nerissa, Portia's confidante, defends 'the lottery' that Portia's dying father devised as a 'good inspiration' in the three 'chests' of gold, silver and lead, by saying 'whereof who chooses his meaning chooses you will no doubt never be chosen by any rightly but one who you shall rightly love' (1.2.24–28). 'Lottery' recalls a similar discussion which opens *As You Like It*, and another reflection on a father's will: it is Orlando thinking of his father's dying charge to Oliver:

> As I remember, Adam, it was upon this fashion bequeathed me by will but poor a thousand crowns, and, as thou sayest, charged my brother on his blessing to breed me well – and there begins my sadness.

Orlando then tells Oliver:

> the spirit of my father grows strong in me, and I will no longer endure it. Therefore allow me such exercises as may become a gentleman, or give me the poor allottery my father left me by testament. (*As You Like It*, 1.1.1–4, 60–63)[4]

The will as testament has been set aside, but the power of the father's will is now felt as a growing strength in Orlando: he wants what has been allotted to him. What is 'allotted' is, according to *OED*, 'distributed in such a way that the recipients have no choice'; the lottery that Portia's father left calls into question whether choice, or will, has any part to play versus chance, a word significantly brought into play alongside choice, as in the couplet presumably written by the father (and therefore having testamentary force), apostrophising the successful suitor: 'You that choose not by the view, / Chance as fair, and choose as true' (3.2.131–32). That may be paraphrased as: have as happy hazards as your choice has made you happy, and choose in your life as truly as you have chosen now. It makes choosing and chancing strangely similar to each other, as everything in this play seems a matter of risking.

In *As You Like It*, if the comma is omitted in the first line, 'I remember Adam' suggests the father as Adam, the prime father, with the prime will. In these comedies, everything begins with the will of the father; Portia has had allotted to her the three caskets which require the suitor to choose the father's meaning: to work out the meaning of a riddle expressed in the caskets and their inscriptions. And so it works out: Portia comments on 'fools' – such as the Prince of Arragon, who has rejected the lead casket, because he will not give or hazard, and the gold because he fears to choose like the 'fool multitude', who only choose by show, and prizes himself on his merit in being able to choose – that 'when they do choose / They have the wisdom by their wit to lose' (2.9.25, 79–80).

Yet despite this observation, which could also apply to Portia if she decided to choose, her original point also remains: she is still the 'living daughter' and not free to refuse the choice that comes to her through the caskets. She does not choose; her will is set going, but is impeded by an anterior will, one that has the force of law, making her a divided subject, and a strange one, aligned with death, as the dead father speaks in the scroll that Bassanio reads. To marry can only be with her father's will, and without her father's will in the matter her fortune would presumably be at risk, because the will of the father is not just over his daughter, but over his own fortune, which he wants to secure in perpetuity. It is noticeable that Jessica, Shylock's daughter, is validated by the play for marrying without her father's will in the matter, and in direct contrast to the 'will of a dead father' to which Portia adheres, Shylock is made – with her collusion – to give half his 'goods' to Jessica and Lorenzo.[5] Freud in his analysis 'The Theme of the Three Caskets' (1913) identifies the lead casket with Portia, with dumbness and with death. That brings out an ambivalence within the woman; it makes Portia ambivalent, as Sarah Kofman argues, because it gives her the power of death.[6] Freud links *The Merchant of Venice* and its three caskets with King Lear and his three daughters; Cordelia, unlike Portia, does not play along with her father's will, which he is making manifest in the opening scene; she chooses 'nothing' in the face of his 'constant will to publish / Our daughters' several dowers' (*King Lear*, 1.1.41–42). But Lear, as blind as the two suitors Morocco and Arragon, does not see the power of death in his daughter, and that refusal keeps him in a revengeful masculine mode from which he is only partially released by madness. In *The Merchant of Venice* the masculine mode is set aside by the inscription of the lead casket, its demand that 'Who chooseth me, must give and hazard all he hath' (2.7.16). Sarah Kofman reads the choice of lead as an acceptance of ambivalence; certainly it requires a refusal of the single will that dominates over the other suitors. Morocco, who says 'Mislike not me for my complexion' (2.1.1), chooses the gold casket because of its complexion, not seeing that all surfaces are double and all realities ambivalent. In the case of King Lear, asserting his single will characterises all his irrational acts.

If Portia cannot choose, nonetheless *The Merchant of Venice* shows her wresting, or taking, authority – will-power – for herself in the face of this law. There are signs of her autonomy in her behaviour with Bassanio when he comes to choose the lead casket. Certainly she does not hold back from revealing her love.[7] She and Nerissa become the male Doctor and the Doctor's clerk, to do what Bassanio and Gratiano cannot do: that is, check the 'will' of Shylock, which Antonio draws on himself – 'Let me have judgement, and the Jew his will' (4.1.83). In the law-court, 'accomplished with that we lack' (3.4.61–62), masculinised as if to equal the father, and occupying a liminal space as in a yet unconsummated marriage, and where, as 'male', she becomes equivalent of the father, she becomes the advocate of mercy (4.1.178–201). But then she becomes the advocate of the law, when Bassanio asks her to 'wrest once the law to your authority; / To do a great right do a little wrong / And curb this cruel devil [Shylock] of his will' (4.1.211–13). But this is not *A Midsummer Night's Dream*, where the will of the father, with its power of law, could be overborne by the word of the ruler. Bassanio's word 'curb' recalls how she spoke about her will in relation to that of her father; and the word 'devil' is aligned with 'will' to suggest where the will originates from. Her will has been curbed, but she will turn that situation into something else by pretending not to curb, but curbing nonetheless, the will of Shylock. The trick that Bassanio wishes her to play as a lawyer she declines to do in the name of law, but then, having led Shylock on to the point where his will is fully manifest, she turns the law upon him, by insisting on its letter being upheld – hence her comment, 'Thou shalt have justice more than thou desirest' (4.1.312). And then she brings in the full will of the law, both in threatening Shylock with death and loss of his goods (4.1.328) and then with another law of Venice which is precisely directed against an 'alien' (4.1.345).

It is justifiable justice against Shylock, except that Portia has created a trap for him to walk into: she could have told him all this as a warning against going further earlier on. Mahood points out that 'like Angelo in *Measure for Measure*, Shylock has willed more evil than he has performed' (18). Antonio is given power to render Shylock mercy, and deals out terms to Shylock which may be construed as measured, but it must be noticed – as one of the indicators that no single reading of this play is possible – that he must, perforce, use the word 'stole' about Lorenzo in relation to Jessica – 'the gentleman / That lately stole his daughter' (4.1.380–81). The word does not flatter the Christians, though it passes without comment. It is hardly possible to feel that things are as fair as they should be, and the same point goes for the condition that Antonio lays down: that Shylock become a Christian. Portia has created a system whereby Shylock is overly punished, and where Antonio enabled to resume the superiority which he showed beforehand over Shylock, and on which Shylock comments, and to which he responds (1.3.98–127).

However neat this justice, it has, in how Portia deploys it, something of a tricking with language such as Lorenzo in another context comments on with 'How every fool can play upon the word' (3.5.36). Is it extravagant to see a response to the will of the father in this subtlety, which plays into the hands of the patriarchate of Venice, and ennobles it, while parodying it, through her adoption, by disguise, of the 'seeming truth that cunning times put on / To deceive the wisest' (3.2.100–1)? She has followed the father to the letter of his will, and it may have secured her the husband she wanted, unless the choice is supposed to be a matter of chance, but she has also assumed an autonomy of her own through the assertion of her own will. She will have asserted both meanings of the word 'will' as it applies to herself in her speech 'O me, the word "choose"'. The victory is the woman's, and it is played out against Shylock in a way which operates most powerfully against him, but it is more than powerful; it is vindictive, reinforcing the point that the Christian position is as vengeful as the system of Judaism it works against. In no sense can a split be made on the basis of law versus mercy, between the Jew and the Christian. Rather Portia's line, 'we do pray for mercy' (4.1.196) acknowledges that one religious system is built on no better premise than the other; both are inadequate, both rely on mercy.

Portia's disposal of Shylock only echoes the way that Jessica stole from her father (5.1.15) disguised as a boy; it is as if Shylock and Portia's dead father are brought into relationship. Portia's trick is succeeded by a further securing of autonomy; the trick with the letter of the law is followed by the ring-trick whereby she presses Bassanio into giving her the ring. It both means that she chooses her husband, retroactively, in the sense that he must come to her on the terms of being forgiven, and it severs Bassanio from the authority of Antonio. It bends Bassanio to her will. To what degree that involves the severance of a homosocial bond between Antonio and Bassanio is a question of interpretation.[8] While the play may seem to put Shylock at its centre, and make him the source of its anxieties, there is a further anxiety generated which associates with Portia's own success through her own sleight of hand. Effectively she asserts the power of the female will to annihilate the male will.

Yet it may be wondered how wrong Bassanio and Gratiano were to give the rings to the lawyer and his clerk even at Antonio's bidding. For in giving the rings to them, they have actually given them to their wives; for Portia and Nerissa have made their identities plural, bisexual. The instinct that gives them the rings is not wrong, because the rings do not thereby stray; but what is interesting is that Portia, and Nerissa, in the last act assert their identity as singular, as absolutely unconnected to the male parts they have assumed. In exercising power over their husbands, they become single figures again, as women only, but, in threatening to sleep with the lawyer (5.1.223–33), i.e. herself, Portia becomes as if narcissistically enclosed in her own sexual being. But, when Bassanio is given the ring again, after the pleading of Antonio, it has another meaning from what it signified when it was given first. As Karen Newman suggests, it no longer expresses a traditional relationship, but 'cuckoldry and thus female unruliness, female genitalia, women's changeable nature and so-called animal temperament, her deceptiveness and potential subversion of the rules of possession and fidelity that insure the male line'.[9] The play ends with an affirmation of marriage, perhaps, but it also involves, on the male side, the acceptance of a limitation, which is also a limitation of Antonio's power.

II 'WHAT YOU WILL'

The Merchant of Venice may be associated with comedies which are ambiguous in their title, *Much Ado About Nothing* (late 1598) and *As You Like It* (early 1599 to mid-1600) and *Twelfth Night*. The initial plot in

As You Like It has already been commented on; Orlando's deprivation parallels the point that Duke Senior, the father of Rosalind, has been banished, and that three or four lords have gone into 'voluntary exile' with him (1.1.97) from the court. Amiens and the other lords sing 'Under the greenwood tree' in celebration of this life; Jaques caps the sentiment with an additional verse to the lyric: 'If it should come to pass / That any man turn ass / Leaving his wealth and ease / A stubborn will to please . . .' (2.6.46–49). The stubborn will may be that of the Duke, and possibly the courtiers who have chosen such a life, but it is the expression of the melancholic and the satirist, and of the malcontent, who leaves the court behind him, so it may be Jaques' will.[10] While good will consorts with wit, as with the punning and quipping 'wit whither wilt?' (4.1.153), which virtually equates the two, by asking the wit what it wills, Jaques shows stubbornness in his affectation of melancholy, and he is criticised for his assumption of the pose of the satirist who speaks out of melancholia, first by the Duke, then by Orlando and by Rosalind (2.7.42–87, 3.2.245–85, 4.1.1–34). And though he speaks of the inhabitants of the forest being brought out there by a stubborn will, he chooses neither to see 'pastimes', nor to return to the court. Instead, he lives 'in a living humour of madness' which means to 'forswear the full stream of the world and to live in a nook merely monastic' (3.2.398–400), like a misanthrope, so that at the end he must acknowledge the stubborn will to be his. In which case he acts outside his will, or shows the will to be divided. Since his aim in staying with Duke Frederick is to observe him, he remains an outside figure whose will is marked by the watching, overseeing eye which pronounces the world a stage, and all the men and women merely players (2.7.139–40). If he is for other than for dancing measures, he makes his will individualistic (5.4.198), and assertive of a single identity whose essence, stubbornness, fosters the will and is fostered by the will.

As You Like It puts emphasis on 'what you will' (2.5.17, 4.1.103). In the wooing of Orlando by Rosalind, which is presented as the wooing of Rosalind as Ganymede by Orlando, Celia is turned into the priest:

ROSALIND: You must begin, 'Will you, Orlando' –
CELIA: Go to. Will you, Orlando, have to wife this Rosalind?
ORLANDO: I will.
ROSALIND: Ay, but when?
ORLANDO: Why now, as fast as she can marry us.

ROSALIND: Then must you say, I take thee, Rosalind, for wife.

(4.1.110–16)

Rosalind picks up on the ambiguity of Orlando saying 'I will', as both an expression of resolution, and as a future action, so that she insists, in 'Ay but when?' on two things: on the will being both immediate, and present, and on willing as being a performative act, by which Orlando fulfils his will by marrying her, so she changes Celia's version to make him say 'I take thee': which becomes a way in which he is indeed betrothed, through the capacity of this language to be both non-specific, and performative. Such punning runs throughout the play as with Rosalind's later words to Orlando, 'if you will be married tomorrow, you shall, and to Rosalind, if you will' (5.2.69–70) which are followed by her words to Silvius, 'I will help you if I can', and to Phoebe, 'I would love you if I could, and I'll be married tomorrow', and to Orlando, 'I will satisfy you if ever I satisfy man, and you shall be married tomorrow', and then back to Silvius: 'I will content you if what pleases you contents you, and you shall be married tomorrow' (5.2.105–12). 'Will you ..?', 'If you will' and 'what pleases you' are variants of the title, and imply a fusion of the simple future tense, (you will, I'll), the declaration of an expectation for the future, and a declaration of intention (you shall, I will), which may defer to the other's will, both here, and at the opening of the last scene (5.4.1–25), when Rosalind again asks the lovers what they are willing to do. But everything depends on a good will, on letting what pleases 'content' the person, not being malcontented, and Jaques shows that this may not be possible, because the will may be stubborn.

Twelfth Night, or What You Will seems to have been preceded by *What You Will* by John Marston (1576–1634), the satirist. *What You Will* was the third of three plays in which Marston seems to have parodied Ben Jonson, *Histriomastix* (1599) being the first, and *Jack Drum's Entertainment* the second.[11] Jonson replied to Marston's *Histriomastix* in his 'comical satire' *Every Man Out of his Humour* (1599), with the character of Clove. At the centre of Jonson's play is Macilente ('lean, meagre, gaunt, barren, thin'), the malcontent scholar , who, 'wanting that place in the world's account which he thinks his merit capable of, falls into such an envious apoplexy with which his judgment is so dazzled and distasted that he grows violently impatient of any opposite happiness in another'.[12] Macilente is to be played by Asper ('bitter'), the Jonson-like satirist who has supposedly written the play; his 'humour' is envy, which makes him a figure of ill-will, destructive towards the humours of all others. In Marston's *What You Will*, which anticipates *Twelfth Night*, the hero, Albano, is presumed to have been drowned; identity is in question, and disguise rules. No-one can be sure of anything: as Albano says, 'Doth not opinion stamp the current pass / Of each man's value, virtue, quality?' (3.1.1247–48).[13] The title *What You Will* appears four times in the play's Induction; including once as a periphrasis for the author ('the what you will') and once to indicate that the play has neither a definite genre nor seriousness; it is 'what you will, a slight toy, lightly composed' (76, 88). In the play, the phrase appears some six times, whereas it comes only once in *Twelfth Night*, (1.5.109); Marston giving the phrase more investment.

In *What You Will*, which is set in Venice, Celia, the 'widow' of Albano, who is really alive, is sought for in marriage. When Albano is spoken of by Francisco, who was dressed up as Albano, in order to frustrate the attempts of a Frenchman, Laverdure, who would marry Celia, Francisco, who is practising Albano's stutter, calls the Frenchman 'an odd phantasm, a beggar, sir, a who-who-who-*what you will*'(3.2.972–73). The word 'who' turns into 'what'; identity disappears altogether. And the joke is continued in Albano's speech, when he is enraged that someone is taking his place with Celia, 'while his father-in-law, his father-in-devil, or d-d-d-devil / f-f-f-father, or who-who-who-*what you will* – ' (3.2.1061–62). Albano does not finish his sentence, but it seems that 'what you will' is a way of completing an utterance when the stutter overmasters him; in other words, 'what you will' as a phrase covers an inadequacy in language; it exists as a euphemism, at least, or a catechresis, advertising the point that language cannot say what it means. And that sense goes into the other scenes where Albano appears.

The phrase also appears when Quadratus, the man of wit and Epicurean, persuades Lampatho Doria (another man of wit, a scholar, echoing Jonson) to woo the flirtatious Meletza:

> MELETZA [to Lampatho]: How it should please you I should respect ye?
> LAMPATHO: As anything, *what you will*, as nothing.
> MELETZA: As nothing! How will you value my love?
> LAMPATHO: Why just as you respect me, as nothing; for out of nothing, nothing is bred, so nothing shall not beget anything, anything bring nothing, nothing bring anything, anything and

nothing shall be what you will, my speech amounting to the value of myself, which is . . . .

MELETZA: What, sweet?

LAMPATHO: Your nothing. Light as yourself, senseless as your sex, and just as you would ha' me, nothing. (4.1.1624–34, my emphasis)

This dialogue, for example with Lampatho's second line, associates the titles *As You Will* with *Much Ado About Nothing*, making 'anything' and 'nothing' equivalents, both produced out of an act of thinking, or willing. Whereas for King Lear, 'nothing will come of nothing' (*King Lear*, 1.89), here, 'what you will', implying the power of fantasy and desire, can make nothing anything or anything nothing. And equally it annihilates sexual difference, recalling the bawdy talk about the woman's 'nothing' in *Hamlet* 3.2.101–9, and what has been discussed of *Troilus and Cressida*: here, the man becomes 'your nothing'; which means, he is ungendered; made like a woman, he becomes 'nothing'. Doing what you will produces much ado about nothing. The woman can use the man as she will; she can even make him a woman. Meletza has already declared that the only person that she will be wed to is 'the true husband, right head of a woman, my will, which vows never to marry till I mean to be a fool' (4.1.1448–49). The woman's will is her wilfulness, and her 'nothing'.

A little later than the Lampatho/Meletza scene, Albano enters, and has his identity doubted and mocked, and himself called all names: he says 'I will even be *what you will*' (4.1.1705–6), a line he repeats when he appears before the Duke, when again his identity is in question: 'Albano Belletoz, thy merchant, thy soldier, thy courtier, thy slave, thy anything, thy *what thou wilt*' (5.1.1994–96). To go from 'slave' to 'anything' to 'what you will' implies a descent indeed in terms of slavery: to become a catamite, at the least, the object of the will of another, when the will is sexual.

Hence, those titles in Shakespeare which leave the subject-matter to the audience, *Much Ado About Nothing*, which calls for an assessment of what the nothing is, *As You Like It*, and *Twelfth Night*. They express an openness which makes everything within language mean both something and nothing together, so they disallow thinking about stable identity and gender, though Portia attempts to stabilise these, by going out of her gender altogether. So 'what you will' suggests that all that exists is the relativity of desire: it is what you want, which also suggests

65

what you lack. 'Will' can mean wilfulness, or bad will, but it can mean the opposite, as with Benvolio, or with the actors performing 'Pyramus and Thisbe' who can say 'If we offend, it is with our good will' (*A Midsummer Night's Dream* 5.1.108). But in *Twelfth Night* the will is complex, and 'what you will' means 'what you desire'; to be at someone else's will means to be sexually available to them.[14] What you will is the object of what the play three times calls 'appetite', as in Orsino's opening: 'If music be the food of love, play on,/ Give me excess of it, that surfeiting / The appetite may sicken and so die' (1.1.1–3). The desire is to destroy the appetite by overfeeding it, but at the same time there is the desire to be overfed, to be made sick. Orsino distinguishes love from appetite and downgrades the latter when he says of women 'their love may be called appetite, / No motion of the liver, but the palate, / That suffer surfeit, cloyment, and revolt' (2.4.96–98). The liver, for Orsino, is the seat of the passions. A woman's appetite goes for what will destroy it; hence the strangeness of the Queen in *Hamlet* whose 'increase of appetite had grown / By what it fed on' (1.2.44–45).

In Olivia's reproach to Malvolio, 'O, you are sick of self-love, Malvolio, and taste with a distempered appetite' (1.5.85–86), the alliance of appetite with the will, discussed in the previous chapter, becomes apparent, for 'Malvolio' derives from 'voglio', 'I will'. It suggests the 'bad will' of the Puritan.[15] Indeed, 'a distempered appetite' could be read as a synonym for a 'malvolio', a bad will, so that Olivia says that Malvolio tastes with a bad will, and that has been brought on by his surfeiting on his overmuch love for himself. His regard for his ego, on which he has overeaten, has made him sick; that sickness creates an evil will in regard to others, so that he now cannot taste, or participate in anything belonging to anyone else. Malvolio expresses extreme ill-will towards Feste, and this runs throughout his reactions to everyone save Olivia, whom he thinks 'affects' him. He is simply exasperated by the 'young fellow' Viola/Cesario, who will indeed be 'affected' by Olivia. And that is something he will later have the opportunity to notice, but does not, when Olivia commissions him to send after Cesario with her ring. He should have guessed what that errand meant. When Olivia asks him 'what manner of man' Cesario is, he replies: 'Of very ill manner: he'll speak to you will you or no' (1.5.147–48). 'What you will' is echoed in this speech, which issues from his ill-will towards this young man whom he cannot speak badly enough of, who has disobeyed his will, by not going away. His blindness is not to have noticed he is up against a woman's will in Viola/Cesario; Cesario's will being that which defeats gender divisions, as, in these comedies, the will does: it is male and female together. His self-love, which is his appetite, his will, turns him against himself (ill-will is expressed towards the self) in the way that he fantasises Olivia making him Count Malvolio; in doing so he can only hurt himself, by becoming a laughing-stock, first in the scene where he is gulled (2.5), then with Olivia and then in the dark room. Even when he gets an explanation of how he has been tricked, his ill-will to others makes him unable to accept what has happened to himself.

Yet Malvolio – Olivia – Viola – as names and spellings suggest recombinations of each other, as in a word-puzzle, a rebus, so that to become a 'Malvolio' seems a constant possibility within the play. Malvolio's exit before the celebration of the marriages at the end of *Twelfth Night* aligns him with two others who do not enter the play's harmony: Feste, and Antonio, whose love for Sebastian which makes him want to be at least his servant draws him into danger, and finally isolates him, as a replay of *The Merchant of Venice*. All three have features of the sad, the malcontent, or malevolent; all complicate the cheerfulness of the comedy of 'what you will'. Malvolio represents a force that cannot be easily eliminated, as when, told he is mad, he clings obstinately – wilfully – to his sanity and demands a rational explanation of what has happened to him. Everyone else in the play accepts the power of illusion, and of wonder; they do not require explanations. Malvolio is not even like Antonio, a figure of loss, who discovers half way through that not only has he lost Sebastian, but when he finds him, that he is married to Olivia. Sebastian requires no explanation before marrying Olivia; is happy to believe 'or I am mad or else this is a dream' (4.1.59). Orsino does not even wait to see Viola changed into women's clothes before proposing marriage. These figures need no rational explanation, nothing to stabilise them; but Malvolio insists on being given such a thing; beginning with his demand for justice with 'Madam you have done me wrong, / Notorious wrong', and ending 'Tell me why' (5.1.318–19, 335), the significance of which is underlined by his speaking it in blank verse, for virtually his first time. He could never have gone mad, if madness, in this play, permits any freedom. He cannot listen to Olivia's 'prithee be content' (5.1.342), with its promise of vindication; while his walking out at the end, rather than being associated either with the weddings or the release of the captain he imprisoned and who helped Viola, is a fiercer example of Jaques' leaving the Forest of Arden at the

67

end of *As You Like It*. Malvolio's final line, and the only one he speaks after hearing everything, 'I'll be revenged on the whole pack of you' (5.1.368) casts doubt upon the comedy of the future associated with marriage; it proposes an alternative time when scores are to be settled.

His words are a deliberate retort to Fabian, who has said that the trick played on Malvolio was done in 'sportful malice', an oxymoron which responds to Malvolio's name, and thinks that it should 'rather pluck on laughter than revenge'.[16] It responds to Feste also, who adds to Fabian's blank-verse explanation his own, in prose, reminding Malvolio of words said to and about him earlier in the play, and culminating in 'the whirligig of time brings in his revenges'. Revenge, for Feste, is what happens outside the power of the personal will, and is the work of time, that which Viola/Cesario appealed to when she realised the chaos that had been produced by her disguise: 'O time, thou must entangle this, not I' (2.2.40). She had already shown her reliance on time when she decides to disguise herself, and says, 'What else may hap, to time I will commit' (1.2.57). Insofar as time has been mentioned by Feste, and Malvolio responds to the point, he expresses what in Nietzsche's *Thus Spake Zarathustra* is seen as 'the will's ill-will' towards 'time and its "it was"' (see ch. 8). Nietzsche calls that the spirit of revenge, and it means the ill-will which is allegorised in Malvolio.

III MALVOLIO / MALEVOLE

Malvolio's anger individuates him, makes him the personal will which neither tolerates the idea that something impersonal, like Time, has defeated him, nor listens to Feste's point that Time takes its revenges on everybody. Perhaps that is what Olivia means when she notices that he is sick of self-love, so that his appetite, his will, is defective, unbalanced, because distempered: he is a man out of his humour. He loves himself, and that individualism makes him the man of ill will. Malvolio's name anticipates by no more than a year that of Malevole in Marston's *The Malcontent*.[17] In that play, Malevole is the name given to the disguised Duke Altofront, who has had his position, and that of his wife, Maria, usurped by Pietro Jacomo. Disguised, he now dwells in the court, which he satirises mercilessly, as an unknown, as a 'malcontent'. The malcontent may be the melancholic, but he is also a political figure, perhaps a machiavel, certainly a schemer, an intriguer, like Iago. 'Discontent is the classic motive' Walter Benjamin writes of the schemer, such as Iago, in seventeenth-century tragedy.[18] In Malevole, it is as though Duke Senior, from *As You Like It*, and Jaques were combined, but confined to the court, not outside it; and the character of Malevole (ill-will) and being a malcontent go together. The new Duke, Pietro likes the discontentedness of this Malevole:

> This Malevole is one of the most prodigious affections that ever conversed with nature, a man, or rather a monster, more discontent than Lucifer when he was thrust out of the presence; his appetite is unsatiable as the grave, as far from any content as from heaven. His highest delight is to procure others vexation, and therein he thinks he truly serves heaven; for 'tis his position, whoever in this earth can be contented is a slave and damned; therefore does he afflict all in that to which they are most affected. The elements struggle within him; his own soul is at variance within herself; his speech is halterworthy at all hours. I like him, faith; he gives good intelligence to my spirit, makes me understand those weaknesses which others' flattery palliates. (1.2.17–30)

After the song which is heard at this point, Malevole appears, and Pietro says, 'now shall you hear the extremity of a malcontent' (1.3.1–2). The build-up of Malevole here makes clear that disguise is not simply a strategy for Altofront; rather, he has become something else, he has doubled his identity. Pietro's speech uses the word 'content', or variants on it, four times; and the word will recall the irony of Shylock's last utterance, after his absolute humiliation and forced conversion, in response to Portia's question, 'I am content' (4.1.389).

As Pietro describes Malevole, he is suggestive of Jaques, but appears to combine the characters of Malvolio, and as regards his function towards himself, of Feste, the fool, since he is what Goneril in *King Lear* calls 'your all-licensed fool" (1.4.175), or what Olivia calls 'an allowed fool', in whom 'there is no slander . . . though he do nothing but rail' (1.5.88–89). Pietro refers to the fallen Lucifer to give a sense of the ill-will of Malevole, and speaks of his 'prodigious affections' – his states of affect, his feelings, which could also include the idea of his will as monstrous, and his 'appetite', which, as in *Twelfth Night*, suggests his desire.[19] The text links 'Malevole' with 'malcontent': the figures of discontent, the malcontents of Elizabethan and Jacobean drama, are ill-willed. Malevole has learned, since trusting too much as Duke of Genoa and being expelled because of it (1.4.7–17), to think differently; his universal satire, and railing, expresses his bad will towards the usurping court of Pietro and against all in 'the presence' in Genoa, and associates with his desire to revenge himself on Pietro, which appears most clearly in his soliloquy at the end of 1.3 (lns. 155–72). His character as at variance with himself is signalled by the 'vilest out of tune music' which is heard at the play's beginning, and it shows itself in his own self-perception:

> In night, all creatures sleep;
> Only the malcontent, that 'gainst his fate
> Repines and quarrels – alas, he's goodman tell-clock! (3.2.10–12)

In Pietro's court, Mendoza, who plans to usurp the Dukedom from Pietro, and is cuckolding him with his wife Aurelia, is also a Malvolio; like the Malvolio who imagines himself becoming 'Count Malvolio' (2.5.32). Mendoza dreams:

> To be a favourite! a minion! to have a general timorous respect observe a man, a stateful silence in his presence, solitariness in his absence, a confused hum and busy murmur of obsequious suitors training him. (*The Malcontent,* 1.5.23–27)

Nor is Mendoza alone: Bilioso is also a Malvolio in his fantasy:

> as I walk up and down the chamber, I'll spit frowns about me, have a strong perfume in my jerkin, let my beard grow to make me look terrible, salute no man beneath the fourth button, and 'twill do excellent. (3.1.108–12)

And Bilioso has a fool, Passarello, and is blind to the lack of distinction between the two of them (3.1.61–68).

The 'strength of fantasy' (4.2.27) works as much in Pietro as it does in Malevole, and in Mendoza; unlike Malvolio's fantasy, fantasies here are negative, working through dreams, undermining, saddening, each ruler in turn. Indeed, when Mendoza is arrested amid all his villainy, during the masque in the final scene – a masque which should remind him of the theatricality all rule – he says, 'What strange delusions mock

/ Our senses? Do I dream? or have I dreamt / This two days' space? Where am I?' (5.7.117–19). Mendoza goes beyond Malvolio, who for all his fantasies of greatness, never leaves off a sense of his own certainty that he is not mad.

The Malcontent shows Malevole opening the eyes of Pietro to see what treachery is in Mendoza, and also what ill-will is in his wife Aurelia, who, told by the bawd Maquerelle, bribed by Ferneze, that Mendoza is no longer interested in her, walks off the set as far as Mendoza goes, with the imperious words 'Hence, worst of ill! / *No reason ask, our reason is our will*' (1.6.78–79). Kay supplies the source for the line, from Juvenal's Satire 6.223, 'where an imperious Roman matron insists on crucifying a slave: *hoc volo, sic iubeo, sit pro ratione volontas* (This I wish, so I command, let my will be my reason)'.

In the comparison between Altofront/Malevole and Mendoza, Malevole is the ruler in disguise who must also be a malcontent, while Mendoza is the figure of malevolence who is also a Malvolio, with all the potentialities for comedy that this affords. It seems no coincidence that Marston's play, while it was dedicated to Jonson as his 'rough comedy' (*asperam thaliam*), was entered at the Stationers' Register, in 1604, as *the malcontent Tragiecomedia*. Perhaps tragi-comedy, of which this was a new example, best fits a play of wills, where the ill-will of the satirist and the avenger confronts the ill-will of the villain Mendoza.[20] In Act 3 scene 3, Mendoza hires Malevole as the malcontent, to murder Pietro: Mendoza wants to usurp what Pietro has already usurped, banish Pietro's wife Aurelia, and marry Maria, the banished Duke Altofront's wife (3.5.38–125). In this, he anticipates Lussurioso in *The Revenger's Tragedy*, who similarly hires the malcontent Vindice, and who aims at taking the Dukedom and who, when he succeeds, banishes the Duchess. Malevole's ill-will is outstripped by Mendoza's, but Mendoza's Machiavellianism is outstripped by Malevole's, who uses the occasion to save Pietro. He disguises Pietro as a hermit, so that this play has *two* Dukes in disguise, one more than *Measure for Measure*, and by the end of Act 4, has brought Pietro to a disillusioned sense of life, and to a position where he is ready to give back the Dukedom to Altofront. In Act 5, Mendoza overreaches himself when he tries to poison Malevole, and his villainy is unmasked in a masque.

The Merchant of Venice removes Shylock before he can be seen as a malcontent, but Don John, the bastard in *Much Ado About Nothing* is, like Antonio in the former play, 'out of measure sad' and marked by 'discontent' (1.3.1,36).[21] From there, through *As You Like It*, and Macilente, it is not far to *The Malcontent* and to Middleton's *The Revenger's Tragedy*, where Vindice's father died 'of discontent, the nobleman's consumption' (1.1.126).[22] Vindice, a revenger as much as Malvolio says he will be, or as Hamlet is, or as Malevole intends to be, is – however satirically, and while in disguise – called both a figure of discontent and melancholy (4.2.26–48).[23] His melancholy is said to have come from going to law; throughout the play it associates with misogyny and hatred of the sexual, which is also associated with the melancholy of Malevole, who reaches towards his reconciliation with Pietro with extreme contempt for the world:

> Think this – this earth is the only grave and Golgotha wherein all things that live must rot; 'tis but the draught wherein the heavenly bodies discharge their corruption; the very muck-hill on which the sublunary orbs cast their excrements. Man is the slime of this dung-pit, and princes are the governors of these men; for, for our souls, they are as free as emperors', all of one piece; there goes but a pair of shears betwixt an emperor and the son of a bagpiper; only the dressing, pressing, glossing, makes the difference. (4.5.110–19)

Everything of the body may be seen as 'slime', and only the soul remains free; for the rest, everything is a matter of clothes, of disguise. The 'difference' resides in that which is created by different disguises. Yet such stoicism, which dismisses difference, is also an expression of ill-will, and cannot be seen as an objective statement; ill-will draws this harsh comedy towards tragedy, tragedy being motivated by ill-will as the mark of the individual.

IV 'MOTIVELESS MALIGNITY'

We move towards tragedy with reference to the ill-will of Iago, in *Othello*, where what may be called Iago's will, which motivates so much of the play – as it seems to be the chief motivator altogether – was called by Coleridge 'motiveless malignity'.[24] The 'discontents' can be assessed, perhaps, starting with Iago's being passed over for the lieutenantship, but the ill-will cannot. In *Othello*, Roderigo says that it is not in his virtue to amend his 'foolishness' in being so in love with Desdemona. Iago reacts to his folly with an expression of the power of the will as the only thing that matters, but the statement here is also an expression of ill-will:

> Virtue? A fig! 'Tis in ourselves that we are thus, or thus. Our bodies are our gardens to the which our wills are gardeners . . . the power and corrigible authority of this [i.e. to have the garden sterile with idleness or manured with industry] lies in our wills. . . . If the beam of our lives had not one scale of reason to poise another of sensuality, the blood and baseness of our natures would conduct us to most preposterous conclusions; but we have reason to cool our raging motions, our carnal stings, our unbitted lusts, whereof I take this, that you call love, to be a sect, or scion.

To Roderigo's objection, Iago continues that love 'is merely a lust of the blood and a permission of the will'; the will giving a licence to both lust and love, though it is both of these things too, as *Troilus and Cressida* showed, and as such it is unlicensed. The speech continues by saying 'these Moors are changeable in their wills' (*Othello*, 1.3. 315–21, 325–30, 340–41).[25] Hence Iago counsels 'be a man', and follows that up by saying, six times, 'put money in thy purse', an expression whose cynicism makes the power of money the power of the will, what gives 'permission', what issues the licence.

The will, then, is a fetish-like structure, as money is for Marx, as associated with the fetishistic qualities that haunt the 'commodity'; a man with money in his purse is a man with a will. When Roderigo has gone out, Iago says 'thus do I ever make my fool my purse'. Not only does he make money from Roderigo, but his own will-power is increased by being able to gull him, because he uses him for his 'sport', a word with sexual suggestiveness. He continues with 'Cassio's a proper man, let me see now, / To get his place and to make up my will, / A double knavery' (1.3.390–92, Q: F reads 'plume up my will'). 'Making up' the will suggests completing it, making it substantial, recognising that it is never full, only a desire. It must be fabricated, given substance by lying (making up); in that sense, in as much as Nietzsche sees the will to be an example of a seduction of language, an instance of a word existing with no referent, Iago, who is a 'corrupter of words', even more than Feste, who calls himself that, sees the will as fictitious. The grammar of that makes 'my will' a synonym for 'the story I will tell'. The pleasure in making up a narrative is the pleasure of desire. To 'plume up' the will, the Folio reading, implies the existence of a narcissism in Iago, like Malvolio: but that narcissism is more sexual in the case of Iago; it is connected to a phallic pride that he wants to sustain. And at the same time, the will in Iago suggests an 'instrumental reason' which Adorno and Horkheimer, explicating the phrase in *Dialectic of Enlightenment*, associate with modernity: the ability to use people, which is central to Iago, and which works through a 'purposeless purposiveness'. That historicises the will in Iago, which is both sexual, and coldly sexless.[26]

Iago's philosophy in 1.3.320–62 – it is virtually one speech, with only a single-line interruption – appears in his persuading Roderigo, over whom he has the power of the will, to exchange 'virtue' – which implies the habit of trying to do well – for the 'will', which is the power of assertion, and seems, as he goes on with love as 'a permission of the will', to be proto-Cartesian in its declaration of the power of the will's control over the body as an object. 'Virtue' is traditional language, but the 'will' which replaces it in Iago's thought is a more modern concept, and marks out a cynicism more modern than that of the other malcontent who has been discussed here, Malvole. For Iago's speech, the power of the will as reason balances anything of sensuality, and it is clear from the way he speaks of the latter that he has an ill-will towards it, and is cynical about love, as just a shoot ('scion') growing out of 'unbitted lust'. The 'lust of the blood, and a permission of the will' puts the will on both sides of the argument, either as rational, or as the blood itself, the uncurbed lust, in which case the will is that aspect of the body which the will itself controls. So if Othello as Moor is changeable in his will, then he has both a defective will in relation to the body, and to the force in the body which controls it.

With Othello, Iago turns his attention onto the woman's will, as when Othello shows signs of being affected by what has been said against Desdemona, and internalising it:

> OTHELLO: And yet how nature, erring from itself –
> IAGO: Ay, there's the point! As – to be bold with you –
> Not to affect many proposed matches
> Of her own clime, complexion and degree,
> Whereto we see in all things nature tends –
> Foh! One may smell in such a will most rank,
> Foul disproportions, thoughts unnatural –

> But pardon me: I do not in position
> Distinctly speak of her – though I may fear
> Her will, recoiling to her better judgement,
> May fall to match you with her country forms,
> And happily repent.
>
> (*Othello*, 3.3.231–42)

Iago seizes on what he makes out to be the strangeness of Desdemona, that she was not attracted to any Venetian. She is both wilful – in how, un-Portia-like, she broke with her father's will – and in her sexuality, her will is rank, and foul, disproportionate, and unnatural. Then he changes the attack; he says he fears that Desdemona's will, meaning again her sexuality; but also her rationality, may go back on itself to coincide with her 'better judgement' (the antithesis between will and judgement was basic to *Troilus and Cressida*). The will might choose a Venetian, not a foreigner and a black – might 'match you with her country forms' and repent. 'Happily' means 'perhaps' but also 'fortunately': it is a last moment of added ill-will in a speech seemingly rational, objective. 'Country forms' contains its own obscenity; Desdemona may happen to compare Othello sexually with the physical forms of men of her own country; 'falls' means she may sink so low as to do that, and 'country forms' recalls earlier lines:

> I know our country disposition well:
> In Venice they do let God see the pranks
> They dare not show their husbands; their best conscience
> Is not to leave't undone, but keep't unknown. (3.3.204–7)

The 'country disposition' means 'the customs of our country' but as an exclusively female reference, it suggests 'the ways of the cunts of our country'; 'cunt-knowledge' ('conscience') maintains secrecy, and 'country forms' suggests 'the methods of similar Venetian cunts'. Iago expresses hatred of the female will, contradicting his earlier sense of the supremacy of what must now be seen as the male will. If Iago is thought of as the expression of instrumental rationality, which uses the other, the language of sexuality is part of that instrumental drive; in Foucault's terms, the impulse to describe Desdemona in terms of a sexuality whose 'pranks' he claims to know and to describe to the outsider, thereby maintaining a superior knowledge, and, while reducing the sexual to the genital zone, pretending that he is not being judgmental, but simply objective, describing things as they are. Iago displays, in this way, the 'will to knowledge' (see ch. 9), while he creates in Othello a voyeur's desire, centred on watching not a heterosexual intercourse between Cassio and Desdemona, but perhaps a homosexual one originating from Cassio towards Iago (3.3.392–428).

Desdemona uses the word 'will' differently from Iago: talking to Cassio: 'What I can do I will, and more I will / Than for myself I dare' (3.4.126–27), and her fear, expressed to Iago: 'If e'er my will did trespass 'gainst his love' (4.2.152). She cannot say the word 'whore' (4.2.161–62), yet she also sings what the forsaken 'Barbary' sang before her, of 'willow', and so unconsciously evokes the will, which is associated, punningly, in the word 'willow' with 'Othello', and which in any case reads almost as a palindrome, with the final 'i' in become an 'o'.[27] It concludes:

> I called my love 'false love', but what said he then?
>   Sing willow, willow, willow.
> If I court more women, you'll couch with more men. (4.3.50–52)

What Desdemona cannot speak about in her conscious language – and what Iago defames in her by speaking of Venetian women's 'country dispositions'- appears here. Freud, strikingly, quotes these last lines to illustrate what he calls 'projective jealousy', where one partner

> projects his own impulses to faithlessness on to the partner to whom he owes faith. This strong motive can then make use of the perceptual material which betrays unconscious impulses in the partner, and the subject can justify himself with the reflection that the other is probably not much better than he is himself.[28]

Desdemona's song allows for the thought of faithlessness, and insofar as the woman's attraction is fantasised by Othello as being directed towards Cassio, his jealousy is homosexual in character; it is necessary to keep the woman's constancy but not quite because of the fear of being cuckolded, as in the case of Bassanio with Portia, the fear of being the wittol, but because of the homosexual fear. As Freud comments, in paranoia and the paranoid person 'it is precisely the most loved person of his own sex that becomes his persecutor' (SE 18.226). The point relates to Othello with

Cassio. In *The Merchant of Venice* the trial of strength between Bassanio and Portia (for it is that) which secures the will of the woman, however provisionally, takes place in the space between marriage and sexual consummation, with the woman working at and against the bond that exists between males; perhaps the same space obtains in *Othello* in a contest between Othello and Desdemona, if we can assume that she dies still virginal.[29] But in that space, in that trial, where Desdemona cannot translate the words of the song which puts the 'willow' at the centre of everything into her and Othello's situation, both male and female are destroyed.

What was accepted and repudiated in *The Merchant of Venice* as a primary male–male tie, becomes in *Othello, the Moor of Venice* protection of the male will to identity, at the price of destroying the woman. Certain stages have been marked out: Portia's discontentment moved her from being a submissive and conventional Romance heroine towards having the power of her own will, which she assumed. In *Othello*, there seems to be a revenge taken against that position. As in other examples, the will becomes centred on a wish to keep fast and stable an identity, where the will, defined as sexual identity, is never more than labile. Such instability produces, characteristically, perhaps out of anxiety, a satiric mode, present in Portia, and in those who are fully malcontents.

Malvolio and Iago contrast with each other. In Malvolio, the self-belief, which is his sickness, produces the determination to revenge which makes him break with the comic mode; he cannot satirise the world he sees, but will break it. Iago, a late example of the malcontent, works differently but also revengefully; his malignity relates to the desire to make up, or to plume up his will: sexual fear, or desire, makes him project a sense of the male will as controlling, and in the woman, as to be controlled: as if the Enlightenment project of instrumental rationalism is fed by a male paranoia here emerging.

77

3

LAW AND WILL IN
MEASURE FOR MEASURE

Near the end of *Measure for Measure*, the Duke condemns Angelo:

> The very mercy of the law cries out
> Most audible, even from his proper tongue,
> 'An Angelo for Claudio, death for death'.
> Haste still pays haste, and leisure answers leisure,
> Like doth quit like, and measure still for measure.
> Then, Angelo, thy fault's thus manifested,
> Which, though thou wouldst deny, denies thee vantage.
> We do condemn thee to the very block
> Where Angelo stooped to die, and with like haste.
> Away with him.[1]

What is meant by 'the very mercy of the law'? Perhaps 'the fullest extent of leniency, or mercy that the law can show'; the law at its most generous to the offender. That implies that the law has both its severe and its merciful aspect, recalling the Duke's words to Angelo, 'Mortality and mercy in Vienna / Live in thy tongue and heart' (1.1.44–45): you have power either to pass the death-penalty or to set someone free. The 'mercy of the law' means that the law inherently condemns Angelo; if a judge looked for some part of the law, which would not condemn, that other part would demand Angelo's death.

Can the law be merciful? Why does the Duke bother to appeal to it, since it is bound to condemn Angelo? The law cannot contain mercy, because that implies something inside the law, overriding it. The law either condemns me or sets me free because I am innocent. It cannot condemn me and then show mercy on me; if it does that, it is not the law. Mercy is opposite to law, not contained in it. If it calls 'from his proper tongue', that suggests that the mercy is inherent to, proper to, the law. But mercy, not contained within the law, cannot speak there from a 'proper', appropriate, tongue.[2]

The Duke appeals to what can only condemn Angelo. Having evoked the law of 'measure still for measure', there is no other choice. The 'law' is that of the Sermon on the Mount: 'Judge not, that ye be not judged. For with what judgment ye judge, ye shall be judged, and with what measure ye mete, it shall be measured to you again' (Matthew 7.1–2). Christ sees that law as the fulfilment of the Old Testament law (Matthew 5.17). 'Mortality and mercy' are not two halves of the law; the law awards only mortality; the principle on which 'mercy' functions is outside the law. The Duke's first speech to Angelo, praising his character as a spirit 'finely touched', uses the image of the torch, derived perhaps from Christ's words in Matthew 5.14–16, inviting Angelo to manifest himself as he is, in all his qualities. It culminates by telling him either to work with the law, which imposes 'mortality', or to act on the principle of mercy. He adds: 'your scope [=freedom] is as mine own / So to enforce or qualify the law / As to your soul seems good' (1.1.64–66). Angelo can, as a matter of 'government' (1.1.3), work with the law, but he need not.[3]

Yet 'mercy' can only be activated because the law pronounces mortality, unless 'vice makes mercy' which would mean that 'for the fault's love is the offender friended' (4.2.112–13). If the law is recognised as self-consistent, mercy reacting to that, must come from another principle; as Claudio says:

> Thus can the demigod Authority
> Make us pay down for our offence, by weight,
> The words of heaven: on whom it will, it will;
> On whom it will not, so; yet still 'tis just.
>   (1.2.119–22)

The passage echoes Romans 9:15,16 and 18: 'For He saith to Moses, "I will have mercy on whom I will have mercy, and I will have compassion on whom I will have compassion". So then it is not of him that willeth, nor of him that runneth, but of God that sheweth mercy'.[. . .] Therefore hath he mercy on whom he will have mercy, and whom he will he hardeneth'. Saint Paul's argument, crucially in Romans 7, asserts the inability of the human will to obey God's law; everything of salvation must be left to God's will as sovereign. Mercy, beyond the law, is part of a will exceeding the will within law-giving. Claudio's speech recognises the supremacy of the 'will' of 'Authority', and this, manifesting Angelo's 'fault', is what is to be investigated here, but in terms hardly flattering to the law: so giving an emphasis differing from much criticism of the play, which, however tacitly, usually agrees on seeing law as the necessary and unquestioned centre.

When Claudio declares the abstract personification Authority 'just' in willing on whom it will have mercy and on whom it will not, he may be ironic, since he has virtually said that the will which is merciful is wilful and selective; but he gives precedence to the power of the will of authority, as impossible to argue with. Yet Isabella questions it when evoking 'man, proud man, / Dressed in a little brief authority' (2.2.120–21) and saying that 'authority, though it err like others / Hath yet a kind of medicine in itself / That skins the vice o' th' top' (2.2.135–37). Nonetheless, she places Angelo's deputed authority under God's authority, which appears throughout as unquestionable and its will sovereign. 'Always obedient to your Grace's will' is Angelo's first line (1.1.25). 'Is it your will Claudio shall die tomorrow?' the Provost asks Angelo (2.2.7), the question evoking the significance of Angelo's name, as nearest God, virtually absolute in power, apparently impregnable. 'Be it as your wisdom will' Escalus tells Angelo (2.1.32). And both Isabella and the Provost recognise the will of the disguised Duke (3.1.157, 178).

But 'the will' cannot bear a single meaning. When Isabella asks for her brother's life, she says 'I am / At war 'twixt will and will not' (2.2.32–33). She pleads for him on the grounds that Angelo:

> might pardon him,
> And neither heaven nor man grieve at the mercy.
> ANGELO: I will not do't.
> ISABELLA: But can you if you would?
> ANGELO: Look what I will not, that I cannot do.
>   (2.2.50–53)

Angelo's responses recall Claudio's 'On whom it will, it will'. Angelo's second use of 'will' implies both 'what I choose not to do, that I cannot do', and 'what I refuse to authorise, or will, that I cannot do', emphasising the supreme decision of his will, which has been aligned, both by himself and the Duke, with the power of the law. But that makes the law arbitrary in character, wilful. The hope 'you might pardon' produces a counter-will – 'I will not do't'. Isabella makes Angelo move from declaring what 'I will' to a three-times affirmed assertion of his position within the law: 'Your brother is a forfeit of the law' (2.2.72), then: 'It is the law, not I, condemn your brother' (2.2.81); and 'the law hath not been dead, though it hath slept' (2.2.91). The last statement says that the punishment exacted by the law, which, as more awake than Barnardine – Angelo's declaration unintentionally hints at a carnival quality in the law – will deter 'future evils'. These by this exaction, will 'have no successive degrees, / But ere they live, to end':

ISABELLA: Yet show some pity.
ANGELO: I show it most of all when I show justice.
For then I pity those I do not know
Which a dismissed offence would after gall,
And do him right that, answering one foul wrong,
Lives not to act another.

(2.2.100–6)

Isabella has gone beyond asking for mercy, seeing that as incompatible with the law; Angelo replies by linking pity to justice, but that, as Blake's 'The Human Abstract' in the *Songs of Experience* stresses: 'Pity would be no more / If we did not make somebody poor' is problematic. It makes pity important to the ruling class in being an expression of superiority. It is questionable how realistic it can be said to be to pity people whom one does not know, and also whether either pity or justice, which Angelo sees as inseparable, are appropriate states to deal with the unknown future. Angelo's speech dramatises the arbitrariness of the will. His assertion of its power as also the power of the law, which he has equated with justice, is succeeded, however, by a new awareness of the will as sexual, and self-dividing: 'I am that way going to temptation / Where prayers cross' (2.2.162–63).[4] Such a self-division is expressed in the self-torment of his soliloquy in 2.4, with its antithesis between tongue and heart, recalling the Duke's speech to Angelo combining 'tongue and heart' as a single entity, belonging to the ideal undivided self. Angelo is like Claudius after prayer; 'My words fly up, my thoughts remain below' (*Hamlet*, 3.3.97):

81

When I would pray and think, I think and pray
To several subjects: heaven hath my empty words,
Whilst my invention, hearing not my tongue,
Anchors on Isabel. Heaven in my mouth . . .
And in my heart, the strong and swelling evil
Of my conception.

(2.4.1–7)

The sexual will, asserting itself perhaps in the half-pun on 'evil'/'will', produces the irony of the loss of his will, the loss of any internal principle of law: hence the self-discovery of his concluding soliloquy: 'when once our grace we have forgot, / Nothing goes right; we would, and we would not' (4.4.32). These words explicitly evoke St Paul whose arguments with the law, which were discussed in the Introduction, inform, implicitly, the play: 'what I would, that do I not; but what I hate, that do I', and 'The good that I would I do not, the evil that I would not, that I do' (Romans 7.15, 19).

We should recap arguments made earlier. St Paul's discoveries about inner sinfulness are usually understood as part of a self-interrogation, recognising that the function of 'the law' is to give him a knowledge of sin: 'I had not known sin but by the law: for I had not known lust, except the law had said, Thou shalt not covet (=desire)' (Romans 7.7), and that the law was given 'that sin by the commandment might become exceeding sinful' (Romans 7.13). The issue for Paul is how to deny that he is saying that the law is sinful, if its enunciation has only awakened desire within himself. If 'the strength of sin is the law' (I Corinthians 15.56), can the law be acquitted of blame for sin? Paul does not, in effect, free law from the imputation of being sin, though he proceeds as if it did. He says that 'sin' has 'taken occasion by the commandment': it awaited its opportunity to show its power when the law came in (7.11) and that the law inspired in him a will to obey, but that this will is countered by sin: 'if I do that I would not, it is no more I that do it, but sin that dwelleth in me' (7.20). Hence:

I delight in the law of God after the inward man,
But I see another law in my members, warring against the law of my mind, and bringing me into captivity to the law of sin which is in my members. (7.22–23)

82

This other law, however, which seems not to be the law of God, is precisely that, though now called the law of sin. The effect of pronouncing the law is to evoke sin, paralysing the will, so that the law of God becomes indeed 'the law of sin'. Romans 7 argues that the Mosaic, and indeed the Adamic law, gives knowledge of sin; making it apparent; and that the law was given that 'sin, by the commandment might become exceeding sinful'.

In bringing out sinfulness, the commandment can only condemn: its message is 'mortality'. So Angelo discovers, when inwardly baffled by his desire to seduce Isabella. At that moment he discovers in himself nothing but sin, such as the 'gravity' in which, he confesses, he takes pride (2.4.9,10). The Duke had invited his character to manifest itself, but it seems that it could only do so in such a way that Angelo ends with 'I crave death more willingly than mercy' (5.1.479). That recalls the 'mortality / mercy' dichotomy; it shows that Angelo wills his death with the force of appetite, as the word 'crave' shows; it makes it the law's function to secure that the will desires not life and mercy, but its enforcement, death. The deathwards-drive is reinforced elsewhere. The Duke's 'Be absolute for death' calls 'life' the desire only of fools, and it assimilates 'Life' and Claudio together as 'death's fool' – but, as in *The Merchant of Venice*, Death is often to be pictured as a fool, or jester – before negating every property of life: such is the tongue of the highest authority in the play (3.1.5,8,11). Isabella confirms that the power of the father, which is, in psychoanalytic terms, the law itself, requires the necessity of death from beyond the grave: when Claudio assents to die, she replies: 'there my father's grave / Did utter forth a voice' (3.1.87–88).

The law is a will to bring out the human will, manifesting its fault-lines; but the will of the law makes its character wilful, marked by the pre-emptory and cruel character of the words 'Thou shalt not', in the full knowledge that the person so addressed is likely to disobey, has no power to do otherwise, and is actually incited to disobedience by the commandment. It works by imposing itself violently so that it must make the person who hears it identify with it as a failure, unless, like Isabella, they go into the convent to be wholly governed by the 'more strict restraint' of the Order of St Clare (1.4.4). If the human will seems ambiguous, so is the law's will, which seems sovereign, but has also the opposite power of appetite.

In Act 2 scene 4, Angelo and Isabella both learn the law's contradictoriness, as both the expression of the divine will, and its opposite. At his most tyrannical, duplicitous moment, Angelo calls himself 'the voice of the recorded law' with the power to 'pronounce a sentence on your brother's life' (2.4.61–62). The voice reads out what is in the record; it affirms the speaker's sense that his will and identity are the same as the law. Isabella, unconsciously recalling Angelo's comment on his tongue as divided from his heart, tells him: 'I have no tongue but one' (2.4.140), attempting to affirm in herself a unity of discourse, tongue and heart together. That affirmation is undermined, however, since she has already admitted to an ambiguity in herself, as motivated by the power of her will, which divides her speech from her actions: 'to have what we would have, we speak not what we mean' (2.4.119). The words echo Saint Paul ('what I would, that I do not') in their self-division. She is rounded on by Angelo:

> I have begun,
> And now I give my sensuous race the rein.
> Fit thy consent to my sharp appetite;
> Lay by all nicety and prolixious blushes
> That banish what they sue for. Redeem thy brother
> By yielding up thy body to my will . . .
> . . .   Answer me tomorrow,
> Or, by the affection that now guides me most,
> I'll prove a tyrant to him.
>
> (2.4.160–70)

The association of the desiring 'appetite' with 'will' and 'affection' (remembering *Troilus and Cressida*, a word with sexual associations), is clearly evident in 2.1.10, 3.1.110. So is Angelo's awareness of the law, in calling himself 'a tyrant', speaking as if he could act above the law, not observing its rule over himself. The definition of 'tyrant' comes from what the Duke says about tyrannous behaviour: a tyrant has a law for others, none for himself (4.2.71–77). Angelo's injustice to Isabella creates her lament:

> O perilous mouths
> That bear in them one and the selfsame tongue
> Either of condemnation or approof,
> Bidding the law make curtsy to their will,

Hooking both right and wrong to the appetite,
To follow as it draws!

(2.4.173–78)

This, as in *Troilus and Cressida*, makes the will synonymous with the 'appetite', a word which has now appeared three times, each time implicating Angelo, who, in the first instance, according to the Duke, 'scarce confesses / That his blood flows' or that 'his appetite / Is more to stone than bread' (1.3.51–53), meaning that he is not capable of being tempted (Matthew 4.3). But Angelo now knows that 'blood thou art blood' (2.4.15); 'blood' as sexual desire being the source of volition, and, as already quoted, he has acknowledged his 'sharp appetite' (2.4.162). As double as the 'tongue', the 'will' is the appetite which hooks both right (Isabella) and wrong (Claudio).[5] Isabella is amazed that when 'one and the self-same tongue' speaks the will is both right (the rational voice of the law) and arbitrary (an affect). Yet Isabella's use of the word implies that the will is only ever an appetite, making the law an appetite too.

The complex and destructive character of that appetite is articulated by Claudio when explaining to Lucio why he is under 'restraint', in a short speech with two similes in it, both of which allude to the appetite, the first referring to 'surfeit', the second to the action of ravening, or eating:

From too much liberty, my Lucio, liberty.
As surfeit is the father of much fast,
So every scope by the immoderate use
Turns to restraint. Our natures do pursue,
Like rats that raven down their proper bane,
A thirsty evil, and when we drink, we die.

(1.2.124–29)

In the second simile, rats devour ferociously that which poisons them, and it causes them thirst; when they drink, they die. Conjoining the simile ('like rats that raven down their proper bane' with the lines on either side, the rats have a devouring nature, they consume poison, thirst, then drink and die. How does this apply to humans? Does it imply a five-stage process, beginning with the opening assumption of a will which pursues an evil which causes thirst (the sexual, producing more desire), which then seeks more solace (drinks), and then dies? But if the 'rat' simile is conjoined fully with the surrounding lines, then the language runs through four stages: humans pursue poison, in, perhaps, wanting too much liberty (freedom from the law), but that creates thirst (the sexual appetite) which is followed by drinking (enjoyment of the sexual) and then death.

The argument within Claudio's speech suggests the libertine pathway he has followed, which is pursued more intensively by Lucio and the bawds. But the sentence beginning 'our natures do pursue', as a gloss on the idea of surfeiting, also suggests an opposite reading: that the 'proper bane', the 'thirsty evil' is the desire that longs for restraint; a pathway which in an undeclared way has been followed not only by the Duke, who seems at home in his monkish disguise, and who 'above all other strifes contended especially to know himself' (3.1.488–89), but by Isabella desiring the convent, and by Angelo, whose desire for 'restraint' shows not least in his praying. The pursuit either of liberty or law carries the sense that both are dangerous. The desire for law is also productive of liberty. Though Claudio, when talking about our natures seeking liberty, is full of self-blame for stepping beyond the law, it seems, from Saint Paul's argument, that the 'all-binding law' (2.4.94), which restrains and literally manacles him, also produces that desire for 'too much liberty'.[6] Since the tendency of the play is to equate the 'will' with 'law', the law becomes desire itself – desire of and over another – and itself the pursuit of liberty even while disavowing that. L.C. Knights writes of Angelo as 'of a will tautened and strained. The Duke speaks of him as "a man of stricture and firm abstinence", [1.3.12] and the unfamiliarity of the word "stricture" ensures that its derivation from *stringere*, to bind together or to strain, shall contribute to the meaning of the line'.[7] With this sense of restriction, which has, perhaps, its own sexual desire contained both sadistically and masochistically within it, may be compared 'strict statutes' (1.3.19), 'strict restraint' (1.4.4) and Angelo as 'strait in virtue' (2.1.9). The straitness produces Angelo's haste: despite his disavowals of interest, Angelo is eager to see execution carried out; he is more than just an efficient machine. And it is not just Angelo for whom restraint is inseparable from the sexual: Isabella thinking of what she would do under threat of death: 'the impression of keen whips I'd wear as rubies / And strip myself to death as to a bed / That longing have been sick for, ere I'd yield / My body up to shame' (2.4.101–4) equally unconsciously shows the eroticism that the law solicits, and which is felt to be a fit response to it.[8] That this forbidding the sexual adds to the pleasure of its repression is clear from Angelo's tortured soliloquies, but it is also expressed in displaced ways: the point relates back to the earlier discussion of 'Kant with Sade'. Desire for restraint, or repression, may also produce something of sexual satisfaction.

The rats in Claudio's speech 'raven' down the bane which is 'proper' to them, because it has been prepared for them in the knowledge that it will kill them, but humans pursue a 'thirsty evil' which is also 'proper' to them, in the sense that it is appropriate, fitting, and finds its natural outlet in drinking, as thirst without drinking also leads to death. This 'thirsty evil' – caused because of thirst, itself a strong appetite, and causing more thirst – returns with Angelo's 'strong and swelling evil'. He has now a sense of himself which contrasts with his earlier sense of his possible 'faults' (2.1.28). Perhaps both perceptions are extreme, neither represent the exchange of measured consideration of the self for another measured consideration. In referring to 'our natures', Claudio's speech implies that poison has been laid down on purpose for humans: if this is how their natures are it seems that 'measure', meaning 'restraint', is not possible in human lives. But his speech also contains another sense of 'measure for measure' – surfeit turns to 'much fast' (two extremes); and every 'scope', a word which recalls the 'scope' given to Angelo by the Duke, by 'immoderate' (measureless) use produces its opposite. What Lucio calls the 'foppery of freedom' becomes 'the morality of imprisonment' (1.2.112–13). With so many scenes set in the prison, 'measure for measure' thus implies a form of justice taking place, but that 'justice' is not necessarily just at all.

Escalus takes a tragic view, reflecting how injustice inheres in the order of things:

> Well, heaven forgive him, and forgive us all!
> Some rise by sin, and some by virtue fall.
> Some run from brakes of ice, and answer none,
> And some condemned for a fault alone.
>
> (2.1.37–40)

Some rise by the power of sin, perhaps becoming judges; some fall by virtue, like Angelo, staking everything on his singleness of will and brought low by Isabella's virtue. The following two lines amplify Escalus's words: some run from breaks (cracks, or faults in the ice), and are safe (they rise by sin too). Some have their virtue destroyed by one fault, like Claudio, rather than by many breaks.[9] 'Fault' contains not only the sense of absence, but of cracks, flaws (*OED* n.4), which suggests a vaginal meaning, and is punned on with 'false'.[10] Perhaps the condemned are so because of a 'fault' in the judge: so Claudio speculates in 1.2.156.

'Fault', a word used more often in this play, in singular and plural forms, than in any other by Shakespeare, appears to characterise what 'our natures' are:

> Go to your bosom,
> Knock there, and ask your heart what it doth know
> That's like my brother's fault . . .
>
> (2.2.138–41)

The word, once implanted, recurs with Angelo's self-questionings, remembering the sexual power of Isabella's 'virtue' – 'Is this her fault, or mine? / The tempter or the tempted, who sins most?' (2.2.165–67). If 'some by virtue fall' perhaps Isabella's virtue is her fault. In the next interview, Angelo returns to the word:

> Since I suppose we are made to be no stronger
> Than faults may shake our frames – let me be bold;
> I do arrest your words. Be that you are,
> That is, a woman; if you be more, you're none.
>
> (2.4.133–36)

He means that in attempting to be 'more' by being a nun, Isabella denies the significance of 'faults' which relate directly to 'our frames'. Escalus's speech allowed for the attribution of faultiness to no single agency: *whose* sin, virtue, or fault is involved in people's risings and fallings does not appear, so it is not clear, from Angelo's words, whether outside faults shake our frames (like Isabella shaking, soliciting Angelo), or internal faults. 'Is this her fault or mine?' cannot be answered. There may be nothing but faults. The will, not single, flawless, may be close in its meaning to 'fault'. 'Is this her fault, or mine?' acknowledges that the will of the law – epitomised in Isabella, whose 'there is a vice that most I do abhor' shows that she identifies with it – tempts the subject's will. Isabella becomes the tempter, the pure agent of desire – like the 'they'

88

evoked in Sonnet 94, a sonnet more often applied to Angelo at the play's beginning than to Isabella:

> They that have power to hurt and will do none,
> That do not do the thing they most do show,
> Who moving others are themselves as stone,
> Unmoved, cold, and to temptation slow . . . . [11]

Isabella's being is an image of the law: cold; but it is that 'coldness' in her soliciting, criticised in her by Lucio (2.2.55), which makes Angelo unable to run from this 'break of ice'. He can hardly be said to sin 'most' in responding to temptation, since this would imply that he had had the power of choice; that his will was other than his appetite, and that he was stronger than the faults which shake our frames.

Like 'fault', 'law', and its cognates, 'laws', 'lawful', 'unlawful' and 'lawless', appears in this play more than in any other by Shakespeare; as does 'justice', with its various cognates. If the law is the will, what is the distinction between it and justice? When the Duke says 'he who the sword of heaven will bear / Should be as holy as severe' (3.1.515–16) that indicates that the law is to be enforced if necessary, even if the idea that the sword is of heaven gives it legitimacy. Enforcing the law is a reminder that law rests on an act of violence which instates it, and which must be repeated, by enacting the law through its power of 'mortality' to sustain it. It is an argument developed in an essay by Derrida, 'Force of Law', discussing issues raised by Walter Benjamin in 'Critique of Violence' ('Zur Kritik der Gewalt'), who stressed that the German *Gewalt* implies both 'law-founding violence and law-preserving violence'.[12] Violence instates the law, and the law is violence; for Derrida, 'the police are the force of law' (277). Derrida's essay is subtitled 'The "Mystical Foundation of Authority"', a phrase taken from Montaigne (*Essais* 3.13, 'De l'expérience'), which might suggest that 'authority' is that whose foundation, or basis for being, takes character from not being questionable, as with the Duke in the play. But it also suggests the opposite: that every act of decision, inherent in passing a judgment, involves a suspension of legal processes, because to give justice is not simply to carry out what the law says, as in Angelo's symptomatic way of thinking, 'the jury passing on the prisoner's life' (2.1.19), but requires thinking of the singularity of the individual case before the court. And all the more so, since, as *Measure for Measure* indicates, the law must condemn: which is an emphasis not found in Derrida. The act of decision or justice takes place outside the ordinary calculations of the law; as a decision, it can lay claim to no basis, no foundation. Derrida writes that 'the operation that amounts to founding, inaugurating, justifying law, to *making law*, would consist of a *coup de force*, of a performative and therefore interpretative violence that in itself is neither just nor unjust and that no justice and no earlier and previously founding law, no preexisting foundation, could, by definition, guarantee or contradict or invalidate' (241). A law is, then, made in a moment of illegality, by which Derrida implies the absence of any founding authority. In contrast, in *Measure for Measure*, despite the moments of *coup de théâtre*, there is no suspension by the Duke of his authority, which finally centres everything.

For Derrida, 'Law is not justice. Law is the element of calculation, and it is just that there is law, but justice is incalculable; it demands that one calculate with the incalculable' (244). Though 'justice' in *Measure for Measure* is sometimes synonymous with 'law', the law is less than justice. 'The deputed sword' may seem to belong to 'ceremony' (2.2.59, 60), but it works unceremoniously, as with the 'haste' that Angelo continually enjoins on the execution of Claudio, and farcically, in the case of Barnardine whom it cannot behead, neither practically nor morally. If it did, it would condemn the executor of the law, since Barnardine cannot be got to crave death more willingly than mercy.[13] Enforcement by the sword sustains government and the rule of law: as St Paul says of the earthly ruler, the 'higher power', 'he beareth not the sword in vain: for he is the minister of God, a revenger to execute wrath upon him that doeth evil' (Romans 12.4). Paul pronounces the ruler a revenger; reacting to what has gone before. *Measure for Measure* shows the law reacting to carnivalistic licence, but the earthly ruler's destiny becomes a revenger's tragedy, since Angelo knows that he has had to be unjust in (as he thinks) putting Claudio to death, because he fears that if Claudio had received his pardon on the basis of Isabella sleeping with the deputy, then he would, in time, have taken revenge (4.4.28). Angelo in his remorse, and awareness of having 'forgot' his 'grace', acknowledges that the law's status has been maintained by an unjust act of violence: founded in violence, the law makes a violent demand, and upholds its authority by getting its revenge in first.

Vienna's 'sinfulness' seems exclusively sexual, but its quality as sin is contingent on the law calling it so ('Lechery?' asks Lucio – 'Call it so' replies Claudio [1.2.116]). Hence Pompey's remark that being a bawd would be a lawful trade if the law would allow it. The law seems counter-intuitive in not recognising the prior existence of bawds (2.1.214–32). No amount of condemnation, short of gelding and splaying all the youth of the city, will avail, according to Pompey's practical wisdom. Elbow has learned the written, 'recorded' law as rules, which dictates responses to people:

> If these be good people in a commonweal that do nothing but use their abuses in common houses, I know no law. (2.1.41–43)

Elbow cannot know except by reference to a written law, whose language Pompey so subverts that he drives Angelo, anxious to maintain the purity of the law's meaning, off the bench. That the law is partial appears in Pompey's comment on the recent legalisation, in England in 1570, of usury (3.1.274–76). Some rise by sin. The law is not a self-evident, ahistorical structure; if it were, Vienna's 'order of law' would not have judged, at a particular moment, in favour of one type of usury, bawdi-ness being the merrier type which has been put down. These examples show that the law is not self-evidently the eternal law of God, but actu-ally more like a comic structure which presents itself as one thing, when personified in Angelo's straightness of character, but which is actually, hypocritically, another. On that basis it could be said that there is no reason why the law should not contain mercy, since it is only a matter of 'seeming' (2.4.151), and has neither 'proper tongue', nor proper being. Nonetheless, the knowledge that the law represents ideology sustained by violence, cannot be avowed within the argument which posits the law as a pure structure which must condemn. The play works within the ambiguity of those two emphases, the law as the name of confusion, and the law as purity, while being the will; and that moti-vates both its comic or tragic possibilities.

In this atmosphere, neither success nor failure in rising or falling are markers of justice, so making more invidious the connection of law and 'justice' with revenge. Angelo recognises that law brings on revenge, and that this must be concealed as a motivation, when carrying out the law, but revenge is inherent in the idea of 'measure for measure'. It was so in *Henry VI Part 3* when Warwick demands that Clifford's head be placed on the walls of York in place of Richard, Duke of York's, for 'Measure for measure must be answered' (2.6.55). Clifford's son had been killed;

Clifford kills Rutland, York's son, and York, and is now killed himself, so evoking a continual tit for tat, 'measure for measure', the phrase establishing the rule of revenge in the history plays. Revenge, as an element of law, is built into Claudio's fear of death: life is succeeded by eternal torture:

> To bathe in fiery floods, or to reside
> In thrilling region of thick-ribbèd ice,
> To be imprisoned in the viewless winds
> And blown with restless violence round about
> The pendent world, or to be worse than worst
> Of those that lawless and incertain thought
> Lie howling . . .
>
> (3.1.125–31)

Claudio does not question that what lies after death means being caught in breaks of ice, condemned for a fault alone. Perhaps the word 'lawless' evokes the zealotry of Christians who go beyond all limits in imagining the afterlife a punishment for this life, but nonetheless the *lex talionis* is part of Christianity, as affirmed by Christ in Matthew 7.1–2, and the Duke's speech, which was quoted at the beginning, in pronouncing it, assumes that punishment is reparation for what has gone before.[14]

Claudio gives his last speeches in his interview with his sister. Making himself 'absolute for death' (3.1.5), he hardly speaks again, and not at all in the last scene, when he is revived. But perhaps the Duke, condemning Angelo, imagines Claudio speaking, like the voice of his father proclaiming a sentence of death: 'the very mercy of the law cries out / Most audible, even from his proper tongue'. This reading identifies 'his' as Claudio, and the crying out like the voice of the murdered Abel demanding vengeance (Genesis 4.10). Certainly Claudio's ghost is both imagined and evoked by the Duke: 'Should she kneel down in mercy of this fact / Her brother's ghost his paved bed would break / And take her hence with horror' (5.1.435–37). And 'An Angelo for Claudio, death for death' confirms the 'law' as retribution, the use of 'death' rather than 'life' emphasising the incongruity: for if Claudio is dead, no equation could possibly balance him with the live Angelo, even if Claudio was to be imagined as a ghost. That is, unless death and life were assumed to be equivalents, as in 'Be absolute for death'. If it is assumed that the Duke is continuing to test Isabella, whose appeal for 'justice'

(5.1.21–37) actually demands revenge, it seems that she has been brought, against all probabilities including the thought of her dead brother's revenge, to surrender it.[15] That is because of what Mariana says, responding to the Duke's declaration that he has manifested Angelo's 'fault' (5.1.413), and discovered 'faults proper to himself' (5.1.110): 'they say best men are moulded out of faults, / And for the most, become much more the better / For being a little bad' (5.1.431–33). If 'best men' – as opposed to 'seemers' – are moulded out of faults, they possess neither a single identity, nor a single will to be appealed to or punished, and make revenge pointless.

Isabella's response, choosing to acquit Angelo of blame for anything he may have thought about her, contravenes Christ on the sinfulness of the thought of adultery, as much as its act (Matthew 5.27,28). Arguing that 'thoughts are no subjects, / Intents but merely thoughts' (5.1.445–46), she makes the 'bad intent', which means the bad will, into that which has neither power nor necessity to be questioned as inherent within a subject put on trial. Her words contradict Hebrews 4.12, which describes the 'word of God' as 'quick and powerful and sharper than any two-edged sword' being 'a discerner of the thoughts and intents of the heart'. Altering without having achieved anything of the 'justice' she craved, Isabella gives up on the idea of measure being followed by measure, which also means surrendering any idea that justice is what Derrida calls 'calculable'.

But if Isabella's plea implies the loss of her will, it is not clear that it has an impact on the Duke, whose 'unknown sovereignty' (5.1.387) is responsible for everything, and the guarantee, by the end, of law-making and justice. Others seem to have lost their will by the end: Mariana, Angelo, Claudio, Juliet, Isabella herself, the Provost – all of them remain silent, not to mention Barnardine; none have a tongue at the end. Isabella responds neither to her brother's new existence, nor to the Duke's offer of marriage. Only Lucio speaks, because he must defend himself against the Duke, who begins by saying he cannot pardon him, despite his 'apt remission', but ends by forgiving him if he marries Kate Keepdown. Uniquely in Shakespeare, the Duke begins and ends the play, so it concludes with one will too many: that of the Duke, who 'pardons' Claudio as if on the basis that the new, unmuffled man on stage replaces the Claudio who has as if 'died'.[16] Angelo can only live on the basis that Claudio is alive: 'By this Lord Angelo perceives he's safe; / Methinks I see a quickening in his eye' (5.1.497–98). 'Measure for

Measure' is not executed, because it is not necessary, but it is not rescinded. Forgiveness depends on the maintenance of sovereignty, even though the Duke has been working virtually against the law, to bring about an outcome where an apt remission can be uttered. It has been 'measure', meaning 'step': circumventing the law, as with the bed-trick – against 'measure'. At the end, forgiveness instates his authority and sovereign will.

The word 'measure' is commented on, in a different context, by Derrida, opening another essay on law and justice, called 'On Forgiveness': 'In principle, there is no limit to forgiveness, no *measure*, no moderation, not "to what point"'.[17] Derrida starts with the caveat 'in principle' because part of his argument is that the word 'forgiveness' is inappropriate, because it supports the will of the person forgiving: 'what makes the "I forgive you" sometimes unbearable, or odious, even obscene, is the affirmation of sovereignty. It is often addressed from the top down, it confirms its own freedom or assumes for itself the power of forgiving' (58). If the Duke is to be thought of as like God, then that shows that theocracy depends on the assertion of the will, which includes the power of forgiveness. The Duke, proposing marriage to her, asks Isabella for a 'willing ear' (5.1.539) but perhaps she is silent because the power of saying 'I will', and the power of the will, has been so questioned by the play. Having been through so much, put under sentence of death, can any of the play's sufferers, so many of them on stage, reassert the will? Can they live without it?

4

The 'Craft of Will' in Shakespeare's Poetry

I Masculine Wills

After the plays, the poetry of rape, or seduction: first *Venus and Adonis* (1593) and *The Rape of Lucrece* (1594), both dedicated to Henry Wriothesley, the Earl of Southampton (1573–1624), and *Shakespeare's Sonnets*, which appeared in 1609, published by Thomas Thorpe, with or without Shakespeare's knowledge or agreement.[1] Kerrigan's edition of the Sonnets made much of *A Lover's Complaint*, which was bound into that Quarto: since then the text has been often discussed.[2] The conflictual masculine will in Shakespeare is exemplified in Bertram in *All's Well that Ends Well*, of whom the soldier says that 'he hath perverted a young gentlewoman here in Florence of a most chaste renown, and this night he fleshes his will in the spoil of her honour' (4.3.14–16). He feeds his lust, which is compared to a hunting dog – he fleshes it – with meat from the prey (the spoil).[3] The hound is stimulated to further hunting by the reward, but what is triumphed over is a spoiled honour.

Venus and Adonis records the woman's attempt to seduce the youth, but 'she would, he will not, in her arms be bound (226).[4] She is 'wilful' – full of will, and also headstrong, and he 'unwilling':

Full gently now she takes him by the hand,
A lily prisoned in a gaol of snow,
Or ivory in an alabaster band,
So white a friend engirts so white a foe:
  This beauteous combat wilful and unwilling,
  Showed like two silver doves that sit a-billing. (361–66)

95

'She by her good will, / Will never rise, so he will kiss her still' (479–80); but by the end, Adonis has been literally unwilled by the boar, despite Venus' plea, 'come not within his danger by thy will' (639). The poem's 199 stanzas speak, inherently, of unfulfilment: Venus' eyes, opened, 'threw unwilling light / Upon the wide wound which the boar had trenched / In his soft flank' (1051–3). The annihilation of sexual difference makes Adonis nothing; but in *The Rape of Lucrece*, it is a question whether the masculine will *is* something.[5]

The poem distinguishes between the irresoluteness of Tarquin, and Lucrece's resolution. No text better shows that the will is not necessarily paired with power, but with desire, that which is lacking; there are over twenty references to it, nearly always in relation to Tarquin. Alerted to Lucrece's chastity by her husband Collatine's ill-judged publishing of her chastity, an edge has been set on his 'keen appetite' (9). Desire is brought on by what is interdicted, and it takes the form of 'envy' (39), which, as *invidia*, suggests the eye that sees and wants what it sees, since it lacks it. One relevant reference in this poem is to the 'wilful eye' (417). Envy desires what cannot be possessed, even through rape. Tarquin rides to see Lucrece at home, the text stressing his 'still-gazing eyes' (84), 'the too much wonder of his eye' (95), and 'his wanton sight' (104). After seeing Lucrece, he retires, in his mind 'revolving':

> The sundry dangers of his will's obtaining
> Yet ever to obtain his will resolving. (128–29)

His will is his lust, and his domination over the woman, and everything must work so that his will gets its will. The poem's first part, till after the rape, shows Tarquin moving towards the deed, like Macbeth, who comments that 'withered murder, / Alarumed by his sentinel, the wolf, / Whose howl's his watch, thus with his stealthy pace, / With Tarquin's ravishing strides, towards his design / Moves like a ghost' (*Macbeth* 2.1.52–56). Macbeth does not see his kinship with Tarquin, whose will is towards Lucrece as everything; the text commenting on the disastrous nature of desire:

> They that much covet are with gain so fond
> That what they have not, that which they possess,
> They scatter and unloose it from their bond,
> And so, by hoping more, they have but less;

Or, gaining more, the profit of excess
Is but to surfeit, and such griefs sustain
That they prove bankrupt in this poor-rich gain. (129–40)

The stanza moralises on the impossibility of possession; even what is possessed is not actually possessed, because it is not theirs. The first line comments on wanting, feeling a lack; 'fond' implies 'overly attached to' and 'foolish'. 'Gaining more' equals 'excess', which means 'surfeiting': a word suggestive of the power of 'appetite', and true of 'surfeit-taking Tarquin' (698) when he rapes Lucrece:

His taste delicious, in digestion souring,
Devours his will, that lived by foul devouring. (699–700)

The will is the appetite that compels him to eat, but the effect of the surfeiting is to eat up the appetite, to end the will, make it disappear, as nothing. The only way he can learn what he has done is when 'self-will himself doth tire' (707). The will has destroyed itself in a process of desiring, eating and surfeiting and sickening: self-will tires the self, with which it is identified, and the will tires itself. The moralising sequence closes:

So that in vent'ring ill we leave to be
The things we are for that which we expect;
And this ambitious foul infirmity,
In having much, torments us with defect
Of that we have; so then we do neglect
  The thing we have, and all for want of wit,
  Make something nothing by augmenting it. (148–54)

'The things we are' suggests the puzzling, irresolvable nature of man, that which the idea of the will tries to resolve by its venturing; the will is the 'ambitious foul infirmity', making ambition the result of envy. The activity of the will is nihilistic; as is seen in the move from 'the things we are' to 'the thing we have' (reducing those things, and making them now into something 'we have') to 'make something nothing'. Plurality is mistaken for singleness, and the effort to add to that, which is the work of the will, turns 'something' into 'nothing', which is also what the will does. Tarquin goes away after the rape 'a captive victor

that hath lost in gain, / Bearing away the wound that nothing healeth'
(730–31). The wound recalls Adonis. Punning on making something
nothing recalls the bawdy talk of Meletza and Lampatho in *What You
Will*. The something made nothing is Tarquin's will, his masculine
desire, and his gender. Rape as asserting masculinity, which is why
Tarquin speaks of his will, makes the woman and man nothing, reducing
'the things we are'. For Lacan, sexual difference is a matter of *das Ding*,
whose perceived loss makes assertion of sexual difference fetish-like in
character; *The Rape of Lucrece* is fascinated by Tarquin's efforts to assure
himself that he has something, though any 'gain' is 'poor rich'. As he
approaches Lucrece, he goes through a soliloquy (190–245) where he
says, as if the rhetoric would make the will (imaged as a fortress under
siege) invincible:

My will is strong past reason's weak removing (243),

this being part of his disputation ''tween frozen conscience and hot
burning will' (247). Yet it cannot be a true antithesis; if the conscience
is frozen, it cannot strive at all against the will; if the will is to have the
effect of melting the conscience, then it does what it would not do: frees
up the conscience, which happens after the rape.

Tarquin opens the locks 'between her chamber and his will' (302); the
portals being 'unwilling' (309). Outside her door, he appeals to 'Love and
Fortune', adding, 'my will is backed with resolution' (352). This, in the
context of the prayer, suggests a weakness of the will; if that must be supplemented by resolution, as a synonym for the will, it becomes a word only,
given substance rhetorically. Seeing Lucrece sleeping:

What could he see but mightily he noted?
What did he note but strongly he desired?
What he beheld, on that he firmly doted,
And in his will his wilful eye he tired. (414–17)

The gaze is that of the 'wilful eye'; later Lucrece says that she has been
'overseen' (1206), and F.T. Prince, who annotates 417 as 'in his lust he
wearied his lustful eye', records the suggestion within the word as it is
used at line 1206, of witchcraft and the evil eye, which is the eye of envy.
The 'wilful eye' notes, desires and dotes; and is both fed full (so Roe) and
tired out by the sum of these activities, which are called 'his will'. His

will exhausts his wilful eye, which cannot look, or have, enough: it tires first, as if again suggesting the will's inadequacy. When Tarquin speaks to Lucrece, he says:

> . . . thou with patience must my will abide,
> My will that marks thee for my earth's delight,
> Which I to conquer sought with all my might.
>   But as reproof and reason beat it dead,
>   By thy bright beauty was it newly bred . . .

> . . . But will is deaf and hears no heedful friends;
>   Only he hath an eye to gaze on Beauty,
>   And dotes on what he looks, 'gainst law or duty. (486–90, 495–97)

Will has an eye, but no ear, and its quality is to 'dote' on 'beauty', a recurrent word throughout this speech; but the doting is ambiguous, because it is destructive, as envy. The speech suggests the wilfulness of the personified 'Will' which he speaks of as though it was separate from him as 'I', and hearing no heedful friends, and working against law; Will becomes that which will have no law, having its own law. Lucrece tells him 'thy will remove' (614), recalling line 243 for contrast, and 'from a pure heart command thy rebel will' (625); but he rapes her, and departs. In his remorse after the rape he feels he stands disgraced, while 'cares' ask his soul (his 'spotted princess', 721) how she fares:

> She says her subjects with foul insurrection
> Have battered down her consecrated wall,
> And by their mortal fault brought in subjection
> Her immortality, and made her thrall
> To living death and pain perpetual;
>   Which in her prescience she controlled still,
>   But her foresight could not forestall their will. (722–28)

The soul's subjects are her passions, whose single 'will' has ruined her temple. The passage emphasises the man's tragedy, his disintegration. If these instances have made the will masculine, that is because at the heart of the text is the tragedy of the will. Lucrece speaks differently: the term 'will' only relates to her when in lines 1181–1206 she declares what will be her 'testament' (1183), her 'will' (1198,1205). In an implicit pun she says Collatine must 'oversee this will', because she has been 'over-seen'. And, after the rhetoric of the will, she writes to Collatine, so that the letter takes on qualities of the last testamentary will, but 'what wit sets down is blotted straight with will' (1299); by her tears, her affectual state; for 'their gentle sex to weep are often willing'.[6] Yet the power of the will there, which works within writing, is significant; and the will by blotting ink creates indecipherability, so that she must follow up the stained letter with her death: 'ere she with blood had stained her stained excuse' (1316). In her will, she had bequeathed to Tarquin 'my stained blood' (1181), but now the ambiguities of 'stained excuse' multiply: she cannot be fully innocent, but is stained. That is where the ambiguities of language work, as with line 401: 'O modest wantons, wanton modesty'. Her will has stained the clarity of her wit, or the clarity of her writing; any form of writing – including writing the will – is a form of staining, so there is never else remaining but the stain. In these ways the blotting and staining of the will moves the writing towards something that cannot be articulated (she dies not speaking Tarquin's name), towards the condition of *das Ding*.

II 'A LOVER'S COMPLAINT'

So on the tip of his subduing tongue
All kinds of arguments and question deep,
All replication prompt, and reason strong,
For his advantage still did wake and sleep,
To make the weeper laugh, the laugher weep:
He had the dialect and and different skill,
Catching all passions in his craft of will.

That he did in the general bosom reign
Of young, or old, and sexes both enchanted
To dwell with him in thoughts, or to remain
In personal duty, following where he haunted;
Consents bewitched, ere he desire have granted,
And dialogued for him what he would say,
Asked their own wills, and made their wills obey. (120–33)

These lines, spoken by a woman in awed admiration of a male seducer, come from Shakespeare's *A Lover's Complaint*, comprising 47 stanzas where the poem's 'I', who is male, listens to a woman complaining to an older man how she was seduced by a young man, whom she describes. The poem, while being a complaint, like Lucrece's complaints to Night and Opportunity (*The Rape of Lucrece* 764–1036), is a tribute to his fascination, recognising his 'craft of will', which is amplified by a later line which acknowledges 'his passion, but [i.e. only] an art of craft' (295); and David Bevington compares his own sympathetic reaction to her to the way he feels about Cressida.[7] The complaint fills the whole poem, prompts the memory of the 'deep-brained sonnets' (209) that were written to him, and the acknowledgement that he could 'swoon at tragic shows' (308). The woman concludes that he could make her fall again; such is his 'craft of will': all his rhetorical powers and persuasion are the exercise of the power of the will; poetry itself is a 'craft' of will, craft implying deceit, and that his charm, appealing to 'sexes both', can seduce both.

Hence 'consents' – meaning consenting people, those assenting to his will – by being bewitched, before he granted them their desire (to be seduced by him) argued the case for seduction that he would make to them within themselves.[8] They 'asked their own wills': i.e. they asked their desires what they wanted, and 'made their wills obey' under the power of his superior 'craft of will': their wills obeyed his will. In *Troilus and Cressida*, reason was supposed to govern the will, but here the will succumbs under the power of another will; indeed 'reason panders will' (*Hamlet*, 3.4.78), aids, not restrains, the will.

Fascination with this idea is inherent also in the Sonnets, which are addressed to a man, and then to an equally compelling woman, possessing the power of the will. One like the seducer is implicitly addressed in Sonnets nos. 1–126, a series of 'lover's complaints' drawing attention to his bisexual charm. This man seems not absent from the 'dark lady' sonnets, 127–152.[9] Though whether the order of poems is Shakespeare's, and so prepared for publication, or whether he even authorised their publication, is unknown; it seems that sonnets were written throughout his career; perhaps those addressed to the woman (127–152) were of the 1590s and some written or revised in the 1600s. But certainly, like other poems, they were written parallel to the writing of plays, not as merely supplementary to them.[10] 'Shakespeare' is the only name discernible from the partial narrative or narratives that make up the Quarto edition, but 'My name is Will' appears at the end of Sonnet

101

136, so implicitly making the text autobiographical; the 'I' who speaks in them has a relationship to Will and, because of the publisher's title, "Shakespeare's Sonnets", to Shakespeare. The significance of the establishment of this poetic 'I' is the subject of Joel Fineman in his work on the sonnets, in *Shakespeare's Perjured Eye* (1986).[11] He points out that the sonnets to the young man make less of 'Will' than here [in sonnets 127–154], which 'not only makes his self-determination into a central and explanatory theme . . . but also speaks this name in such reverberating and resounding fashion that it becomes . . . a sound informing almost all the other words he speaks' (290). Indeed, the only sonnets which invoke 'Will' and which are written to the young man – assuming that only one man is addressed throughout – are 57, 58, 89; those addressing the woman – if she is one woman – are 134, 135, 136 and 143. And there is little similarity between the two senses in which 'will' appears in the two groups.

Fineman's work on the Sonnets associates with a later essay on *The Rape of Lucrece*. *Shakespeare's Perjured Eye* was to be the prelude to a book on Shakespeare's Will, left unfinished at Fineman's death. He sees the poetry of sonnets 1–126 as part of an idealising poetry of praise, derived from the sonnet tradition of Dante and Petrarch, so that there is nothing of heterogeneity within the ideal figure. In the same way, the male tradition in which Collatine praises Lucrece to Tarquin as 'chaste' produces another situation which comes 'after praise'.[12] What comes after is the rape of the woman, outside the homosociality of the circle where praise is given. With the Sonnets, after no. 126, the epideictic language is forsworn for 'an imagery of phenomenal heterogeneity, the conflicted physicality of which embodies an interruption in or wrinkling of familiar imagery of visionary sameness, identity, reflection, likeness'. A visionary recreation of the woman cedes to a linguistic one, and that poetic voice:

> establishes the first-person speaker of the sonnets, whom the sonnets will sometimes call 'Will' as the internally divided, post-idealist subject of a 'perjur'd eye' (sonnet 152). . . . This subject, 'Will' . . . possesses a specific characterological profile, e.g. he – for this subject is conceived as male – experiences his own phenomenal substantiality as a materialised heterogeneity; he is subject of an unprecedentedly heterosexual, and therefore misogynist, desire for an object that is not admired; he speaks a language that effectively speaks against itself

and derives from the experience of such speaking a specific sense of space and time. ('Temporality', 29)

The Sonnets record, then, a movement from homosexuality which is homogeneous, and idealist, towards a heterosexuality founded on an opposition to the woman as other; in the assertion of this otherness, an identity for the self is constructed, which Fineman says is marked by 'an altogether unprecedented verbal desire for what is not admired' ('Shakespeare's Ear' in *The Subjectivity Effect*, 223).[13] Fineman offers a form of 'queer theory' which sees the birth of heterosexuality as a poetic discourse as founded on the supersession of a normative homosocial/homosexual thinking, which prompts its own emulation with regard to the woman in *The Rape of Lucrece*; or else, it suggests that heterosexuality is based on the power of emulation rising from sexual difference, which does not exist within the non-differentiated mirroring relationship of the poet and the young man. Especially with *The Rape of Lucrece*, Fineman sees writing as analogous to rape, a violence associating with the sense that the politics of heterosexuality is misogynistic. Tarquin and Lucrece speak the same language, so much so that *The Rape of Lucrece*'s title, its double genitive ('of') threatens to make the woman the rapist as much as the object of rape ('Temporality', 44). Fineman discusses the folding over of language, in a chiastic structure, in a literary device Puttenham called a 'cross-couple', the 'syneciostic trope' where 'two contrary words' are tied as it were like a pair of couples, and made to agree ('Temporality', 31–32).[14]

Bringing contrasts together allows him to find M and W as inversions of each other, and suggestive of Shakespeare's name, William, the letters being a signature (48); hence there is a continual pattern in *Lucrece* of reversals, and of 'folds' ('Temporality', 43). So punning on Tarquin 'all in post' from Ardea to Collatium in the first line, and Collatine publishing details about Lucrece, and Lucrece writing back to Collatine, he detects, following Lacan's reading of *The Purloined Letter*, a structure which forms the literary subjectivity of the one who was 'author of the rape' 'because he is the "orator" and "publisher / of that rich jewel" (lns. 30–34)'. Hence, Fineman argues, we see how

Shakespeare conceives the formation of literary subjectivity in general, so that the poem's particular elaboration of a postal circuit whereby Collatine becomes a sender who receives his message back in an inverted form (inverted by the movement of re-turning or re-versing repetition) describes the way in which *all* Shakespeare's strong literary characters acquire their specifically psychologistic literary power. ('Temporality', 55)[15]

Collatine had begun by naming Lucrece as 'chaste', (ln. 8), but now pronounces Tarquin's name (1786); this symmetry, which makes him more like Tarquin than he could ever have wished to be, and the consequent effect it has on him, produces a typical, in Shakespeare, 'misogynist erotics', where characters

> discover the same internal sense of present broken self and retrospective temporality as is summed up in 'I no more can see what once I was' [line 1764]; and they all turn into textured subjects when they learn first-hand how 'by our ears our hearts oft tainted be'. [line 38]'
> ('Temporality', 66)

Collatine has now become the subject of desire, defined as 'a longing for a visionary origin that the very act of speaking renders lost' ('Temporality', 67): the subject can say 'Will', as an expression of desire, but not 'I am' ('Temporality', 68). He is the Lacanian subject, and lost as to his identity.[16]

This material in Fineman is suggestive, if overly-schematic; I will return to it via those sonnets which invoke the will.[17] First, 57 and 58, which are often considered as linked, because of the 'slave' image which opens both, and in the first is underlined by the address to 'my sovereign' in line 6, and by the language of line 8, which includes in it the imagined tone of a superior dismissing his servant:

> Being your slave, what should I do but tend
> Upon the hours and times of your desire?
> I have no precious time at all to spend,
> Nor services to do, till you require:
> Nor dare I charge the world-without-end hour
> Whilst I, my sovereign, watch the clock for you,
> Nor think the bitterness of absence sour
> When you have bid your servant once adieu.
> Nor dare I question with my jealous thought
> Where you may be, or your affairs suppose,

But like a sad slave stay and think of naught
Save, where you are, how happy you make those.
  So true a fool is love, that in your will,
  Though you do anything, he thinks no ill. (57)

The opening question, with its rhetorical, even exaggerative opening, 'Being your slave', suggests that there may be an alternative answer to be given; there are other things he should do, or be. The poem suggests a series of reproaches, apparent in the negatives of lines 3,4,5,7,9, 11 and 14, and in the word-play of 'sad slave stay . . . save'. The final couplet, where the Quarto capitalised 'Will', moves from the image of the slave to that of the fool, and brings out the implicit criticism of the addressee, the young man: Booth (233) paraphrases: 'Love thinks there is no ill in your will [i.e. in your whim], no matter what you do in your will [i.e. in your lust, when you are driven by desire]' and 'Love in your William . . . is so true a fool [or makes William so foolish] that it [or he] thinks no ill, no matter what you do'.

If the second reading is adopted, Will has been objectified; the poem begins with 'I', but ends with the slave, or the fool, as the way he objectifies himself, referring to his name in the third person, alienated from the 'I' of the poem. And the defence of the young man depends on a repression: the 'I' has already said 'Nor think the bitterness of absence sour', and 'Nor dare I question with my jealous thought' before coming to an end with 'he thinks no ill'. So the poem, which is apparently a justification of the young man, is also a complaint, and an implicit accusation of ill-will in the other, as the whole poem with its sense of wasting hours and times, accuses the other of being wilful in his 'desire', a word synonymous with 'will'. 'The times of your desire' means 'desires which alter from time to time'. The poem is an expression of 'my jealous thought'; since 'thought' implies melancholia (see 'sad' in line 11), the poem is also an expression of melancholy, which relates, perhaps, to the sense of exaggeration.[18] The couplet concludes by saying that 'in your will / (Though you do anything) he thinks no ill'; but the poem is, nonetheless, the expression of ill-will, it is what his melancholy thought thinks. And 'thought' begins Sonnet 58:

That god forbid, that made me first your slave,
I should in thought control your times of pleasure,
Or at your hand th'account of hours to crave,

Being your vassal bound to stay your leisure.
O let me suffer, being at your beck,
Th'imprisoned absence of your liberty,
And patience, tame to sufferance, bid each check,
Without accusing you of injury.
Be where you list, your charter is so strong
That you yourself may privilege your time
To what you will; to you it doth belong
Yourself to pardon of self-doing crime.
  I am to wait, though waiting so be hell,
  Not blame your pleasure, be it ill or well. (58)

This begins by evoking Eros (recalling 'so true a fool is love' (57), but love is not mentioned here), who made him the slave and the other free. There are many expressions for that freedom the young man has: 'your times of pleasure', 'your leisure', 'your liberty', 'your charter' and the ability to do 'what you will' – recalling *Twelfth Night* – and last, 'your pleasure'. Do sonnets 57 and 58 give expression to the sufferings, and the sufferance of Antonio, who is, literally imprisoned, in that play? In which case, 'what you will' becomes the permission given to Sebastian by Antonio. The third quatrain speaks entirely of the young man: the 'I' returns in the couplet, which is more critical than in 57. Here, 'what you will' is declared to be 'either ill or well'. Booth shows the pun on 'well' and 'will'.[19] The poem expresses a will to control on the part of the 'I', acknowledging the power of the will of the other.

Sonnet 89, associating with both 88 and 90, makes a justification of the lover.[20] What he wills, in terms of his refusal of the 'I', will be justified by the 'I' of the poem: in the first quatrain, perhaps the faults are in the poetry, which is accused of lameness:

Say that thou didst forsake me for some fault,
And I will comment upon that offence;
Speak of my lameness, and I straight will halt,
Against thy reasons making no defence.
Thou canst not, love, disgrace me half so ill,
To set a form upon desired change,
As I'll myself disgrace, knowing thy will.
I will acquaintance strangle and look strange,
Be absent from thy walks, and in my tongue,

106

Thy sweet beloved name no more shall dwell,
Lest I, too much profane, should do it wrong,
And haply of our old acquaintance tell.
  For thee, against myself I'll vow debate,
  For I must ne'er love him whom thou dost hate. (89)

The second quatrain uses the ill/will rhyme that appeared in 57, and in it, the ambivalence which exists between justifying the lover and pleading with him appears in the placing of the word 'love', which is the name of the person addressed as 'thou' in the first line. There is an acknowledgement that the lover desires change, and that leads into the phrase 'knowing thy will'. That may be paraphrased as 'knowing what you want', 'knowing your lust', and 'knowing your William'. In the last case, that implies the separation of the 'I' from the 'William' who is to be cast off; the young man has desire, but not the 'I', who is cast off in a way which makes him think he may be too profane – as Hal called Falstaff (*2 Henry IV*, 5.5.48). The seventh line 'knowing thy will' concludes a sentence, so that 'I will acquaintance *strangle* and look *strange*' begins a new sentence which runs over from the second to the third quatrain; the word 'will' has been repeated; first expressing the attitude of the young man, whose name must be excluded; the second giving the determination of the 'I' who will look strange.

III THE WOMAN'S WILL

The tone of servitude, of conceding 'what you will', changes in those using the trope of 'Will' which are addressed to the woman. The first group of the Sonnets posits Time as the enemy, following the Petrarchan and Renaissance tropes, whereas in the second Time is unmentioned; not Time threatens the relationship between the 'I' and the woman, but difference between wills. Sonnet 134 sees a development from a dramatic situation which was worked out in 133. There, it seemed that the woman had enslaved his friend. Duncan-Jones (380) paraphrases 133: 'the speaker rebukes the mistress for enslaving his next self, his friend, as well as himself, and tries to negotiate better terms by enclosing the friend's heart in his own bosom'. The 'sweet'st friend' (133.4) is his 'next self' (133.6), now 'slave to slavery'; so that 'Of him, myself, and thee, I am forsaken' (133.7). The sonnet's last six lines ask that 'my friend' be imprisoned in his heart, so that with whatever 'rigour' the woman uses him, he will still have the consolation of protecting the friend. 'Will' does not appear in Sonnet 133, except as 'wilt', in the last couplet, which expresses the 'rigour' that she will use: 'And yet thou wilt, for I being pent in thee / Perforce am thine, and all that is in me' (133.13–14). Sonnet 134 starts with the acceptance of a position which is stated starkly throughout, in a poem virtually devoid of adjectives: the friend belongs to the woman as the lover does; she has power over both through her will, but as in 133, he wants the friend back:

So now I have confessed that he is thine,
And I myself am mortgaged to thy will,
Myself I'll forfeit, so that other mine
Thou wilt restore to be my comfort still.
But thou wilt not, nor he will not be free,
For thou art covetous, and he is kind;
He learned but surety-like to write for me,
Under that bond that him as fast doth bind.
The statute of thy beauty thou wilt take,
Thou usurer that put'st forth all to use,
And sue a friend came debtor for my sake;
So him I lose through my unkind abuse.
  Him have I lost; thou hast both him and me;
  He pays the whole; and yet am I not free. (134)

It is as if the 'friend' (ln. 11) was a proxy wooer, making an appeal on the behalf of the 'I', and has now been enslaved to the 'will' of the woman. She will not give him back (note 'wilt' in lns. 4 and 5). The friend pays everything, but the speaker is also in debt to the woman, in a sexual sense, though it is not possible to free the friend from blame, since 'nor he will not be free' implies that he has become a willing captive to the woman. Yet the poem is a series of strategies, Vendler argues, 'for blaming the woman, rather than the young man for the affair' (Vendler, 571).

If the young man was guiltless, it would be possible to see this proxy wooing, like that of Don Pedro for Claudio with Hero, or Cassio for Othello with Desdemona, or in a nineteenth-century context, Paul Rée for Nietzsche with Lou Andreas-Salome – as a form of standing surety for the speaker as the wooer. It would make the friend like Antonio in

The Merchant of Venice, though more heterosexual than him, in relation to Bassanio whom he loses to Portia, while the woman is both Portia, only more unscrupulous than her, since possessing the power of the will, while, since she is a usurer who puts forth everything to use, she is also a Shylock, and 'covetous' with it. And the friend is now under a bond, both to the sonnet's 'I', and to the lady, like Bassanio to Portia, or, like Antonio to Shylock. The friend is under a legal bond, while it is as if he has entered into bonds (chains). In *The Merchant of Venice* Antonio has surrendered his friend Bassanio to Portia, and is left desolate, which is apparent at the end of the play; in the sonnet, the speaker sounds like a Bassanio who recognises that his friend (Antonio) has lost out to a powerful and voracious woman. Antonio pays the whole, 'and yet am I not free', says the 'I', because being also 'mortgaged' to the woman's will. 'Him I lose' is followed by 'Him have I lost'; he is not restored. That is the tone of Antonio speaking, though it could also be Bassanio at the end, wholly indebted to Portia, since marriage to her excludes Antonio. But there is no possession of the woman in this sonnet.

After declaring the woman's success comes Sonnet 135, which uses 'will' thirteen times, and 'wilt' once. Sonnet 136 supplements it, using 'will' seven times. Both read as forms of ingenuity, and misogynistically – like Iago – in the way they make the woman's sexual appetite voracious, and do not let up on the genital meaning of the 'will'. It is tempting to align the Sonnets with the speeches of Iago, but there is a difference, which may be expressed by noting a sexual fear or anxiety in Iago, which in *King Lear* becomes vaginaphobia; as Lear fantasises: 'there's hell, there's darkness, / There's the sulphurous pit' (4.6.124– 25).[21] In the Quarto reading for *King Lear* 4.6.263, Edgar, having killed Oswald, who is carrying a letter from Goneril to Edmund, reads the letter and discovers that it shows her planning to eliminate her husband, Albany, and to replace him with Edmund in the marriage-bed. Edgar's comment is, in the Quarto, 'O indistinguished space of woman's wit', and, in the Folio, 'O indistinguished space of woman's will'. The Folio's emphasis shifts from her scheming, expressed in her letter, to her lust, her genitals, 'the forfended place'. Sonnet 135 begins with the woman's wilfulness, and continues with her sexual will, unless it is assumed that the three wills of the first two lines refer to three different men she possesses (including two men from 134):

Whoever hath her wish, thou hast thy Will,

And Will to boot, and Will in overplus.
More than enough am I that vex thee still,
To thy sweet will making addition thus.
Wilt thou, whose will is large and spacious,
Not once vouchsafe to hide my will in thine?
Shall will in others seem right gracious,
And in my will no fair acceptance shine?
The sea, all water, yet receives rain still,
And being in abundance, addeth to his store,
So thou, being rich in Will, add to thy Will
One will of mine to make thy large Will more.
  Let no unkind no fair beseechers kill;
  Think all but one, and me in that one Will. (135)

The trope of 'Will' associates with another which so expresses excess ('to boot', 'overplus', 'more than enough', 'still' (twice), 'addition', 'large and spacious', 'all water', 'abundance', 'addeth to his store'. 'rich', 'add', 'large will more' (repeating from 'large and gracious') as to identify will with excess.

The 'I' whose name is Will uses wit to achieve, and to assert, his own will, in the face of the woman and 'others', i.e. other men, other wills (7). The outrageousness in the wit is how it plays his will against hers, which it has created in the poem. In comparison to her excess, he says 'more than enough am I'. She has a will (sexual appetite) in excess; so does he; or else he says that she has as much of him, Will, as she wants: in that sense, lines 3 and 4 replicate 1 and 2. The second quatrain consists of two rhetorical questions posed to her, almost like a prayer (the point is made by Vendler, who sees a potentially deliberately blasphemous note in these four lines). The two questions are requests for physical love. They are followed in the third quatrain by giving a comparison which leads into the 'so . . . ' of line 11, which makes her will comparable to the sea: a natural force, like it: her will is 'in overplus' and the sea is 'all water' and 'in abundance' able to receive more water. The simile gives the sense in lines 11 and 12 that if she adds him, as Will, to her will, that can only make her large will more; there will be increase of appetite. Since she is 'rich in will', which sounds as if she is marked by a generous ('gracious') superfluity, the prayer which is implicit in those two lines asks her to increase her will. So the couplet concludes, asking that no 'unkind' (i.e. no unkind woman) will kill any beseechers; the line thus contains a double negative in it; or else it reads 'Let no unkind "no"' kill any beseechers. Or 'let "no" unkind, no fair beseechers kill', which is Burrow's reading. But it then, reversing the word 'no' into 'one', joins all beseechers – with probably a pun, as Booth suggests, on 'besiegers' – into one. All males are contained in him; as he says, 'think all but one'. (And she must also think that all is all but won in the siege.) He is contained in that male will which would beseech the woman for her favour, the 'one' is 'me'. And he wishes to be contained in that one will, which is universal in its scope (returning to the image in lines 8 and 9).

Sonnet 135 has changed from the tone of 133 and 134; whereas before, the speaker thought about the friend, now he does not appear, unless his name is Will and he is alluded to in lines 1 and 2 and line 4, as 'sweet will', and in line 11. But the speaker boasts a universal competency ('more than enough am I'), which he equates with the woman's will. His 'one will' knocks out all others. If the woman adds that 'one will of mine' to her will, she will make her large will more, as the sea's abundance is increased. The last line establishes an absolute narcissism – 'Think all but one, and me in that one Will', where the speaking I says he sums up all those who will, and says that he, called 'me', is contained in 'that one Will'. But equally, for that to happen, he would lose his identity, as the unique lover. Is 'that one Will' the woman, as personified by her will? And she is the universal will? –the world as will, as expressed by the rain going into the sea? Vendler refers to the sonnet's 'conspicuous urbanity': it attempts seduction, while knowing she has other lovers; and yet everything said about the woman is misogynistic, and little better in 136:

If thy soul check thee that I come so near,
Swear to thy blind soul that I was thy Will,
And will, thy soul knows, is admitted there;
Thus far for love my love-suit, sweet, fulfil.
Will will fulfill the treasure of thy love,
Ay, fill it full with wills, and my will one.
In things of great receipt with ease we prove
Among a number one is reckoned none.
Then in the number let me pass untold,
Thou in thy store's account I one must be;
For nothing hold me, so it please thee hold
That nothing me a something, sweet, to thee.

Make but my name thy love, and love that still,
And then thou lov'st me for my name is Will. (136)

The Sonnet asks for acceptance of his will in relation to her; she should tell her blind soul (who will not know), 'I was thy Will'. The first two lines urge her soul to become blind, not to know what is happening to her, to become split in herself. The reassurance appears in line 3: your soul knows that 'will' – i.e. a male organ – is allowed in, so the name of the individual will does not matter.[22] 'Will will fulfill the treasure of thy love' imposes, by its repetitiousness, an obligation on Will; will does not have freedom in regard to 'the treasure of thy love', which, suggests the pudenda, like 'things of great receipt' in line 7, and 'thy store' in line 10. The repetitiousness is enforced by the next line, which, punning on 'Aye' and 'I', sounds like a protestation, affirming what has been repeated already, that he will fill her full with wills; summed up in his one will, which sums him up. For the quatrain continues with a play on one being nothing, because 'a number' implies more than one, since a number must be divisible. While that means that he can pass uncounted, unremembered, amongst the number of wills that enter her 'account', that also negates him. The prayer follows over the next three lines: though he must be her, held as one in the account she makes, let him be held as nothing. But, supplementary to that: he is dependent on her, that she will call that nothing which is himself as something to her. 'Sweet' may be part of his address to her, as in line 4, or it may be attached to himself – he desires that he may be held as something sweet to her.

If 'among a number, one is reckoned none', then the 'I' has no identity, and the rest of the sonnet faces that possibility. Sonnet 135 laid an emphasis on 'overplus', and the sonnet's desire was that the poet's will might be hid in that abundant will of the woman. So, 'vouchsafe to hide my will in thine'. The male's desire is to be lost; she must think that all means just one (i.e. his will) and that his will is to be absorbed, lost in her. Yet that has already been shown by 134.14 to be an impossibility: the friend 'pays the whole, and yet I am not free'. If 'whole' includes 'hole', the 'w', which is a marker of Shakespeare's signature, supplements emptiness (the point arises from Fineman's analysis).[23] Then paying the whole, which suggests that the friend giving sexual service to the woman, implies trying to fill absence, an impossibility; and it emphasises that in these 'Will' sonnets, identity is what is miss-

112

ing, and the 'Will' must be brought in, as a supplement, to attempt to fill an absence.

'Make but my name thy love' he prays; but if one is reckoned none, has he a name? If she loves his name, that confirms her identity, because his name is Will: it coincides with what she loves: the will. The price of loving her is to be nothing else than the will – to be the name of male and female genitalia. He is the name of the sexual desire and being of both sexes. As an individual will, he has no identity, but because his name is Will, he can assert an identity, and give a sense of the individual subject. But to name something is an expression of desire, or a will to control; names are not the consequences of things but construct an identity, and to name a thing, or a person, is part of the will to knowledge, where naming is misnaming, and alienating. 'My name is Will' may sound as if it is attempting to be triumphalist, but 'Will' is not the same of a single subject, or a single sex, and the statement is a confession which attests to a name being conferred. Conferring a name, which testifies to the imposition of power, wounds: the wound covers an absence.

What gives Will identity is that the woman's will is not 'nothing'. One is reckoned none, which makes him, as a man, nothing; but the woman as nothing is not nothing and if she holds him (sexually), she makes him a something. Making 'something nothing' happened in *The Rape of Lucrece*; the woman has the power to reverse that; for she has power to hold him as something sweet to her. The point is the reversal of Tarquin's world, which produced nihilism in asserting sexual difference, in the power of the will; but now, gender-difference cannot be made definite, in that both man and woman are equally something and nothing.

Since the writer's name accidentally is 'Will', that supplements the point that he gets an historical identity from being the bearer of the name of the will; acceptance of that means accepting alienation. It means recognising that he has an identity which is always other from what he is, because it is locked up in the woman, in the power of the other. Sexual difference locates desire (the will) within the other. The point appeared in Sonnet 20, which presented the young man as sexually perfect, the 'master-mistress of my passion', 'not acquainted / With shifting change': the pun on 'quaint' being obvious.

And for a woman wert thou first created,
Till nature as she wrought thee fell a-doting,

And by addition me of thee defeated,
By adding one thing to my purpose nothing. (20.9–12)

The 'master-mistress' was originally meant to be a woman, or to be 'for a woman', like Viola for Olivia, but Nature, like Venus, or Olivia, fell in love with this Adonis, and therefore added one thing to him: the male organ (the will); the opposite of the boar who subtracted it when he lovingly 'sheathed unaware the tusk in his soft groin' (*Venus and Adonis*, 1116). 'To my purpose nothing' means 'it added nothing', which is a declaration of heterosexuality, or of homoeroticism, 'the one thing that nature added is, for my purposes, equivalent to a woman's sexual parts' (Duncan-Jones). Certainly, the 'one thing' is the same as 'nothing', being virtually an anagram of it; the male and female wills are seen as equivalents, as in the reversal whereby in *Venus and Adonis*, the woman can be seen as the figure of the poet who would woo the woman, making Adonis figure the woman.[24] And indeed, Venus says that he is 'more lovely than a man' (*Venus and Adonis*, 9), which implies that she desires him as other than man. It seems that gender identity is, in this lover's complaint, always alienating: always creating difference: the man praised is alienated from the man, and it seems, from women: their treasure is to use his love; but is the woman thereby less alienated? One sex gets the man's love, the other, physical enjoyment.[25] In which case, the Venus / Adonis lack of fulfilment runs throughout the poetry, and disallows a separation between the differently sexed addressees of the Sonnets; the will is no will, in the sense that it cannot establish a differentiation which can be a source of fulfilment.

The last 'Will' sonnet is 143; its octet giving a simile of the woman chasing 'one of her feathered creatures', a plumed-up cock, while her neglected child calls after her.

So runn'st thou after that which flies from thee,
Whilst I, thy babe, chase thee afar behind:
But if thou catch thy hope, turn back to me
And play the mother's part: kiss me, be kind.
So will I pray that thou mayst have thy Will,
If thou turn back and my loud crying still. (143)

The woman desires another; the neglected lover calls him 'thy hope', and in the couplet, 'thy Will'; she chases one Will while another calls after her; but 'thy Will' also means 'your desire', and may refer to himself. He desires, in this last 'Will' sonnet, that she will 'play the mother's part': this wish for the lover as maternal figure seems the ultimate concession that the male can make, and represents, within the misogynistic terms of the debate, his defeat as Will and her triumph over him, if not over the one she desires. If she plays that part, he will pray that she has her will; but the condition that she should be the mother is reiterated, as 'turn back' is repeated. Evans (261) says that he is 'content to cast himself in the role of the often satirised "happy cuckold"'; but that is because he cannot be the object of her will; hence the tactic which is also a desire, of conceding her as the mother.[26]

These poems' anger, and verbal ingenuity, and perhaps resignation, comes from seeing the woman as making the 'I' a thing; his identity and being depends on her since 'one is counted none'; he cannot make up an identity. Similarly, Viola and Iago use the language of negation. Viola has already told Olivia, that she is not a 'comedian', but 'by the very fangs of malice I swear – I am not that that I play' (1.5.174–76). Malice is associated with serpents (the Arden note to the line makes this point); Viola's utterance identifies herself nearly with malice, the Malvolio spirit, the opposite of the comic, but it also refuses the suggestion. Later, pressed by Olivia, Viola says 'You do think you are not what you are'. Olivia replies 'If I think so, I think the same of you'. Viola answers: 'Then think you right, I am not what I am' (*Twelfth Night*, 3.1.137–39). Olivia thinks that she is in love with a man, but is not; or, she is in love with a woman and does not think it. Or she does not understand that as a woman she is playing the part of a man in wooing, because she is wooing a woman as a man would woo, but in fact she is not wooing a man.

Olivia's rejoinder cannot comprehend Viola's declaration of non-identity, a statement of sexual difference: Viola says 'I am not what I am' because not 'pricked out': as she says when required to duel: 'A little thing would make them tell me how much I lack of a man' (3.4.290–91). She is not what she is because though she seems to be a something (with 'a little thing'), she is nothing, being a woman. Iago says 'I am not what I am' (1.1.65) in the context of saying 'Were I the Moor, I would not be Iago' (1.1.57). If he was Othello, he would not have Iago round him in a position of trust; and if he stood in Othello's place, it would then be seen that there was no Iago; that the character is a nullity, depending on the differential relationship between Othello and himself to give him validity. Male, his misogyny is driven by the knowledge that the woman makes his something nothing. Hence the need to make up/plume up, his will; to give himself being; hence, too, the need to unpluck Othello, and Cassio, in the desire to eliminate any apparent difference between them.

For David Schalkwyk, the excess in sonnets 135 and 136 is 'the wilful, male impulse to obliterate all distinctions in the headlong pursuit of sexual gratification'.[27] The reading seems overly critical of the 'I', unless it is considered that the rhetorical drive in these sonnets is the same as that which accompanies the drive of Sonnet 129: 'Th' expense of spirit in a waste of shame / Is lust in action', commenting on male desire, in as angry a way as Claudio's self-accusing in *Measure for Measure*. That sonnet closes with the 'hell', which is the woman's will, but which as an image produces its strangest effects in 144.[28] This links the friend and the woman, suggesting her will-power, which works through not tempting the 'I', but the friend, doing so 'to win me soon to hell'; creating a jealousy that will make the 'I' succumb:

> Two loves I have, of comfort and despair,
> Which like two spirits do suggest me still.
> The better spirit is a man right fair,
> The worser spirit a woman coloured ill.
> To win me soon to hell my female evil
> Tempteth my better angel from my side,
> And would corrupt my saint to be a devil,
> Wooing his purity with her foul pride.
> And whether that my angel be turned fiend
> Suspect I may, yet not directly tell;
> But being both from me, both to each friend,
> I guess one angel in another's hell.
>   Yet this shall I ne'er know, but live in doubt
>   Till my bad angel fire my good one out. (144)

Every rhyme and suggestion – still/ill/evil/devil/tell/hell – is there save 'will'; it is as if the will is implied throughout as that which works every-where but unseen, producing suspicion, requiring guesswork, making the 'I' in the middle live in doubt about the friend: is he still a love? Is she? Have both betrayed him? Whereas in 134, the friend woos for the 'I', here, the woman woos. She and he are both 'loves' of the 'I', and since she has the power to make the friend like herself, so that both are called angels in line 12 – the craft of her will appears when she annihilates those distinctions and oppositions. Sexual difference, as the power of the 'will', is as much a fetish as the will that attempts to establish identity.

PART TWO

The Posthumous
Life of the Will

5

DICKENS AND TROLLOPE

I TROLLOPE AND THE LAWYERS

At length the important hour arrived, and the will was produced in the midst of the expectants, whose looks and gestures formed a group that would have been very entertaining to an unconcerned spectator. But the reader can scarce conceive the astonishment and mortification that appeared, when the attorney pronounced aloud, the young squire sole heir of all his grandfather's estate, personal and real. My uncle, who had listened with great attention, sucking the head of his cudgel all the while, accompanied these words of the attorney with a stare and *whew*, that alarmed the whole assembly. The eldest and pertest of my female competitors, who had been very officious about my grandfather's person, inquired with a faltering accent, and visage as yellow as an orange, 'If there were no legacies?' and was answered 'None at all'. Upon which she fainted away. (Smollett, *Roderick Random*)[1]

Mr Protocol, accordingly, having required silence, began to read the settlement aloud in a slow, steady, and business-like tone. The group around, in whose eyes hopes alternately awakened and faded, and who were straining their apprehension to get at the drift of the testator's meaning through the mist of technical language in which the conveyancer had involved it, might have made a study for Hogarth. (Scott, *Guy Mannering*)[2]

Smollett's positioning as a 'group' the people waiting to hear the will read out after the funeral implicitly makes them the subject for a satirical painting, as Scott also does and explicitly, by referring to Hogarth. *Guy Mannering* gives the inspiration to the picture by David Wilkie

(1785–1841), 'Reading the Will' (1821), which suggests how generic the scene of reading the will became in eighteenth and nineteenth century texts. The scope for comedy is in how the relatives are poised to be disappointed, and how hatred for the testator will emerge. Living and dead are equally satirised. In Wilkie's picture, the lawyer, fat and comfortable with himself – not T.S. Eliot's 'lean solicitor / In our empty rooms'[3] – sits at a table in the middle. The will, with its seals, is a huge document, one of several reminders of the departed: his picture in an oval frame on the wall behind, his empty chair to the left of the picture, and the enormous strong box, now opened to extract the will. The son, hands in pockets, stands in the position his father must have taken, before the fire, to the far left of the picture: he is one of twenty people listening to the lawyer reading. Everything speaks simultaneously of life going on, and everyone having their own plans and their own lives to lead, including the widow, and of the dead man whose absence, which means his loss of will-power, is apparent in the will, the portrait, the strong box, the chair, and the dog beneath it.[4] People in the room are attentive and inattentive: this Hogarthian reading of the will suggests the inability of the will of the dead to command the living, and suggests also bustling lives, and futures for the mourners, where the patriarch's will is that which permits him to be forgotten.

There is the implication that the person writing the will must imagine it being read. If there is the desire to know the primal scene, that which in Freud has the power to authenticate everything, by being the pure origin, so the subject who wills projects itself forward to the posthumous scene, of the definitive reading. The writer of the will cannot imagine his total exclusion from this event: nobody can imagine a world where they do not exist. Hence the will involves the ego who will be there after death. The *amour-propre*, which is masked as public duty, is what Dr Johnson laughed at, in the idea of his friend Mr Langton making a will, with the pretensions it implied about asserting identity. Boswell reports how Johnson:

called him the *testator*, and added, 'I dare say, he thinks he has done a mghty thing. He won't stay till he gets home to his seat in the country, to produce this wonderful deed: he'll call up the landlord of the first inn on the road; and after a suitable preface upon mortality and the uncertainty of life, will tell him that he should not delay making his will and here, Sir, will he say, is my will, which I have

just made, with the assistance of one the ablest lawyers in the
kingdom; and he will read it to him (laughing all the time). He
believes he has made this will; but he did not make it' you, Chambers
[Sir Robert Chambers, of the Temple], made it for him. I trust you
have had more conscience than to make him say, 'being of sound
understanding'; ha, ha, ha! I hope he has left me a legacy, I'd have his
will turned into verse, like a ballad'.[5]

What the person willing cannot know is also how his will, as a posthumous document, can be contested. But as a Benthamite Wills Act of
1837 insisted that wills be written, and gave apparent rights to the
testator over what happened to his property, so changing direction from
the idea that what was sacred was the property and its right to be held
in the family, so it becomes a motif for Dickens, or Trollope, or George
Eliot, and a way of singularising identity.[6] Similarly, in the 1850s,
making, proving and contesting the will became a real-life scandal in
the case of Turner.[7] Trollope's novels frequently arise from a will, whose
importance is to secure the right of primogeniture, property in the hands
of the right male.[8] Even in *Orley Farm* (1862), 'the Great Orley Farm
Case', as Trollope calls it, the farm which has been 'stolen' by Lady
Mason, who forged a codicil to her husband's will, so that the farm will
go into the possession of her and his son Lucius, must revert to Joseph
Mason. He is an older son by a previous marriage, the rightful male
owner, and he and his wife are detestable. It seems that a will attracts
forgery, and then, as with Lady Mason, perjury. The question of the will,
the forgery and the perjury, leads towards the trial of Lady Mason, where
she is acquitted, perhaps because, as Lucius Mason thinks, 'that lawyers
are all liars' (2.22), playing with language, as forgery and perjury also
play, though these save neither her nor the farm.[9] Behind this favouring
of the male succession there is in the will a desire to deny death within
the patriarchy: writing on *Orley Farm*, Kieran Dolin quotes Sir Frederick
Pollock and Frederic Maitland's *History of English Law Before the Time of
Edward I* (1895), that 'to us it must seem natural that when a man dies
he should leave behind him some representative who will bear his
persona. Or again we may be inclined to personify the groups of rights
and duties, which are, as it were, left alive, though the man in whom
they once inhered is dead, to personify the *hereditas*'.[10] Yet Trollope
recalls the actions of Rebekah to favour Jacob over Esau (50.203, see
Genesis, 27), and so introduces another – and older – set of precedents

123

which give autonomy to the mother over the father. Coral Lansbury aptly summarises the situation, with the sense that the prior injustice was from Sir Joseph Mason's, Lady Mason's father's creditor: 'She had never been a willing partner to the marriage contract but she had fulfilled her obligations conscientiously. When Sir Joseph failed to provide for their son, her outrage led her to commit a forgery. The contract she had observed so faithfully had been broken by her husband and she therefore felt justified in seeking redress'.[11] Lady Mason feels that her husband had not done 'justice' to Lucius (45.46). At the end, the 'justice' is that she is acquitted but knowing her guilt, concedes the farm, while Mr Mason is angry that 'justice' – by which he means revenge (78.390–91) – has not been done, even though he has the farm back, though he must pay money to get rid of his lawyer, Dockwrath (79.406–7). Justice cannot be a unitary matter; it must recognise sexual difference, which is what Trollope's novels register, and fear, as with the question of the theft by Lizzie, widow of Sir Florian Eustace in *The Eustace Diamonds* (1873): in keeping the diamonds which the will of Sir Florian's grandfather had been left to the eldest son, and so on in perpetuity, is she is possession of an 'heirloom'? – 'a chattel that, under a will, settlement, or local custom, follows the devolution of real estate. Hence, any piece of personal property that has been in a family for several generations' (*OED*). Or are the diamonds 'paraphernalia': 'articles of personal property, esp. clothing and ornaments, which (exceptionally at common law) did not automatically transfer from the property of the wife to the husband by virtue of the marriage' (*OED*)? So the barrister Mr Dove thinks, enraging the family lawyer, Mr Camperdown, who wants the diamonds kept in the family.[12]

But in *Cousin Henry* (1879), Cousin Henry has stolen a will which dispossessed him of the property that had belonged to his Uncle Indefer, and the lawyer, Mr Apjohn, has to read out what he feels is the penultimate will and testament, rather than the last will, which made over the property to a woman, not to a male heir. Uncle Indefer had decided, on his death-bed, that on this occasion, and exceptionally, the property should not go to the unworthy male. Being wily, Apjohn tracks the proper will down, hidden in a book in the library, and so ensures that the will of the deceased is carried out: not deferred. Mr Apjohn is puzzled why the earlier will was not destroyed by Uncle Indefer, to which the other lawyer replies that 'there are men who think that a will once made should never be destroyed'.[13] And the last will and testament that Uncle

124

Indefer has made, leaving the estate to Isabel, not to the male heir, has represented a fight of his 'conscience' – almost the first word of the novel – over his principle, which is 'that a landed estate in Britain should go from father to eldest son, and in default of a son, to the nearest male heir' (9). The different wills represent his split loyalties, to Isabel and to the principle of patriarchy which identifies Trollope's politics as Liberal/Tory.

The will is, in Trollope, though a material thing, something with the quality of the fetish, hauntingly religious, unconfinable to paper, unmodifiable – especially by a woman such as Lady Mason – undestroyable: Cousin Henry lacks courage to destroy the last will which dispossesses him; he keeps it in the library, amongst the sacred books, and is terrified by it: his inability to deal with the will, which controls his will, figures his unsuitablity to run the estate. In making the lawyer the effectual detective, Trollope is more innocent than Dickens could ever be, more upholding of law and privilege, and with more of a sense of the link between the lawyer and his professionalism which guarantees the survival of the dead man's will.

Similarly, Wilkie Collins, David Wilkie's godson, makes much of the 'family lawyer', as with Mr Gilmore and Mr Kyrle, family lawyers for the Fairlies, and Mr Merriman, lawyer for Sir Percival Glyde, in *The Woman in White* (1860) and Mr Bruff in *The Moonstone* (1868–69), who witnesses the experiment Ezra Jennings carries out to ascertain Franklin Blake's innocence, and concludes: 'in a legal phrase, you have proved your case'.[14] The family lawyer is to protect the family; acting as a means whereby the values of the country house (Limmeridge and the Verinder house, in these novels) are protected against illegitimacy and fraud, and against the slur of slander, and he is as much the defender of the house against the police, and their accusations, as a representative, in himself, of the court of law, which must hear a case and judge.[15] Dickens's lawyers such as Mr Tulkinghorn and Mr Jaggers are both seen in relation to propertied interests: Chesney Wold and Sir Leicester Dedlock (*Bleak House*) and Satis House (*Great Expectations*). When the lawyer narrates, as Gilmore and Bruff both do, that says implicitly that the narrative is self-evidently true, and its statements valid in a court of law. The way that a will, disputed, unresolved, contested, produces the trial suggests a new legalism, which makes George Eliot, in *Adam Bede* (1859), align her realism to court-room practice: 'I feel as much bound to tell you, as precisely as I can . . . as if I were in the witness-box narrating my experience on oath'.[16] Collins follows this when *The Woman in White* announces that nothing 'will be related on hearsay evidence'; hence the plural narratives of the book, when the characters telling the story in sequence 'relate their own experience word for word'.[17] At stake, making the court the forum for establishing the truth of narrative, which Collins's conservatism requires, is the sense of a failure of the will, which must be supported, supplemented. The will, which is both a marker of change occurring through death, and of continuity, of succession, becomes the origin of narrative, insofar as this becomes the supplying of evidence to provide retrospectively what was deficient in that will, and will-making.

For the implications of considering the will as the source of action, I turn to Dickens.[18] One draft title of *David Copperfield* (1849–50), Dickens' most autobiographical novel, was *The Last Will and Testament of Mr David Copperfield*.[19] The posthumous child, as he is, projects himself forward posthumously, making his life what he wills to be recorded of him, and, as posthumous, mentally putting himself beyond the grave in the sense that there will be no more to be known of him after he has concluded the writing. He writes as if already dead. But the novel reads as a series of variations on wills, as with various of Mr Micawber's letters, which speak as though the death of the author had happened; on willing, and on the power of the will, as with the Murdstones destroying Clara Copperfield through their training of her. Thus, 'Barkis is willin' (5.75), Barkis memorably says, though it might be thought that being willing was more the response of the woman than how the man proposed marriage. Mr Peggotty goes to drink in the public house called 'The Willing Mind' (3.51). Mr Wickfield, the lawyer, does not use the word 'will', but – following on from an idea of Dickens of a man who would always uncover an action by asking 'What's his motive', considers everything in terms of a person's 'motive' (15.229), which he searches for.[20] His obvious 'motive' is his affection for his daughter, and its inadequacy becomes apparent, as being obsessive in one way, towards Agnes, and will-less in another, as he turns to drink, and concedes the ascendency to Uriah Heep, embodiment of *ressentiment*.

Wickfield's parallel is Mr Spenlow, and David Copperfield is warned off making love to his daughter, Dora. Mr Spenlow, the proctor in Doctors' Commons, makes dark threats to David about his will, as if suggesting that if he persists in seeing Dora, or wants to become a son-in-law, he will change his will which, presumably, is at present in her favour. A proctor spends his time proving wills, and Mr Spenlow says that he has professional experience of:

> the various unaccountable and negligent proceedings of men, in respect of their testamentary arrangements – of all subjects, the one on which perhaps the strangest revelations of human inconsistency are to be met with. (38.539)

Mr Spenlow adds that his own affairs are settled. The next day he is discovered dead, and his business-partners search for his will. David Copperfield tells the partners that he definitely had made a will, because he said so; they agree that this means that none was made, concurring that 'there is no subject upon which men are so inconsistent and so little to be trusted' (38.565). 'Inconsistency' contrasts with a resolute will, or a man who makes his will, who has a settled determination on what to do with it. Perhaps the man who checks wills, and proves them, knows what they are worth. Perhaps their effect is to make him resist the thought of his own death, which writing the will would bring on, or perhaps he has never had will enough to make his will, or too much to make it. But as Mr Wickfield has not enough motive, so Mr Spenlow has not enough consistency, yet this reveals both isolatable 'motive' and 'consistency' to be inadequate ways of thinking about what wills or motivates. And certainly, 'inconsistency' is not just separate from, oppo-site to the will, but part of it; the will itself is both inconsistent, self-contradictory, and this also appears in actual wills, and is revealed when they are read out, so that a will becomes a way to read the testator's character.

In *Bleak House* (1852–53), everything centres on the Jarndyce versus Jarndyce case, which started because 'a certain Jarndyce, in an evil hour, made a great fortune, and made a great Will'.[21] The will has been disputed; Tom Jarndyce has blown his brains out, so everything is now 'in chancery', until rightful possession can be established, so that every-thing lies in ruins, like Tom-all-Alone's, itself 'in chancery' (16.273), and the case is the 'family curse . . . the horrible phantom which has haunted us so many years' (24.393).[22] If, as Hillis Miller wrote at the beginning to his Introduction to the Penguin edition of *Bleak House* in 1971, '*Bleak House* is a document about the interpretation of documents', that statement can be supplemented: the documents are a will, and the papers about it that the will accumulates, and all interpretation, then, is about what someone has willed, with the sense that to will something, to want something to happen, like God's great act of creation – 'He spoke, and it was done' (Psalm 33.9) – means to create division.

The costs incurred by the legal proceedings in Chancery eat up the legacies involved. Pursuit of the will, a pursuit of the past and of the future, makes Richard Carstone – 'ruined by a fatal inheritance' (60. 881) say 'I – I wish I was dead' (45.677); it saps the will; in the same way, Caddy Jellyby, after wishing Africa was dead, says 'I wish I was dead . . . I wish we were all dead' (4.93, 94). Chancery, which controls all those who are in some ways victim of the failure of the will to assert itself, 'has its decaying houses and its blighted lands in every shire . . . its worn-out lunatic in every madhouse and its dead in every church-yard' (1.51). Similarly, Mr George, imprisoned, writes a desposition of what he knows of the facts of the case for which he has been imprisoned, in case he cannot speak in his defence – but 'I have no longer a will of my own in this case' (55.809). The loss of will affects everything: even the gas lit in the fog 'has a haggard and unwilling look' (1.50).

Studying literature and legal discouse, Dieter Polloczek argues that 'incarceration' is the dominant motif of *Bleak House*. He first refers to the medieval legal tradition of Civil Death, whereby a person, such as a criminal, can be legally presumed dead while alive, so that their property becomes the possession of another's, such as the Court of Chancery. So it is an allegorical detail when the Jarndyce will is found among the waste paper collected by Mr Krook, the pseudo-Lord Chancellor (ch. 62): if Mr Krook had taught himself to read before he was spontaneously combusted, he would have got round to reading the will (62.896). The will is in the possession of this mock Court of Chancery. Dickens shows his sense of what wills associate with when, in *Our Mutual Friend*, the Harmon will is concealed in the rubbish heaps of the Holloway area of London. The other idea Polloczek focuses on is that of Substituted Judgment, devised by John Eldon (1751–1838), Lord Chancellor between 1801 and 1827, who from 1816 onwards was extending the authority of Chancery to administer the fortunes of so-called mental incompetents, as if they possessed their reason.[23] Polloczek comments on *Bleak House* through these two more-than-tropes, which, he argues Dickens knew, and was not in any sense out-of-date in discussing. Hence Mr Kenge the lawyer can say that Jarndyce and Jarndyce provides a case where 'every difficulty, every contingency, *every masterly fiction*, every form of procedure . . . is represented over and over again' (3.68).[24] So 'both the legal fictions [Civil Death and Substituted Judgement] can be used to manipulate established relations between death and inheritance', for they are 'possibilities to manipulate standards of ownership by means of declaring death'; they 'allow judges and lawyers to use death as a trope so that they can re-interpret literal inheritance', such as that provided by the will.[25] As early as *Pickwick Papers* (1836–37), Chancery was referenced when Pickwick in the Fleet prison sees a man who has been victim of a Chancery suit for twenty years, and speaks of himself as a 'dead man, dead to society' (41.564), so much so that when he dies, 'he had grown so like death in life, that they knew not when he died' (43.594).[26] The man has been virtually buried alive – a Dickens motif, structuring the Dr Manette narrative in *A Tale of Two Cities* – his fate to be forgotten through the agency of a system which deals with disputed wills by removing people from life into an official non-existence. Removed from the power of the will, which would operate in his favour, the non-person is now will-less. The same novel shows a cruder form of the exertion of power after a will has been made: with a cobbler – anticipating M. Manette – ruined by having money left to him in a will which is contested by the deceased's nephews and nieces, who, after having the legacies paid to them, bring an action to set the will aside. 'After that, we went into Chancery, where we are still, and where I shall always be. My lawyers have had all my thousand pound long ago, and what between the estate, as they call it, and the costs, I'm here for ten thousand, and shall stop here till I die, mending shoes' (*Pickwick Papers* 43.588).

Nicholas Nickleby (1838–39) comments indirectly on the idea of the legal fiction, which so transforms reality into the unreality of language, which nonetheless has the force to bind. Dickens refers to the King's Bench prison, where some debtor prisoners can live, however squalidly, outside, within the 'rules' of the prison, and not in the prison itself, while others who can raise no money starve in jail. 'There are many pleasant fictions of the law in constant operation, but there is not one so pleasant or practically humorous as that which supposes every man to be of equal value in its impartial eye, and the benefits of all laws to be equally attainable by all men'.[27] Legal fictions have a life of their own: they mean the civil death of prisoners. The second comment comes from Mrs Nickleby, whose confusion of mind parallels, not exceeds, the crazed nature of the legal fiction analogous to which the chancery prisoner of *Pickwick Papers* has been imprisoned: 'if they don't want this young lady to be married, why don't they file a bill against the Lord Chancellor, make her a chancery ward, and shut her up in the Fleet prison for safety' (55.678). 'Incarceration' is the dominant motif in *Bleak House*, and all Dickens, and for its relation to the will, I turn to *Little Dorrit* (1855–57).

II THE FAILURE OF WILL: *LITTLE DORRIT*

'And now, Mr Clennam, perhaps I may ask you whether you have yet come to a decision where to go next.'

'Indeed, no. I am such a waif and stray everywhere, that I am liable to be drifted where any current may set.'

'It's extraordinary to me – if you'll excuse my freedom in saying so – that you don't go straight to London', said Mr Meagles, in the tone of a confidential adviser.

'Perhaps I shall.'

'Aye! But I mean with a will.'

'I have no will. That is to say,' he coloured a little, 'next to none that I can put in action now. Trained by main force; broken, not bent; heavily ironed with an object on which I was never consulted and which was never mine; shipped away to the other end of the world before I was of age, and exiled there until my father's death, there, a year ago; always grinding in a mill I always hated; what is to be expected from me in middle-life? Will, purpose, hope? All those lights were extinguished before I could sound the words.' (*Little Dorrit* 1.2)[28]

The prison in *Little Dorrit*, like the Marshalsea, includes the will as imprisoned, and the will as a prison and prison-creating. In comparison, the image for *Middlemarch* (see ch. 6), is the web, which may act as a prison, but may also indicate the possibility of forming relations, and seeing relatedness, especially in narrative, providing interconnections frustrated by the personal will expressed in the deed of willing. In the opening of *Little Dorrit*, the forty-year old Arthur Clennam re-enters Europe after twenty years in China, a period he regards as imprisonment, which is, indeed, analogous to the Chancery prisoner, where 'the iron teeth of confinement and privation had been slowly filing him down for twenty years' (41.564). The prison connects with those technologies of power Foucault alludes to in *Discipline and Punish*, illustrated in

Panoptical forms, which enframe and dominate the will, making it passively willing, within the regime of the 'docile body'.[29]

Clennam tells Mr Meagles, the banker, that he has no will. His education and career, the combination of nineteenth-century Evangelicalism and Utilitarianism, of religion serving the interests of acquisitiveness, a spirit marked by both Mr Gradgrind and nineteenth-century colonialism, has done that for him. There is no imagination to be 'lit up' in him. Michael G. Cooke emphasises the presence of the will in Romanticism, as with Coleridge, in the *Biographia Literaria*, seeing the 'secondary Imagination' as 'an echo of the former [the primary IMAGINATION], co-existing with the conscious will, . . . It dissolves, diffuses, dissipates, in order to re-create; or where this process is rendered impossible, yet still at all events it struggles to idealise and to unify'.[30] Clennam shows the Romantic imagination in defeat.

When the novel reveals, through Mrs Clennam, what happened in the past which so left Arthur Clennam without will-power, it appears that another, literal, 'will' is involved. Blandois can blackmail Mrs Clennam, since he possesses the codicil to the will that old Gilbert Clennam dictated to Mrs Clennam. Forty years earlier, Gilbert Clennam had directed his nephew, Arthur's father, to marry Mrs Clennam. Unknown to him, the nephew had already 'married' a singer, who became Arthur's real mother. Mrs Clennam's discovery of her husband's secret has made her possess Arthur as though he were hers, and made her repress the codicil in the will by which Gilbert Clennam later attempted reparation to the singing girl, and, failing her, willed money to Amy Dorrit, as next in line; curiously, Amy's reception of the money depends on her not being the daughter, but only the niece of Frederick Dorrit, patron of the unnamed singing-girl: this undercuts patriarchy.

Clennam has deduced that Mrs Clennam's 'ascendancy' over his father made him go out to China, as a form of separation, and tells her, attempting to get her desire to recognise him, 'it was your will that I should remain with you until I was twenty and then go to him as I did' (1.5.47). The split between two parents which has divided up his life is part of the failure of will in himself. Everything in Clennam's life speaks of incitements to feel guilt; thus when he works for Doyce and Clennam, and is at his most integrated, he sees a 'shaft of light' produced in the architectural arrangements of the factory 'which brought to [his] mind the child's old picture-book where similar rays were the witnesses of Abel's murder' (1.23.267). Memory creates the instability of not knowing whether he is Abel, or Cain; while the language of witnessing suggests the power of surveillance, the sense of being on trial, like Cain, with whom Blandois is compared (1.11.124).

Mrs Clennam is confined to a wheelchair, part of her self-punishment for what she has done in suppressing the codicil: she has unconsciously chosen a 'civil death' for the past fifteen years. F.R. Leavis reads this confinement in terms analogous to Sir Clifford Chatterley in Lawrence's *Lady Chatterley's Lover*: as symbolic of life become machinic, will-bound; Leavis speaks of her 'mechanism of will, idea and ego', and says that her 'Calvinistic religion enables her to transmute the service of her will – of her possessiveness, pride, jealousy, vengefulness and life-hatred – into the service of God, and this gives a poised, judicially stern and quasi-rational authority to her ruthless dominance'.[31] The insight, carried over from Leavis's readings of Lawrence, is obviously significant, though perhaps this insistence on Mrs Clennam being the symbol of the will-bound underestimates how the woman has been injured. But certainly she stands as opposed to Arthur, the man without a will, who thinks she is his mother: she is not, and that resentment towards her husband and his uncle has made her repress the patriarch's codicil.

In a reading of *Little Dorrit* earlier than Leavis's, Lionel Trilling focuses on society in relation to the individual will. He calls the prison 'the practical instrument for the negation of man's will which the will of society has invented' (viii). That 'negation', of course, is repression: it is the argument of *Civilization and its Discontents*. He continues with reference to Freud's conception of 'the mind', as based on 'the primacy of the will' but whose organization is split: it parodies a criminal process where the mind is 'at once the criminal, the victim, the police, the judge, and the executioner'; so that, 'having received the social impress, it becomes in turn the matrix of society' (viii). The criminal process of law, so much validated in the nineteenth-century novel, parallels the split nature of the subject, as super-ego, ego and id: tormenting, tormented, and inciting to a torment it resists in itself. If the Victorian novel turns to the court room to establish the will, and the 'corrrect' interpretation thereof, Trilling's use of Freud shows that process as unable to establish anything save to produce a situation more schizoid than before, while interpretation can only ever be split, because the will is internally divided. If making a will is a split process, what would resolve this splitting replicates its division. Hence at the centre of *Little Dorrit* is a prison where the Father of the Marshalsea, as if judge in the prison, exercises a

Lear-like tyranny, which implicates Amy Dorrit, who must fictionalise her own working-life (she is not allowed to admit to the father that she goes out to work) and Clennam, who visiting Dorrit, must collude in the deception. Money given to Mr Dorrit cannot be gifts to someone with nothing; it must be as a 'testimonial' (1.8.83), as if speaking to the good character of the man, like a witness. Is the giver of a testimonial a testator? The word means both a witness and the maker of a will. A testimonial becomes an act of deeding, an expression of the will, leaving something to Dorrit, as well as something to supplement the will of the person who is presumed to have rights, privileges and dues, as the Father of the Marshalsea.

At the other end of 'society' is the sense of the Merdles as, in Trilling's words, 'having received the social impress', becoming 'the matrix of society' (vii). With them, the will creates the prison to negate the will. In the chapter 'Moving in Society', Fanny and Amy Dorrit visit Mrs Merdle, the 'Bosom' whose function is to 'move in society' and whose son by a former marriage is 'monomaniacal in offering marriage to all manner of undesirable young ladies' (1.21.247–48). Mrs Merdle is buying Fanny off from seeing her son. She tells the Dorrit sisters that 'Society . . . is so difficult to explain to young persons . . . . I wish Society was not so arbitrary, I wish it was not so exacting'. Here, the parrot, as the voice of Society, shrieks, being parodic of her, and also as the torturing voice of the superego, and the protest of that which has been caged, imprisoned. 'We know it is hollow and conventional, and worldly and very shocking, but unless we are Savages in the Tropical seas . . . we must consult it' (*LD*, 1.20.239). As she keeps Fanny out of Society, she blames Mr Merdle for not going into Society, for not being '*dégagé*; and being too preoccupied with his business, and not having 'the tone of Society' (*LD*, 1.33.396,397), and here, as if to voice the power of the superego, the Chief Butler terrifies him beyond the power of his own guilt, which convicts him as a swindler. Merdle, required by Mrs Merdle to have 'better conformation of himself to Society' (*LD*, 1.33.398), which suggests that neither of them can be quite identified by Society, but both are driven by it as an abstraction, possesses nothing in himself, and his suicide is the fulfilment of his anomie. He has never 'got anything for himself' (*LD*, 1.21.247), and illustrates the absolute failure of any kind of pleasure under the legalistic eye of the law. He feels as much guilt as Clennam, the criminal without a crime.

Trilling speaks of 'the social will, the will to status' (x) in the novel, and calls Blandois, self-pitying and egotistical, embodiment of the 'unmitigated social will'. This describes Nietzsche's *ressentiment*, the term of *The Genealogy of Morals* used to characterise Christian slave-morality. This, out of its lack of power in relation to its persecutors, advertises its passivity as humility; and being weak, and being aggrieved, means having a grievance, which implies taking action, that is, revenge.[32] The Nietzschean history of the nineteenth century is this *ressentiment* internalised as a dominant rule. As Blandois tells Cavalletto, illustrating *ressentiment*, 'I am a man . . . whom society has deeply wronged since you last saw me. You know that I am sensitive and brave, and that it is in my character to govern. How has society respected those qualities in me? . . . Such are the humiliations that society has inflicted on me, possessing the qualities I have mentioned . . . But society shall pay for it' (*LD*, 1.11.132). The social will shows itself as reliant on 'some version of Blandois's pathos: they [the people who make it up] are confirmed in their lives by self-pity, they rely on the great modern strategy of being the insulted and the injured'. Trilling refers to the title of a Dostoyevsky novel, *The Insulted and the Injured* (1861), a text about Petersburg, influenced by Dickens's *The Old Curiosity Shop*, since one of its focuses of attention is the thirteen-year old epileptic waif Nelly. As the narrator, a poor novelist himself, says about Nelly's refusal of help, that 'she was savouring her own pain, and revelling in this *selfish orgy of suffering* if I may put it that way. This rubbing of salt into the wound and taking pleasure in the act were familiar to me; it is the last refuge of the many who've been offended and humiliated . . . '.[33] This 'egoism of suffering', as Constance Garnett translated it, is at the heart of a novel fascinated by two things, which come together in this paragraph: the weak – poor folk – are the objectively humiliated and insulted, but their technique for enduring this is a masochism which is productive of *ressentiment*. As Prince Valkovsky, the Sadeian aristocrat, tells Ivan Petrovich, the narrator, about the wife (Nelly's mother) he has seduced:

> if I gave her the money, I might even make her unhappy. I'd have deprived her of the pleasure of being totally miserable *on my account* and of cursing me for it for the rest of her life. Believe you me, my friend, there is supreme pleasure to be derived from the kind of misery where one knows oneself to be quite blameless and generous, and totally justified in calling the wrongdoer a scoundrel.

He calls it 'an ecstasy of hatred' (3.10.257). Forgiveness is an act of the ego, as when Nikolai Sergeich Ihhmenev forgives his daughter, Natasha, for her unmarried relationship with Alyosha, 'no matter that we are humiliated, no matter that we are insulted' (4.9.328). He enjoys the romantic luxury of being able to forgive, as a way of pretending that he has some autonomy, and he likes to label himself as insulted, because, as Nietzsche would argue, that allows him to think that he is these things out of his own will.[34]

The most extraordinary reference in *Little Dorrit* to the strategy of acting being insulted and humiliated occurs in the chapter 'Spirit' (1.31), showing the Dorrit family's patronage of Old Nandy. They regard the Marshalsea College (1.31.365) as more elevated than his home, the workhouse. Mr Dorrit considers himself humiliated that his daughter has been seen 'coming into this College out of the public streets – smiling! smiling! – arm in arm with – O my God, a livery!' (1.31.370). At that point, he receives a letter from Clennam, which contains a banknote; appeased, he patronises Nandy over tea, to which Clennam also comes. Tip, Dorrit's son, a wastrel though also a product of the humiliations of the prison, suddenly arrives, and shows himself angry with Clennam in front of the rest of the family for not giving him money when it was requested; he has not been treated 'like a gentleman'. Everything depends on the insulted and injured Tip being able to identify and parade some specific humiliation which will allow him to demonstrate his egotism. His anger shows 'a proper spirit', this being a synonym for the aggrieved will.

Mr Dorrit, furious, sees this display of 'spirit', which acts as though Tip has been humiliated and insulted, and which is the purest *ressentiment*, as 'parricidal': literally so, because Tip is in a way to offend Clennam and stop him sending any more banknotes. Tip's actions, in not showing servility to Clennam, means the destruction of the Father, because it shows up his own practice of begging which is disguised as seeking testimonials. It comments on how he lives by needing to solicit money; hence, confronted with how he is humiliated and insulted, he calls it 'unnatural', 'not filial'. And then as the action of someone:

> not a Christian. Are you – ha – an Atheist? And is it Christian . . . to stigmatise and denounce an individual [i.e. Clennam] for begging to be excused this time, when the same individual may – ha – respond

with the required accommodation next time? Is it the part of a
Christian not to – hum – not to try him again? (1.31.375–77)

Christianity depends on vindicating the Father's will, and spirit,
anything else being unnatural. But the 'spirit' of the Father, as with all
patriarchy, starting with Christianity, is servile, being dependent on
receiving testimonials.[35] To recall the Blake poem, cited in relation to
Measure for Measure, 'Pity would be no more / If we did not make somebody poor': the social system requires producing the humiliated and the
insulted in order to patronise them, and so receive their gratitude. The
poor have no other recourse than to the *ressentiment* this engenders. For
Blake, the inclination to insult is the principle of patriarchy; in
Nietzsche, the insulted and injured must make patriarchy a system of
beneficence. Dickens, quite exceptionally, identifies the dignity of the
Father of the Marshalsea with that of the Father in Christianity: as if
both depend on acting a role of servility: both operate with a calculating
slave morality which acts as if injured and aggrieved. The difference is
that Dorrit has been made to feel guilty – and humiliated and insulted
– because he is in debt.[36]

So, if not in Blandois, 'the subversive pathos of self-pity' is sometimes
justified: Trilling speaks of the human will as 'perplexed by the disparity
between what it desires and what it is allowed to have' (xi), which causes
its unhappiness, its masochism. That invokes Freud's *Civilization and its
Discontents*, where society is founded on the need to give up satisfactions
both sexual and aggressive, and on the inculcation of guilt. That self-
pity is true of Clennam. But Dickens does not suggest that it is possible
to have no will. Even for Clennam to say 'I have no will' is a desire, not
a statement of fact; he does not want a will, because of what he has
suffered from his parents, and here, not to have a will is a masochistic
desire; but it is also a rationalisation; he colours up while speaking to
Meagles, perhaps acknowledging the sexual meaning of the will.
Negating the will in the self concedes that there is something else at
work, in him and beyond him, which cannot be articulated.

Trilling argues that the novel works towards rejecting the social will;
its energy being directed 'to finding the non-personal will in which shall
be our peace' (xv), while Amy Dorrit is 'the negation of the social will'
(xvi), but at the price of lacking aggression. This reading, as Nietzschean
as Freudian, has made the will self-divided, and dividing the self, and,
in its social form, as vicious, both cruel and sentimental. If it works by

law, its law is also a form of cruelty, and cruelty is the 'spirit' of the Father. It is a consistent note in Trilling, who, ten years before writing on *Little Dorrit*, had, in 1943, discussed E.M. Forster in terms of his 'relaxed will', his tolerance, noting, especially in Forster's literary criticism, his 'deep suspiciousness of the rigid exercise of the intellect':

> A world at war is necessarily a world of will; it is a world at war. Forster reminds us of a world where the will is not everything, of a world of true order, of the necessary connection of passion and prose, and of the strange paradoxes of being human. He is one of those who raise the standard of Achilles, which is the moral intelligence of art, against the panic and emptiness which make their mark when the will is tired from its own excess.[37]

It also seems that the spontaneous will is so little present, that it is not possible to make a will. So, the turnkey of the Marshalsea prison wants to leave money to Amy Dorrit, and asks every 'professional gentleman' coming in and out of the prison how to do it. The advice is invariably 'Settle it strictly on herself' but the questions come back: supposing she had a brother or a father or a husband who wanted to make a 'grab at the property'. The lawyer says the money would be settled on her and they would have no legal claim, but the turnkey, as if he has read Trollope, is fearful of the power of patriarchy asserting itself:

> 'Stop a bit,' said the turnkey, 'Supposing she was tender-hearted and they came over her. Where's your law for tying it up then?'
>   The deepest character whom the turnkey sounded, was unable to produce his law for tying such a knot as that. So, the turnkey thought about it all his life, and died intestate after all. (*Little Dorrit*, 1.7.70–71)

So, in *Little Dorrit*, it seems that, as Agamemnon in *Troilus and Cressida* knows, 'the ample proposition that hope makes / In all designs begun on earth below / Fails in the promis'd largeness' (1.3.3–5). The will to make a will fails. And in Dickens, it may be said that the making of the will seems negative: so Mr F, in spite of making a 'beautiful will' also dumps his aunt upon Flora as a 'legacy' (1.13.157), and as, in *Our Mutual Friend*, Mr Harmon has created marriage conditions for his son, John Harmon, which involve marriage to a woman he has never seen, and the bad will apparent in that 'will of a dead father', which he necessarily rebels against. The idea of a person being left as part of a will evokes *The Merchant of Venice*.

III RESPONSIBILITY

'I have no will', means Clennam has neither desire, nor aim for the future, nor drive (what is called will-power, for which *OED* gives 1874 for a first citation, making it a synonym for 'moral force'), nor sexual desire. In the chapter 'Nobody's Weakness', Clennam decides not to fall in love with Pet Meagles, objectifying himself, as 'nobody', 'nobody within his knowledge'. The chapter concludes making his desire to be 'nobody' a death-drive:

> And he thought – who has not thought for a moment, sometimes? – that it might be better to flow away monotonously, like the river, and to compound for its insensibility to happiness with its insensibility to pain. (1.16.200)

Two further chapters, 'Nobody's Rival' and 'Nobody's Disappearance', cancel out all desire for Pet save of a nostalgic kind; his impulse is towards a civil death, long before he gives himself up to the desire for exclusion within the Marshalsea. That too, as a will to nothingness, as *The Genealogy of Morals* suggests, is a will.

Clennam's state compares with John Stuart Mill, whose posthumous *Autobiography* (1873) describes his mental condition in the 1820s, where his 'self-consciousness' brings about a state of paralysis, a dejection emanating from the sense that nothing is worth it; if he was to achieve all his objects in life, it would bring no joy or happiness. Following Carlyle in his 'anti-self-consciousness theory', Mill thinks, 'ask yourself whether you are happy, and you cease to be so'.[38] He was rescued from this melancholia, associated with his and his father's Utilitarianism, by reading Wordsworth's poems, 'a medicine for my state of mind' because 'they expressed, not mere outward beauty, but states of feeling, and of thought coloured by feeling, under the excitement of beauty. They seemed to be the very culture of the feelings which I was in quest of' (*Autobiography*, 125). Thus marvellously equipped, Mill evokes the doctrine of 'philosophical Necessity'; that character is the 'helpless slave of antecedent circumstances', a product of Utilitarian thinking, which would make the concept of will otiose. He concludes:

> I perceived that the word Necessity, as a name for the doctrine of Cause and Effect applied to human action, carried with it a misleading association; and that this association was the operative force in the depressing and paralysing influence which I had experienced: I saw that though our character is formed by circumstances, our own desires can do much to shape those circumsances; and that what is really inspiriting and ennobling in the doctrine of freewill is the conviction that we have real power over the formation of our character; that our will, by influencing some of our circumstances, can modify our future habits or capabilities of willing. (143–44)

The habit of willing is moulded by the reading of poetry, specifically Wordsworth. Mill escapes, but not Clennam, whose disposition is to rationalise his lack of ability to act onto the idea of everything being 'nobody's fault', which was a draft title for *Little Dorrit*.[39] According to Charles Kingsley in *Alton Locke* (1850), referring to some 'Owenite "it's nobody's fault" harangues in the debating society' which are heard in the context of a 'victim of circumstance doctrine', this phrase, 'nobody's fault', was associated with Robert Owen (1771–1858).[40] He was introduced by James Mill to Bentham, so 'nobody's fault' belongs with Utilitarianism, which refuses to accept any irrationality within the self, such as having a 'will'. Blandois, the murderer, turns the phrase about being a victim of circumstance against the landlady of the Break of Day, at Chalons. Disguised, he hears himself being discussed by the company, and says:

> it may have been his unfortunate destiny. He may have been the child of circumstances. It is always possible that he had, and has, good in him, if one did but know how to find it out. Philosophical philanthropy teaches . . . (1.11.127)

The landlady interrupts him with her disbelief in 'philosophical philanthropy', which would treat criminality as a matter of a person's bad circumstances. She does not know it is Blandois speaking, nor the nature of his irony, that he is giving a rhetorical self-justification, like Mrs Clennam, when she is confronted with his blackmailing of her. The landlady believes there are people who have no good in them, who must be 'detested without compromise' (1.11.127). Such would also show the power of the will, and, as with Schopenhauer, this evil will must be resisted, save that the landlady's anger is as passionate as Blandois, and equally interested in revenge.

'Nobody's fault' does not negate the idea that there is a fault some-where, but refuses to name doer or fault. The anonymity compares with Miss Wade, presumably illegitimate, saying about Tattycoram: 'she has no name, I have no name' (1.27.330). Pancks says of Miss Wade:

> I know as much about her as she knows about herself. She is some-body's child – anybody's – nobody's. Put her in a room in London here with any six people old enough to be her parents, and her parents may be there, for anything she knows. (2.9.540)

Clennam will never know that he has never been in the same room as both his parents. A wise child knows its own father, but, it seems, a wiser one knows its mother. Miss Wade is, literally, 'nobody's fault', like Arthur Clennam, also illegitimate. The 'fault' which produces the ille-gitimate child implicates both parents, but it leaves the child without a name, *filius nullius*, a bastard in common law, the child of nobody. Her ignorance of her parentage and origins, means that there will be some-thing to read in any situation which she cannot know, which disqualifies her from reading, because she cannot interpret a social situation. She rationalises the paranoia this induces in her autobiography, which fills one chapter of the novel (2.21), her 'history of a self-tormentor'. It is a masterpiece of paranoid interpretation, that being what is meant by self-torment. Freud writes: 'the self-tormenting in melancholia, which is no doubt enjoyable, signifies . . . a satisfaction of trends of sadism and hate, which relate to an object and which have been turned round upon the subject's own self' ('Mourning and Melancholia', *SE*, 14.251). So it is with Miss Wade, and her title – her only name – is her self-reflection on being insulted and humiliated. It links having no name, which means having no father, with having no will, in the sense that the will comes from the father, as in normal testamentary wills. Yet the father can make many wills, as in *Our Mutual Friend*, in an attempt to impose his anger and ill-will on the future; hence John Harmon speaks of the many wills made by 'my unhappy self-tormenting father' (4.14.873). The son must repudiate the father's will and desire to spoil the future by changing his identity.[41] In *Little Dorrit*, the name of the father is the will of the father; the dispossession of both is the loss of history. Clennam, victim of civil death in China, lacks a history and is searching for one, which means, did he but know it, searching for a will. Miss Wade's 'history', written to explain what she means by hating (2.20.660), is no objective history, but a Freudian case-history, of her interior interpretations, of interrogating motives and torturing herself, a testimony to her 'egoism of suffering'.

Her autobiography poses most fully the *David Copperfield* question, 'what's his motive? That question is paranoid, and involves other questioners: Blandois, wanting to know Mrs Clennam's motives; Mr F's Aunt, in the accusatory force of her madness; Dorrit when released from the Marshalsea and wondering what people know about his history; Clennam wondering what lies behind the imperative 'Do Not Forget', and encountering another defensive and wilful paranoia in his mother who wants to represent her motives out loud when blackmailed and believes, like Miss Wade, that they are justified. 'What's his motive?' is the supreme question in the will to knowledge, yet a necessary question, if it suggests that behind the motive which can be represented is the legitimacy of considering unconscious motivations. We go from the will as knowable to the will that cannot be read. It is George Eliot's progression, as her fiction moves towards *Daniel Deronda*.

6

GEORGE ELIOT AND THE 'MURDEROUS WILL'

There can be no Good Will. Will is always Evil; it is persecution to
others or selfishness.

(BLAKE)[1]

His mind was destitute of that dread which has been erroneously
decried as if it were nothing higher than a man's animal care for his
own skin: that awe of the Divine Nemesis which was felt by religious
pagans, and though it took a more positive form under Christianity,
is still felt by the mass of mankind simply as a vague fear at anything
which is called wrong-doing. Such terror of the unseen is so far above
mere animal cowardice that it will annihilate that cowardice: it is the
initial recognition of a moral law restraining desire [. . .] 'It is good',
sings the old Eumenides, in Aeschylus, 'that fear should sit as the
guardian of the soul, forcing it into wisdom – good that men should
carry a threatening shadow in their hearts under the full sunshine;
else how shall they learn to revere the right?' That guardianship may
become needless, but only when all outward law has become needless
– only when duty and love have united in one stream and made a
common force.

(GEORGE ELIOT, *Romola*)[2]

I *THE MILL ON THE FLOSS*

The fiction of George Eliot (1819–80), more than Dickens, or Trollope,
concerns itself with the law, whether this is moral, or official, with
lawyers, illegitimacy, wills and the will. Perhaps it can be said that Eliot

thinks of mobilising the will, turning it towards 'the growing good of the world' (*Middlemarch*, Finale, 896), and away from any death-drive, or giving up on the will, or refusing to attend to the moral law, or failing to notice it. Only in a qualified way does she see the moral law as oppressive, in the way that Lacan discusses Kant with Sade, though the quotation from *Romola* suggests that it may ultimately be replaced. She recognises an ambiguity about the law. How far it represents a corrupt system, how far it is necessary is a question at the heart of Eliot, and apparent in her treatment of lawyers. She recognises the need of transgression: as Romola wonders:

> The law was sacred. Yes, but rebellion might be sacred too. It flashed upon her mind that the problem before her was essentially the same as that which had lain before Savonarola – the problem where the sacredness of obedience ended, and the sacredness of rebellion began. To her, as to him, there had come one of those moments in life when the soul must act on its own warrant, not only without external law to appeal to, but in the face of a law which is not unarmed with divine lightnings. (56.468–69)

The idea of having to act doubly, in self-contradictory mode, in a moment of crisis, fascinates Eliot more and more. The idea works against the patient statement of principles, articulations of moral law, of rational principle, that she wishes to give in her fiction. Eliot has a double attitude to the will, either as opposed to rationality or as formed by it; either possessive, destructive, and egotistical, or as usable. The sense of the will as possessive she could have taken from Blake.[3] She is interested in what happens when someone makes a will: we can bring out these points by concentrating on several of her novels, particularly *The Mill on the Floss*, *Romola*, *Felix Holt*, *Middlemarch*, and we will see a persistence of thinking that deepens towards the investigation of what will-power means in *Daniel Deronda*.[4] Even the early 'Janet's Repentance' in *Scenes of Clerical Life* (1857) has it: dealing with the fraudulent and drunk Dempster the lawyer brings out an 'inevitable incompatibility of law and gospel'.[5] Dempster's opposition to Evangelical Anglicans, such as Mr Tryan, brings out his religious legalism, while with his wife Janet, he is a 'huge crushing force, armed with savage will' (14.342). She is also tempted by drink, and her confession to Tryan evokes Romans 7:

[The temptation] was always coming, and it got stronger and stronger, I was ashamed and hated what I did; but almost while the thought was passing through my mind that I would never do it again, I did it. It seemed as if there was a demon in me always making me rush to do what I longed not to do. . . . I shall always be doing wrong, and hating myself after . . . (18.356–57)

The passage, inverting the Pauline view of law creating desire, implies law's incapacity to do other than increase the desire to drink, but insofar as Janet changes, Eliot commits herself to no determinism, but to the possibility of willing.[6] She is more interested in the consequences of actions. In *Adam Bede* (1859), Mr Irvine, who has been reading Aeschylus, tells Arthur Donnithorne, that a man who struggles against temptation into which he falls at last is to be pitied, 'in proportion to his struggles, for they foreshadow the inward suffering which is the worst form of Nemesis'.

Consequences are unpitying. Our deeds carry their terrible consequences, quite apart from any fluctuations that went before – consequences that are hardly ever confined to ourselves. And it is best to fix our minds on that certainty, instead of considering what may be the elements of excuse for us.[7]

Eliot does not retreat from the word 'terrible' throughout her fiction, and the discussion of Nemesis, or destiny, which reappears in *Romola* and *Felix Holt*, gives to her work the sense that it is marked by a sense of events repeating themselves.

A second lawyer, Wakem, appears in *The Mill on the Floss* (1860), as the nemesis of Mr Tulliver, whose litigiousness appears from the beginning.[8] Wakem is seen in Book 3 chapter 7, and Tulliver writes in the Bible a testamentary account that he will never forgive Wakem. Tom signs it as a witness, and, as son, an executor, and as a legatee of that expression of the will (3.8.280–81).[9] This novel, called 'a history of unfashionable families' (4.3.303), has an implicit dialogue on the value of the will. Mr and Mrs Glegg show their Protestant adherence to keeping accurate accounts with God in their need to have an 'unimpeachable will' (4.1.285), and in the imperative, that there must be no 'dying without wills' (6.12.474). In addition, there is Glegg's 'reticence' about his will (1.12.135) and his wife's obsession about hers, and how it must not be altered to provide for the Tullivers (2.3.225); an obstinacy which, however, pays off at the end with Mrs Glegg's surprising reaction to Maggie's apparent lapse: she will not admit bad conduct in one of the family, because 'that would force you to alter your will' (7.3.518). The testamentary will, as the marker of the personal will, calls back the self to itself, gives it a guarantee of stability; its value appears in Tom's anxiety that his Aunt Moss should not pay back the money that Tulliver gave her because it would be against his father's will (2.3.230). At that stage, Tom's father is still alive, but incapacitated, and here the will of the dying man, and the last will, to be read posthumously, come together.

In contrast to these, Maggie, without 'that knowledge of the irreversible laws within and without her which, governing the habits, becomes morality, and developing the feelings of submission and dependence becomes religion' (4.3.300), turns to Thomas à Kempis (c.1380–1471). She reads in 'the old monk' – giving the voice of Catholicism now, not the Protestantism of her family – 'if thou seekest this or that, and wouldst be here or there, to enjoy thy own will and pleasure, thou shalt never be quiet' (4.3.301). It is a doctrine which means that 'renunciation means sorrow, though a sorrow born willingly' (4.3.303). When Maggie renounces, as she does, 'she threw some exaggeration and wilfulness' into her self-renunciation (4.3.305), and those several senses of the will – (a) that it must be given up, and (b) that it is used in the process of giving up, so that it must exist whether or no, and (c) that its use is not without self-assertion, gives so much of what interests Eliot. Maggie, not 'seeking her own will' (5.1.309), tells Philip Wakem that she has been discontented because she cannot have her own will, and 'our life is determined for us – and it makes the mind very free when we give up wishing' (5.1.314). She accepts as absolutes the laws that the Dodsons are anxious to keep and be on the right side of, in their Protestantism, and which the lawyers, like Wakem, are rascals enough not to let lay hold of them. Her behaviour attempts to work around that, but it makes her to be 'borne along by the tide', 'without an act of her own will' (6.13.484). Her brother Tom, with the Dodson spirit, is opposite, with a mind:

> strongly marked by the positive and negative qualities that create severity – strength of will, conscious rectitude of purpose, narrowness of imagination and intellect, great power of self-control and a disposition to exert control over others. (6.12.475–76)

Maggie's will can hardly 'recoil' from Stephen Guest (6.14.492), but the debate within her is about law: 'if the past is not to bind us, where can duty lie? We should have no law but the inclination of the moment' (6.14.496). She leaves him, saying 'it has never been my will to marry you' (6.14.497). At the heart of the text is an antithesis between a desire for law, and the slippages, and the drift, of language, which means that no state can fully know itself, or, as the force of the river indicates, impose its own will.[10]

II TO *FELIX HOLT*

The weak will appears in *Silas Marner: The Weaver of Raveloe* (1861), with Godfrey Cass, whose father never 'checked his own errant weakness and helped his better will' and who accuses him of having no will, like his mother ('a woman has no call for one') (9.124,125).[11] He is echoed by Tito Melema in *Romola* (1862–63), whose double life is reflected in the child he fathered on Tessa, the woman he questionably 'married', in a mock-ceremony, while being betrothed to Romola. He does not acknowledge the child, but after his death, Romola does. Tito Melema, as the Florentine (though he is Greek) in political ascendancy in the Florence of the 1490s, is analysed in terms of a failure of the will: 'Tito longed to have his world once again completely cushioned with good-will' (34.306). This longing is his reaction to the discovery that Baldassare, who cared for him in his childhood, and whom he abandoned, is in Florence, and implacably revengeful towards him (he will kill him). Tito has acted unscrupulously towards him in a failure of sympathy, and of recognition because he wants life to be easy, and easy towards him (that was the case with Godfrey). Hence Tito's acts take the form of finding the path of least resistance. Throughout, he learns, contrary to his will for universal goodwill, 'that inexorable law of human souls, that we prepare ourselves for sudden deeds [in this case, the impulse, which happens in an emergency, to call Baldassare a madman] by the reiterated choice of good or evil which gradually determines character' (23.223). 'Law' in the quotation is crucial: beyond any moral law which dictates, is another, which, unlike that, is unavoidable, and which makes action in a crisis not exceptional but the accumulation of all previous decisions taken beforehand. The issue is stated more flatly later; here the 'law' has become an internal 'moral tradition':

Our lives make a moral tradition for our individual selves, as the life of mankind at large makes a moral tradition for the race, and to have once acted nobly seems a reason [the word may be compared with 'law'] why we should always be noble. But Tito was feeling the effect of an opposite tradition: he had won no memories of self-conquest and perfect faithfulness from which he could have a sense of falling. (39.348)

In contrast to Tito – 'he had simply chosen to make life easy to himself' (23.224), is Savonarola, saying that 'for four years I have preached in obedience to the divine will' and declaring himself 'willing' for martyrdom, while he is equally sure he knows what God's 'will' is (24.227,229).[12] It produces Eliot's comment on his religion and previous intervention in Florentine politics, that 'it is probable that his imperious need for ascendancy had burned undiscernibly in the strong flame of his zeal for God and man' (25.235). The quotation is full of synonyms for the will; and the dominance in one case and the deficiency in the other polarises Savonarola and Tito. The former challenges Romola when she attempts to leave Tito in what he calls 'self-will and anger'":

The higher life begins for us, my daughter, when we renounce our own will to bow before a divine law. (40.360)[13]

Later, he is challenged by Romola who is appealing for her godfather's life, and asks that 'private ill-will should not find its opportunity in public acts' of revenge (59.488). The words indicate Eliot's reliance on Shakespeare for writing political themes, while the episode, along with chapter 40, recalls Isabella's first interview with Angelo in *Measure for Measure*, as much as the issue of the law being itself a will – discussed earlier in relation to that play – returns here, to damaging effect. Eliot comments on Savonarola, with his 'power-loving and powerful nature' that:

feelings [of resentment towards Romola] were nullified by that hard struggle which made half the tragedy of his life – the struggle of a mind possessed by a never-silent hunger after purity and simplicity, yet caught in a tangle of egoistic demands, false ideas, and difficult outward conditions, that made simplicity impossible. (59.490)

The words could be part of an analysis of Angelo's will, save for the absence at this stage in Eliot, of a sense of the will being sexual. Nonetheless, unlike Tito, Savonarola is capable of tragedy; his utterances, which in this scene conclude with him saying he is 'willing to die' for God's kingdom on earth (59.492), are ironic and un-ironic.

The question of paternity, which Godfrey Cass must, and Tito does not, confront, and Eliot's relationship to tragedy, further appears in *Felix Holt, the Radical* (1866).[14] The setting is the Midlands, in 'Treby Magna', and around the time of the First Reform Bill. This passed into law on 7 June 1832, creating a new General Election that October. The context of writing was the Second Reform Bill, which passed into law in 1867. And law is the subject, including the idea of Rufus Lyon, the Dissenting Minister, that:

> true liberty can be naught but the transfer of obedience from the rule of one or of a few men to that will which is the norm or rule for all men. And though the transfer may sometimes be but an erroneous direction of search, yet is the search good and necessary to the ultimate finding. [. . . when] one law shall be written on all hearts, and be the very structure of all thought and be the principle of all action. (13.143)

The single will becomes a general will, and one law replaces legalism and becoming the basis of the religion of humanity: in such a way Eliot joins together an interest in both law and in wills.[15] The dual theme relates to the book's two plots which become one; but the private plot has more power, despite the difficulty in following the legal implications.

Mrs Transome, of Transome Court, has had an illegitimate son, Harold, by the lawyer Mr Jermyn, of whom it is said 'moral vulgarity cleaved to him like an hereditary odour' (9.109). Harold, unknowing, comes back from abroad, from Smyrna, and intends, Childe Harolde-like, to stand as a Radical in the elections, having 'the energetic will and muscle, the self-confidence, the quick perception, and the narrow imagination which makes what is admiringly called the practical mind' (8.104). Matthew Jermyn becomes his election agent. Felix Holt is the young working-class radical who loves Esther Lyon, supposed daughter of Rufus Lyon, the town's Dissenting Minister. Esther is actually heir to Transome Court, without knowing it, because of her father, Maurice

Christian Bycliffe. In 1729, John Justus Transome had entailed the estate on his son, Thomas, and Thomas' sons, on the condition that if that male line failed, it would go in 'remainder' to the Bycliffes. Thomas sold his rights to a lawyer-cousin, Durfey: Mrs Transome is a Durfey, who calls herself a Transome (29.263). During the Napoleonic wars, Maurice Bycliffe attempted a suit against the Transomes and was foiled by Jermyn, who managed the estates for his own benefit, and who knew of a still surviving male Transome, Tommy Trousem. Trousem dies in the Treby riots (ch. 33), bringing to a close the rights of the Transomes to live at Transome court. Maurice Christian Bycliffe, unknown to Jermyn, had married Annette Ledru in France: Esther is the daughter. Esther's identity is revealed through a servant of the aristocratic Debarrys, living near Treby Magna, Henry Scaddon, who swapped identities with Bycliffe in France, in order that Bycliffe could get back to England to challenge the Transomes.

Harold wants to proceed against Jermyn for his corrupt practices in relation to the Transome estate, unaware that the lawyer is his father. Jermyn wants to blackmail Harold into silence through disclosure that someone unknown has a claim to the estate (21.204, 35.308). But Harold discovers the identity of this person – Esther – through Scaddon/Christian, and Philip Johnson, Jermyn's assistant. Esther, after staying at Transome Court, rejects the world of the Transomes for life with Felix Holt. The making of the Transome will suggests that there was a will to keep the property even if there is no Transome to succeed to it.[16] The will has excluded women completely; it is only interested in the male line. The Transome line was sold by the son, while the father who made the will was still alive, to the Durfeys, who have no entitlement; they are parasitic on the Transomes, whose name they take (Introduction, 9). Equally, however, the Transomes have been parasitic on the Durfeys, in exchanging what is to be inherited for money: the legality of the line becomes more and more questionable, and now the heir apparent is the illegitimate Harold. As the males die out, Esther becomes the heir, but she is not interested in what also would exclude her. But the Transomes are doubly illegitimate, both in the literal sense with Harold, and in the sense that they do not belong to the property.

The Introduction (9) says that Lawyer Jermyn 'had made the wills of most people thereabout'. Eliot imagines a coachman pointing out Transome Court, 'a place there had been a fine sight of lawsuits about' (9). The word 'court' suggests the grand house, and the law court, in the same way that the name Mr Grandcourt, in *Daniel Deronda*, suggests that marriage to such a man is a matter of a legalism and bondage which cannot be comprehended: when Gwendolen says 'yes' to Grandcourt, the word comes 'as gravely . . . as if she had been answering to her name in a court of justice' (27.348).[17] Law is a matter of lawyers who corrupt it: the coachman 'would not say that Lawyer Jermyn was not the man he would choose to make his own will some day' (9). That very sentence, from a non-legal mind, with its double negative, warns the reader against the law whose interpretation can always go either way, always equivocating. The interesting point in this novel is that the lawyer also falls.

The passage introducing Transome Court leads into speculation on 'wrongdoing' which carries with it 'some downfall of blindly climbing hopes, some hard entail of suffering', before speaking of the 'tragic mark of kinship', which connects a life to the 'far-stretching life that went before'. The symbolism of the will begins to appear as the hinge between generations, that which allows or disallows a future for 'the life that is to come'. The will is the link that creates causality, and the will, as possessed by the individual, is called 'thy most anxious will' (15.155). The sense of one life 'cursed by its woeful progeny' is said to have 'raised the pity and terror of men ever since they began to discern between will and destiny'. The legal will has modulated into the human will, and its control by legal wills, which confer destiny, and the paradigm to understand this is tragedy, as interpreted by Aristotle, who speaks of 'pity and terror' which strike people since they began to discern between 'will and destiny'.[18]

The Introduction concludes: 'many an inherited sorrow that has marred a life has been breathed into no human ear'. The last paragraph moves into an echo of the wood of the suicides in Dante (*Inferno*, 13), and it is a near approach in Eliot to the sense that dreams bear signs of trauma:

> The poets have told us of a dolorous enchanted forest in the under world. The thorn-bushes there, and the thick-barked stems, have human histories hidden in them; the power of unuttered cries dwells in the passionless-seeming branches, and the red warm blood is darkly feeding the quivering nerves of a sleepless memory that watches through all dreams. These things are a parable. (Introduction, 10)

Eliot uses the Transome will to speak of inherited sorrow; it conveys a human history which is readable from it, and it generates a 'sleepless memory'. The wood is where past repressed (unuttered) events are worked out in secret suffering. In calling the wood a parable, the present becomes the working out of the past, including hereditary conditions. Eliot speaks of the 'hard entail of suffering' (Introduction, 10) and the Transome property 'entailed' onto Thomas Transome (29.263). An entailed inheritance is 'limited and regulated as to its tenure and inher-itance by conditions fixed by the donor: thus distinguished from *fee simple* or absolute ownership' (*OED*, 'tail', *adj.*). Another example of being 'entailed' is Daniel Deronda, who thinks he is the illegitimate son of Sir Hugo, and that he has an 'entailed disadvantage' (*Daniel Deronda*, 16.215). An entailed property means that the donor keeps a control over it, which may, as with the Transome property, be evaded for a time, but finally cannot be.

When Mrs Transome re-meets her long-absent son, 'in the moment when their eyes met, the sense of strangeness came upon her like a terror' (1.15). It is the first intimation of 'hereditary, entailed Nemesis'; and the feeling of 'dim terror about the future' recurs (2.35, 42.370). Mrs Transome has the sense of her past disconfirming her present. She knows 'there were secrets which her son must never know' (1.16).[19] 'It had come to pass now – this meeting with the son who had been the subject of so much longing; whom he had longed for before he was born, for whom she had sinned . . . the moment was gone by' (1.21). Eliot plays on the dual sense of the Biblical 'it had come to pass' – time brings the moment, but the moment goes, leaving the woman feeling the resentment that everything has passed into the past. She has 'the presentiment of her powerlessness' (1.24) to look forward to. The chapter's last long para-graph concludes:

> Mrs Transome, whose imperious will had availed little to ward off the great evils of her life, found the opiate for her discontent in the exertion of her will about smaller things. She was not cruel, and could not enjoy thoroughly what she called the old woman's pleasure of tormenting, but she liked every little sign of power her lot had left her. (1.29)

The exercise of will is on account of the passing of time; and Harold as the expression of her will focuses her 'discontent'. In the next chapter she sees Jermyn and Harold together, and recalls how 'she had been imperious to one of these men, and had rapturously pressed the other as an infant to her bosom, and now knew that she was of little consequence [the word implies her future state] to either of them' (2.35–36). Even love-making was an expression of will. Mrs Transome is made to feel her inadequacy when thinking about Esther, who, now discovered to be the heir, is staying at Transome Court. She tells her servant, Denner, that Esther will never be able to control Harold, if they marry:

'Not true that she will ever master him. No woman ever will. He will make her fond of him, and afraid of him. . . . A woman's love is always freezing into fear. She wants everything, she is secure of nothing. This girl has a fine spirit – plenty of fire and pride and wit. Men like such captives, as they like horses . . . they feel more triumph in their mastery. What is the use of a woman's will? – if she tries, she doesn't get it, and she ceases to be loved. God was cruel when he made women'. (39.344)[20]

The gender-question is significant; a woman has, or can have, no will, as is the fate of the Transome women who cannot inherit, and if the woman has a will, it is useless. It makes Mrs Transome decide that 'if I could choose at this moment, I would choose that Harold should never have been born' (39.346); her version of the wisdom of Silenus, which *The Birth of Tragedy* (3.27) comments on. The sentiment repeats one felt by both parents in an earlier moment which focuses for Mrs Transome her powerlessness and Jermyn's corruption, which she can do nothing about, but which she fears will cause Harold's anger against him (9.111). Now, she wishes that Harold had never been born: it has given Jermyn power over her. It is a displaced comment on her own feeling about herself, for she adds that 'every fibre in me seems to be a memory that makes a pang' (39.346). Her powerlessness comes from the sense that Nemesis has not come to her *after* the event; it was *in* the event; as she tells Jermyn, 'If I sinned, my judgment went beforehand – that I should sin for a man like you' (42.370). Incident and its 'punishment' have become inverted: what she went through contained its judgment already. The past returns in different ways, as when Jermyn reminds her of words she had said much earlier 'a clever lawyer can do anything if he has the will; if it's impossible, he will make it possible' (42.367). The 'clever lawyer' excludes the woman; and the punning on 'the will' that she makes – the legal will, will-power, sexuality – is essential; but at the end, the will eludes all the men in this part of the novel, as of course it eludes the woman, Mrs Transome.

The relationship of this situation, of the collapse of the dynasty of Transomes, and the failure of relationships for Mrs Transome, to classical tragedy, is stated in chapter 47. Here, Jermyn, about to be ruined by Harold, goes to see him, though the two are not on speaking terms; he wants him to call off the pursuit. Harold strikes him across the face with his whip, and Jermyn tells him that he is his father. And Harold, looking in the mirror, 'saw the hated fatherhood reasserted' (47.421) as an example of the power of heredity, and inheritance: he is his own father. The moment is Oedipal, since the violence was his attempt to annihilate the father, an unconscious act, since the action precedes the knowledge of what relation Jermyn is to him; and it is Oedipal since the father's words, laying bare the mother's secret, are the ruin of the son.

The quotation from *Agamemnon* opening chapter 48: ''Tis law as stedfast as the throne of Zeus – / Our days are heritors of days gone by' (48.422) makes links with Aristotelian tragedy; for Harold, the comment 'all the pride of his nature rebelled against his sonship' (48.423) brings out his imperiousness of his nature – like mother, like son – in the act of attempting to repudiate where he has come from. He must learn 'the hard pressure of our common lot, the yoke of that mighty resistless destiny laid upon us by the acts of other men as well as our own' (49.425). Such a conclusion, which suggests no determinism, but shows how each will is hedged about and contradicted by other wills, emphasises how this part of the plot can admit no heterogeneity, nothing that will alter the will-power within Transome Court: Esther, a figure from the outside is wanted not for her difference but in order that she might be assimilated to that order.

III *MIDDLEMARCH*

Was inheritance a question of liking or of responsibility? (*Middlemarch*, 37.407)

She yearned towards the perfect Right, that it might make a throne within her, and rule her errant will. (*Middlemarch*, 80.846)

The first sentence quoted here illustrates Dorothea's scruples over the poverty of Will Ladislaw, impoverished because his mother had chosen someone who was poor. Dorothea's sense is that an inheritance cannot be given away to someone with less natural right to it, simply because of a personal dislike. The second sentence, from later in the book, focuses on the other meaning of the will, and shows the unconscious within desire, as Eliot narrates the aspiration of Dorothea. She has been weeping on the floor all night, having had the shock of seeing Ladislaw and Rosamond together – and drawing the wrong conclusion from that coincidence. Dorothea yearns that she shall be controlled as to her will – she wants no 'pitiable infirmity of will' such as Lydgate sees in Mr Farebrother's gambling (18.218) – and Eliot's sense that the will is to be surrendered appears in Dorothea's perception that 'she was part of that *involuntary*, palpitating life' which she can see outside her window (80.846, my emphasis), and must participate in it in its non-wilful character.

These quotations recall F.W.H. Myers' record, whether accurate or not, of a conversation with George Eliot, on the words 'God', 'Immortality' and 'Duty' – 'how inconceivable was the first, how unbelievable the second, and yet how peremptory and absolute the third'.[21] It is curious that, since Dorothea is in love with Will Ladislaw, and knows it, that the word 'will' should appear when Dorothea yearns for renunciation. But no stranger than that the man she loves should combine Will and Law in himself, and that Ladislaw should also contain an anagram for will. That ambiguity runs throughout Eliot. Desire for duty, for adherence to the law, is fuelled by a repression of desire, which does not quite recognise itself, so, when she yearns towards the perfect Right, opposed to the will, she invokes Will.

Middlemarch shows the necessity of setting aside desire for duty, while not quite seeing that these two are not opposed, as the name Will Ladislaw combines at its beginning and end the two contraries which are the theme of Lacan on Kant with Sade: law and desire. Hence the critique of Nietzsche, discussing Eliot, that 'they are rid of the Christian God and are now all the more convinced that they have to hold on to Christian morality . . . For the English, morality is not yet a problem'.[22] It is interesting, in the light of this to know that George Eliot, who studied German – unlike Casaubon (*Middlemarch*, 21.240) – read Schopenhauer in 1873, before writing *Daniel Deronda*. And she must have known his work before, because the *Westminster Review* carried discussions of him, beginning in 1852.[23] *Daniel Deronda* is the novel least concerned with Christian pieties: Christianity seems only to be criticised in it. The ambiguity, however, between Dorothea's desire to do the right thing, and her sense of the power of her will, which she must repress, is basic to the way she is idealised: the text cannot recognise that the yearning is also a matter of will.

Middlemarch is concerned with the present as posthumous, the dead past blighting lives: hence the stress on last wills and testaments, with which people seek to control after their death. Nearly eighty, Peter Featherstone reminds Fred Vincy 'I can alter my will yet' (12.137), thus affirming the will's arbitrary nature: if the will can alter, what was 'the will' worth? Featherstone thinks he has the power of 'the dead hand' ('mortmain' in legal terms) which would hold the living in the power of the dead: expressed, with Peter Featherstone, in his death-grip: 'his right hand clasping the keys, and his left hand lying on the heap of notes and gold' (33.354). Featherstone has written the programme for his burial, an act almost equivalent to writing a will, but

> he certainly did not make clear to himself that his pleasure in the little drama of which it formed a part was confined to anticipation. In chuckling over the vexations he could inflict by the rigid touch of his dead hand, he inevitably mingled his consciousness with that livid stagnant presence, and so far as he was preoccupied with a future life, it was with one of gratification inside his coffin. (34.358)

Middlemarch is interested in the lawyer, who has responsibility to encode the will and to pronounce on it. His presence speaks of the power of *ressentiment*, as the dominant nineteenth-century force which protects property, and guards its own against the other by the force of words, which are intended to capture, and work against, the 'magnificent formlessness' of life.[24] In chapter 35 the lawyer, Mr Standish, reads out the first and second wills of Peter Featherstone, which means that the shifts in Featherstone's thinking are displayed, and the way in which he tries in his wills to manipulate people – raising expectations and dropping them – but finally determining that the will is instrumental in continuing his name through the 'erection and endowment of almshouses . . . to be called Featherstone's Almshouses' (35.372).[25] In the ensuing discussion over the will's arbitrariness, and that of the person who made it, Caleb Garth wishes 'there was no such thing as a will' (35.372). In comparison to Featherstone's, Mr Casaubon's 'will', oppressing Dorothea and rejecting Ladislaw – the son of his mother's sister, Julia (9.100–4, 37.401) and therefore his second cousin – is his 'egoism' (48.519). Casaubon's codicil is designed to prevent Dorothea marrying Ladislaw (chs. 49 and 50). Similarly, he expects Dorothea to continue his work: the 'Synoptical Tabulation' left for her guidance expresses the point: 'he willingly imagined her toiling under the fetters of a promise to erect a tomb with his name upon it. (Not that Mr Casaubon called the future volumes a tomb: he called them the Key to all Mythologies)' (50.535). That is his legacy: Dorothea must reject it.

Mr Bulstrode, the banker, too, must remember his past life when Raffles, who has reappeared from that past, attempts to blackmail him. Eliot opens the chapter comprising his memory with an epitaph from *Rasselas*: '"Inconsistencies," answered Imlac, "cannot both be right, but imputed to men they may both be true"' (61.660). We have returned to the inconsistency of Mr Spenlow, in *David Copperfield*. Bulstrode, in his past, had married the widow of Mr Dunkirk, a rich pawnbroker, and suppressed her daughter's existence from her to marry the widow, and possess the money. The daughter, Sarah, had gone on the stage in reaction to her parents' occupation: there is a similarity here in this suppression to the Clennam will in *Little Dorrit* which, if it had not been suppressed, would have benefited the singer (another stage artist) who was the mother of Arthur Clennam. Sarah married the son of a Polish refugee who was married to the Julia who was Casaubon's aunt (37.400–1).[26] Sarah's son is Will Ladislaw, and Raffles, who had worked for old Mr Dunkirk, can now blackmail Bulstrode on account of his repression of the rights of the daughter. Arthur Clennam's sense of a past injustice which must be repaired has influenced George Eliot: in *Romola*, it produces the wife's intuition that Tito has been unjust to someone unknown, as when she says to her husband, 'Have you robbed someone else [he has already disposed of her father's library] who is *not* dead?' (*Romola*, 36.321).

Eliot dissociates Bulstrode from being a 'coarse hypocrite' who 'consciously affect[s] beliefs and emotions for the sake of gulling the world'; he is much more like Angelo in *Measure for Measure*, the play which, ending in a trial onstage, Eliot associates herself with, since it is evoked twice in the epigraphs to *Middlemarch*, in the book significantly called 'The Two Temptations'. The first is chapter 66 (720): Angelo's words ''Tis one thing to be tempted, Escalus, / Another thing to fall', and the second chapter 71 (769), a fragment of the official investigation of Froth and Pompey in the same scene.[27] So Bulstrode is:

> simply a man whose desires had been stronger than his theoretic beliefs, and who had gradually explained the gratification of his desires into satisfactory agreement with those beliefs. If this be hypocrisy, it is a process which shows itself occasionally in us all . . . (61.667)

Bulstrode has united his 'inconsistencies' into one, repressed, Evangelical outward form, by the process of willing, whereby his desires – what he wills – are expressed in terms of his beliefs, also willed. He has enriched himself at the expense of the daughter who should have inherited the money from the pawnbroking business, and Eliot, noting the sophistries by which Bulstrode has let himself believe his yearnings are God's, comments:

> this implicit reasoning is no more peculiar to Evangelical belief than the use of wide phrases for narrow motives is peculiar to Englishmen. There is no general doctrine which is not capable of eating out our morality if unchecked by the deep-seated habit of direct fellow-feeling with individual fellow-men. (61.668)

Later, knowing that Raffles is ill, Bulstrode 'knew that he ought to say, "Thy will be done" and he said it often. But the intense desire remained that the will of God might be the death of that hated man' (69.750).[28] The prayer from which he quotes continues, 'Lead us not into temptation' (Luke, 11.2–4) – temptation, as with Angelo, being the subject of this part of *Middlemarch*. And as Raffles remains ill, 'Bulstrode felt himself getting irritated at the persistent life in this man, whom he would fain have seen sinking in to the silence of death: imperious will stirred murderous impulses towards this brute life, over which will, by itself, had no power' (70.761). Hence the action that Bulstrode takes with Raffles: he lets him die.

Will Ladislaw has been kept back from the inheritance owed to his mother, and Dorothea will lose hers if she becomes his wife, under the terms of Casaubon's will. But the will, as a form of law, with the intention of maintaining estates (land and property and classes) the way they were, secures the opposite effect. *Middlemarch*'s meliorism works by eliminating such forms of entrapment by the past. The difficulties posed by this are a subject of *Daniel Deronda*.

IV *DANIEL DERONDA*

Becoming a governess is the fate – Gwendolen calls it the 'horror' (28.355) – which is spared Gwendolen Harleth in *Daniel Deronda* (1876). The fate, which she wills is worse, since she chooses to marry Henleigh Grandcourt. The novel is of all Eliot's most interested in the power of the will.[29] But the will now includes, for Eliot, its Shakespearian sense of the sexual. Its titles begin with 'The Spoiled Child' (one never tested by having to make choices, and above all, childish), and it continues with 'Maidens Choosing' and 'Gwendolen Gets her Choice'. The 'spoiled child' kills her sister's canary (3.53), and fancies a tragic existence, since she says, 'all the great poetic criminals were women' (6.85), as if tragedy was definable as criminal lawlessness. Beyond Gwendolen's world is a larger one which, in the aspect which cannot be defined through the mechanisms of social interaction, includes the Liszt-like musician Herr Klesmer (*klesmer*, in Yiddish, is popular music). The novel uses Rossini, and Beethoven, and implies that music points to a power which exceeds the individual, who must submit himself or herself to it.[30] Beyond that again is the Jewish world, a part of the novel, which despite the fascination of double-plot novels, I do not discuss here, because of its different mode, where Deronda's discovery of his Jewishness and what he makes of that in his commitment to found a Jewish community implies that a will has been imposed on the text, to discover that something is true that it is hoped is true.[31] Because of the sense that there is something of a 'rigid will' in the writing of the Jewish part of the novel – however much this intersects with the Gwendolen Harleth sections – I concentrate on the other part which, as with the epitaph to chapter 16, muses on choice:

> men, like planets, have both a visible and an invisible history . . . the narrator of human actions [must] thread the hidden pathways of feeling and thought which lead up to every moment of action, and to those moments of intense suffering which take the quality of action. (16.202)

The word 'will' appears many times in the text, applied to Gwendolen, who has 'fire and will' (3.54) even after the canary-incident, and is too strong for her mother (9.129). Grandcourt is an opposite force, as the equivalence of the initials show: GH, HG. He has 'a peremptory will' (12.162), and knows, from Lush, that Gwendolen is 'a young lady with a will of her own'; and that she thinks marrying him will not require 'any subjugation of her will' (13.168). Called 'wilful' (13.176), as having 'forcible will and daring' (21.276), she has learned from Herr Klesmer that she cannot 'command fortune by force of will and merit' (26.334).

The personal and the testamentary meanings of 'will' are played on with Grandcourt, who in the process of the novel makes his will. That implies that he is future-less, and that his existence is death. In relation to Mrs Glasher, 'he would never settle anything except by will' (30.387); she 'depended on his will' (30.389); he feels that 'his will must impose itself without trouble' (30.396). In how language is used in this dialogue with Lydia Glasher, everything depends on the ambiguity of the will meaning (a) what he will leave, and (b) his will as supreme. After marriage to Gwendolen, there is more reference to his legal will (44.615), which is paired with the point that 'he had no imagination of anything in her but what affected the gratification of his own will' (44.616). The parallel between the will he exerts and the will he has written are enforced again in 48.645, 646; the contents of the will are administered to Gwendolen by Lush; they are predictably mean, an expression of egotism. Sir Hugo says:

> even a wise man generally lets some folly ooze out of him in his will
> . . . if a fellow has any spite or tyranny in him, he's likely to bottle off
> a good deal for keeping in that sort of document. (59.783)

It is the document, as a substitutionary form of communication, like Lush, that is the point. It makes the will something to be supported by forces beyond the self; similarly, Sir Hugo can comment on 'that posthumous grudgingness towards a wife' (64.827); an instance of the legal will as revengeful, as 'ill-will'.

'Terror', as with Mrs Transome, is a crucial word in the novel, starting with the epigraph: 'Let thy chief terror be of thine own soul'. The will seems not in control, acting, rather, as a reaction-formation. Eliot moves towards a sense of character as being not 'a process and an unfolding', as in *Middlemarch* (15.178) but an 'iridescence':

the play of various, nay, contrary tendencies. For Macbeth's rhetoric about the impossibility of being many opposite things in the same moment referred to the clumsy necessities of action, and not to the subtler possibilities of feeling. We cannot speak a loyal word and be meanly silent, we cannot kill and not kill in the same moment; but a moment is wide enough for the loyal and mean desire, for the outlash of a murderous thought and the sharp backward stroke of repentance. (4.72)

This is a crucial passage. 'Tendencies' contradicts, in its non-specificity, the singleness and determination of the will, and so the singleness of 'character'; though a tendency may be also a milder form of the will, and contrary tendencies mean an always divided will. The passage gives the sense of the novel outgoing tragic drama in its response to character through the allusion to Macbeth's words. He is defending himself for having done something which, in his planning with Lady Macbeth, he had not intended doing: he has killed the grooms who were guarding Duncan, and whom he and his wife were framing. Having killed them, he must justify his murderous act – not just his murderous thought – to others and to himself:

> Who can be wise, amazed, temp'rate and furious,
> Loyal and neutral in a moment? No man.
> Th'expedition of my violent love
> Outran the pauser, reason. (*Macbeth*, 2.3.105–8)

Macbeth, having killed the guards, must now reflect on why he did so, and has no satisfactory answer. The issue points either to a divided will, as with the antitheses (e.g. wise/amazed) within this quotation, or to something which precedes the will, an impulse to kill which cannot be rationalised. Or, as the whole speech indicates, Macbeth's irrational impulse comes from seeing Duncan's dead face. Two chapters later, Gwendolen is acting in a *tableau vivant* the part of Hermione, the statue who comes to life in *The Winter's Tale*. At the moment of her descent from the pedestal, the movable panel 'of an upturned dead face, from which an obscure figure seemed to be flying with outstretched arms' (3.56) flies open, and Gwendolen stood 'without change of attitude, but with a change of expression that was terrifying in its terror. She looked like a statue into which a soul of Fear had entered' (6.91).[32]

'Terror' is again significant; Gwendolen is like a statue of the tragic muse, in the hysteria-inducing state that Henry James's governess in *The Turn of the Screw* is confronted with, but now tragedy is not a matter of a pose, or of an actress's skills, but of how much of the self depends upon repression, even of an incident like the killing of the canary; the opening panel suggesting the Freudian return of the repressed. And what of the content of the picture? Gwendolen's reaction repeats the action of the fleeing figure, just as her terror terrifies, but it does so because she is *both* the dead face, *and* the fleeing figure: the paralysed statue and in flight from that. This chapter of Fear ends with Gwendolen's customary asser-tion of self when 'she found again her usual world in which her will was of some avail' (6.95), but in the following chapter, when Rex tries to take her hand, she recoils (7.114), not bearing to be touched. This expe-rience shocks her, and marks her out as 'the spoiled child' (7.115) for whom the move towards the sexual, towards being touched, or having 'love' made to her, is impossible. This hysterical reaction to being touched brings out, retrospectively, the horror before the opened panel as sexual, a recoil from masculinity, which requires her to return to the 'almost painful clinging' to her mother at the end of the chapter. The kiss on the hand that Grandcourt gives responds to her 'Yes', which contains an 'indefinable prohibition'; it is a 'yes' which 'entailed so little at this moment'(27.348): the pun suggests how little she is thinking that her will must be bound up with responsibility and in thinking how another's will imposes an 'entail'.

But in bed, in the following chapter, while 'looking on darkness which the blind do see' – the quotation from Shakespeare's Sonnet 27.8 implies the complex thought of the poet at night considering the young man, and its reference is at least, in part, sexual – 'she was appalled by the idea that she was going to do what she had once started away from with repugnance' (28.356). The complex reference is to her dash away from England and Grandcourt to Leubronn after her interview with Lydia Glasher at the Whispering Stones. That episode itself, which seems to recall the enchanted forest with its 'unutterable cries' of the Introduction to *Felix Holt*, was preceded by the observation that Grandcourt is not with the archery party that day, and it makes Gwendolen wonder: 'Can he be starting away from a decision?' (14.187). At that moment, Eliot permits a comment on an ambiguity of will in Grandcourt, that his will is inseparable from apathy:

'Starting away', however, was not the right expression for the languor of intention that came over Grandcourt like a fit of diseased numbness, when an end seemed to be in easy reach: to desist then, when all expectation was to the contrary, became another gratification of mere will, sublimely independent of definite motive. (14.187)

Grandcourt does not 'start away'; does not complete things because of a wilfulness which is in him independent of motivation, from something to make him start away. In that way, he cannot be terrified – has not the imagination to be – and he contrasts with the two women. The episode of the Whispering Stones is uncanny, partly because of the name of the place; it suggests comparisons with Macbeth meeting the Weird Sisters, who cause 'terror', since 'it was if some ghastly vision had come to [Gwendolen] in a dream and said, "I am a woman's life"' (14.190), both Lydia's and Gwendolen's. The image evokes the picture of chapter 6 – Lydia as the dead face, Gwendolen fleeing away – and it supplies, again, twice, when Gwendolen is lying in bed, the word 'terror'.

Here had come a moment when something like a new consciousness was awaked. She seemed on the edge of adopting deliberately, as a notion for the rest of her life, what she had rashly said in her bitterness, when her discovery had driven her away to Leubronn: that it did not signify what she did: she had only to amuse herself as best she could. [See 15.194 for the connection]. That lawlessness, that casting away of all care for justification, suddenly frightened her: it came to her with the shadowy array of possible calamity behind it . . . [with] the vague conception of avenging powers. (28.355–56)

The first sentence here fuses the incident of chapter 14, when she had met Lydia, and the moment of lying in bed; so it evokes awareness of the sexual in relationship to Grandcourt; both because she thinks of Lydia with Grandcourt, and then of her own sense of her impending marriage, and her fear of that, and she ends up by again going to her mother's bed. It adds to Lush's sense that Grandcourt's marriage is on both sides a 'perverse wilfulness', and that Grandcourt, too, is 'led on by an ominous fatality' (28.361–62), which recalls the point that he is not a man who can act when given some spur, or motivation to do so.

Gwendolen chooses Mr Grandcourt, knowing that he belongs, properly, to Lydia Glasher, and to her children. The letter she receives from

Lydia, which refers to Grandcourt's 'withered heart', ends: 'You took him with your eyes open. The willing wrong you have done me will be your curse' (31.406: the words echo in Gwendolen's consciousness in 35.478). Does 'willing wrong' mean 'the wrong you intended – because your eyes were open – to do to me'? Or 'the will to wrong me'? Or 'the wrong which you were happy to do'? Or 'the willing in you which was, as wilful, inevitably, wrong'? Whatever the sense, when Grandcourt enters:

> the sight of him brought a new nervous shock, and Gwendolen screamed again and again with hysterical violence. . . . [Grandcourt] saw her pallid, shrieking as it seemed with terror, the jewels scattered around her on the floor. Was it a fit of madness? In some form or other the Furies had crossed his threshold. (31.407)[33]

'Terror' which entered into Gwendolen, and arrests her as she sees Grandcourt, as she was earlier arrested in chapter 6, now leads to the 'Furies', to an out-of-control state, beyond the will. The Aeschylean image suggests that Gwendolen, as the unconscious agent of Lydia Glasher, who is also present in the form of her jewels, will be a feminine revenge on Grandcourt though not before Gwendolen herself has been cursed by the 'willing wrong'.

After marriage, Gwendolen's nature still has 'strength in the will to reassert itself' (35.477), but in seven weeks:

> her husband had gained a mastery which she could no more resist than she could have resisted the benumbing effect from the touch of a torpedo. Gwendolen's will had seemed imperious in its small girlish sway; but it was the will of a creature with a large discourse of imaginative fears: a shadow would have been enough to relax its hold. And she had found a will like that of a crab or a boa-constrictor which goes on pinching or crushing without alarm at thunder. Not that Grandcourt was without calculation of the intangible effects which were the chief means of mastery . . . (35.477–78).

The animal unalarmed at thunder indeed suggests Grandcourt's wilfulness; perhaps there is an echo of Macbeth's desire to 'sleep in spite of thunder' (*Macbeth*, 4.1.86), which of course, he cannot. Gwendolen learns that 'he would do just what he willed, and that she had neither devices at her command to determine his will, nor any rational means of escaping it' (35.480). His function is to annihilate 'any opposing will in her' (44.608). The action moves to Genoa, for the final boating accident, where Grandcourt goes out sailing, taking Gwendolen – whom he fears is seeing Deronda covertly – 'with the gratified impulse of a strong will which had nothing better to exert itself on' (54.745). They stand on the pier moving, as the lookers-on think, 'like creatures who were fulfilling a supernatural destiny', as if they are under the power of a superior will, like Macbeth, under the power of a 'supernatural soliciting'. Here, Gwendolen is declared to 'be like a statue' (54.745). That immobility, which recalls the Hermione episode, suggests how she needs to be recalled to life.

On this voyage out, Gwendolen:

> was afraid of her own wishes, which were taking shapes possible and impossible, like a cloud of demon-faces. She was afraid of her own hatred . . . quick, quick came images, plans of evil that would come again and seize her in the night, like furies preparing the deed that they would straightway avenge. (54.745–46)

It is what has been described with Macbeth: an impulse to kill which precedes the will. The Furies, which crossed Grandcourt's threshold, and are now inside the house, are both incitements to murder – like Macbeth's weird sisters – and to revenge after murder: a continuation of violence. Suddenly Gwendolen lets her hand fall from the tiller to say 'God help me' (54.746). The chapter ends, cutting to a separate Deronda episode, but that concludes with him seeing Gwendolen brought back from the boat, with Grandcourt dead, and Gwendolen driven to an agonised confession to speak about the 'dead face' (56.753) and to articulate her sense of being a murderess. The 'dead face' of Grandcourt fuses with the dead face seen in chapter 6. She says 'and I wished him to be dead' and then adds how she had kept a stiletto with her, and while she wanted to kill him, motivated by 'the temptation that frightened me, the longing, the thirst for what I dreaded', says how she thought 'he would kill me if I resisted his will' (56.758). She says how she killed Grandcourt in her thoughts:

> evil wishes were too strong. I remember then letting go the tiller and saying 'God help me!' But then I was forced to take it again and go

on; and the evil longings, the evil prayers came again dim and blotted everything else dim, till, in the midst of them – I don't know how it was – he was turning the sail – there was a gust – he was struck – I know nothing – I only know that I saw my wish outside me. (56.761)

Paratactic utterances, pauses acknowledging gaps in knowledge, like the pauses that attend Gwendolen's first meeting and dialogue with Grandcourt (ch. 11) acknowledge that there are things which are unknowable. They indicate breaks, intermittences, within identity, the will. The narratives of chapters 54 and 56 never quite fit. Does seeing her wish outside her reify the will, or is Grandcourt falling the visualisation of her wish? Parataxis reappears in the next paragraph when Grandcourt comes up above the water and calls for the rope:

and he cried again – and I held my hand, and my heart said 'Die!' – and he sank; and I felt 'It is done – I am wicked, I am lost!' – and I had the rope in my hand – I don't know what I thought – I was leaping away from myself. (56.761)

The sentence evokes self-hatred, followed by 'I was leaping away from my crime', both recalling the earlier phrase 'starting away', and the figure in the picture running away from the dead face, which is actually the empty, flaccid face of Grandcourt as he was while alive (11.145), as much as when he is dead. The statement shows the power of self-accusation; thinking a 'crime' has been committed, she aligns herself with it. Leaping away is also literal, for she leaps into the water; but whether to save Grandcourt, to get out of the situation or drown herself, is not clear. The significant part of the utterance is its gaps. They indicate that the self in its 'iridiscence' cannot give a confessional account of itself, and they imply the impossibility of thinking sequentially, within a narrative that allows for causality. They make it impossible to decide whether the passages between ellipses may be spoken of as other than gaps themselves: does 'I held my hand' mean that Gwendolen thinks she did this deliberately? Does it suspend such judgment, making her like the statue that she was when she saw the tableau reveal itself? The gaps and the speech may change places: what is the value of the silence, and what the value of the speech? Which tells more? The gaps, in spatialising utterance, allow for the differences to emerge between the 'I' who speaks, and the 'I' of the 'I held my hand' (the 'I' and 'my' are different), and the difference between 'my hand' and 'my heart' and the 'I' of 'I felt', all making it impossible to see a single agency here. If David Carroll is right to see the episode in the light of Romans 7, that must be quali- fied, for Eliot works beyond St Paul.[34] It is not now a psychomachia between law and desire, but desire and dread. Nothing speaks for the law, for the dread in Gwendolen is not of the moral law of *Romola* chapter 11 (see the epigraph to this chapter). In *Daniel Deronda* it is part of her fear of life which appeared in an hysterical reaction to the sexual; if that is the moral law, it is now wholly repressive.

Nor is it clear how the forces in this episode operate; this is brought out by the gaps' disconnectedness; the fragments that Gwendolen's speeches fall into are the ruins of egoism, and of the claim of the realist novel to be able to say that it knows. The bad thoughts and evil wishes, which become singular in the expression 'I saw my wish outside me': do these relate to the terror which, as if from outside, enters Gwendolen, or to the Furies which crossed Grandcourt's threshold? Do they flow inwards, from Lydia Glasher, for instance, to destroy him? Are the jewels – which have passed from him to Lydia to Gwendolen – the 'Terror' which have come to take revenge on him? If Gwendolen sees her wish outside her, as before she had seen the dead face and the figure fleeing from it, is that saying that she was glad to see Grandcourt overboard? – since she says that the gap before he came up for the first time was 'long enough for me to be glad'? But if the wish is outside, then the inner will is not sufficient; identity is not a matter of inward character; it is as much formed by what is outside.

It seems that unconsciously Gwendolen has been taken over by the Furies, with the puns on the idea of madness included; while inner iden- tity and will-power as agencies have been brought into question. So too, Grandcourt calls for the rope 'in a voice – not his own'. Drowning, in nineteenth-century ideology, seems to be feminising; if this is a femi- nine death, that associates with something in the name Henleigh, at least in its first syllable. Grandcourt's drowning contrasts with Mirah's near-drowning in chapter 17. If the feminising hint is relevant, it suggests something sexless in Grandcourt's will: Gwendolen is sure she is not pregnant, and that Grandcourt's will favouring his illegitimate son, Henleigh, will be implemented (57.764). In which case, the Casaubon/Dorothea and Grandcourt/Gwendolen marriages may have something in common.

The power of thought to accuse the self recalls Eliot's interest in

Measure for Measure.[35] Grandcourt's mode of being within the boat, even how he stands, is a form of temptation, underscoring the impossibility of answering the question, 'the tempter or the tempted, who sins most?' Everything here indicates the impossibility of speaking of the will in discrete terms. Gwendolen feels guilty, but Deronda feels that 'there had been throughout a counterbalancing struggle of her better will'. But this is the characteristic moralising of the male who has been placed in the confessor's position, and idealised by Eliot because he has the assurance of his Jewish identity and of his position as a potential leader. If the concept of single identity has dissolved into something else – character as contradictory – there cannot be the judgmental voice of a single 'I' such as Deronda, nor of the 'I' who narrates: the process of working out what can be said about Gwendolen and Grandcourt makes 'realism' impossible.

In the chapter following her confession, Gwendolen speaks of her 'murderous will', a phrase associating with an earlier part of Deronda's meditation, 'murderous thought' (57.763, 56.762). Deronda muses on how Grandcourt could not, despite Gwendolen's remorse, have been saved and tells her: 'that momentary murderous will cannot . . . have altered the course of events. Its effect is confined to the motives in your own breast. Within ourselves our evil will is momentous, but sooner or later it works its way outside us'. The 'motives in the breast' recalls Isabella's defence of Angelo: that intentions cannot be judged; and recall how Isabella calls thoughts 'merely thoughts'. Outside, Deronda says, the will may be 'the vitiation that breeds violent acts', or 'self-abhorrence', producing 'better striving' (57.764).

Murderous thought; murderous will. The passage recalls Bulstrode's 'murderous impulses' towards Raffles, and it goes back to the passage quoted from the end of chapter 4 (page 160), Macbeth's speech and Eliot's commentary that his rhetoric about 'the impossibility of being many opposite things in the same moment' refers to 'the clumsy necessities of action, and not to the subtler possibilities of feeling'.

We cannot speak a loyal word and be meanly silent, we cannot kill and not kill in the same moment; but a moment is wide enough for the loyal and mean desire, for the outlash of a murderous thought and the sharp backward stroke of repentance. (4.72)

Macbeth's point is that it is a deficiency in the human that when he must be two things at once – wise and amazed – he cannot. Actually, he demonstrates the opposite, that he is deeply divided. Throughout, he wills the existence of his 'violent love' – which includes his love of violence, which is one form of the will – wanting it to outrun 'the pauser, reason'. Earlier, he spoke of 'my thought, whose murder yet is but fantastical' (1.3.138), within the context of having been tempted, through the ambiguous words of the Weird Sisters: the primary temptation is to murder his thought, his reason. Angelo with his self-divided thoughts and Macbeth with his, are parallels. Macbeth, perhaps, does not know why he has killed the guards, an irrational act, certainly not what he and his wife had intended to do. Eliot's reference to 'the subtler possibilities of feeling', in that passage just cited again from chapter 4, which allow for 'the loyal and mean desire', is difficult. Are these two things, or, as a hendiadys, is desire (the will) both 'loyal' (on the side of the law, as with *loi*), and 'mean' together? – as much as 'murderous thought' and 'repentance' are put together?

We note the chiasmic structure of the two halves of the phrase, starting with loyalty and ending with repentance, outlashing and outrunning. As with Mrs Transome, judgement precedes the sin. Effect and cause, punishment and crime so inverted suggest that no identity can be founded on the idea of a stable will which wills actions and consequence. The passage recalls *Measure for Measure* as much as Eliot thinks of Macbeth's actions in murdering the guards, which, as a false statement of his loyalty, he says he repents of (*Macbeth*, 2.3.103–4). Eliot is absorbed by the the inconsistency of 'thoughts' with themselves, and in thinking about 'the moment', she leads into Nietzsche's discussion (see ch. 8) of the contents of 'the moment' (the *Augenblick*) being reversible.

The loyal and mean desire expresses a divided will, split because of ambivalence towards the person to whom these feelings are directed, while 'we cannot kill and not kill' is puzzling: it may mean 'we cannot kill someone and the same time refrain from killing' but it also implies the suicide of the one who murders, and in implying that, puts volition and its consequences outside the subject's control. The ambiguity of language is the ambiguity within willing: when I will, I will not, but when I will not to do something, I carry with it the will to do it as an unconscious other. The 'outlash' of the murderous thought recoils in the same moment into a 'backward stroke' which lacerates the thinker. Perhaps the 'lash' is already as masochistic as sadistic, and points to an ambivalence within motivations, even inside the murderous will.

PART THREE

THE WILL TO TRUTH

7

SCHOPENHAUER
Music, Nietzsche and Freud

Music is as *immediate* an objectification and copy of the whole *will* as the world itself is, indeed as the Ideas are, the multiplied phenomenon of which constitutes the world of individual things. Therefore music is by no means like the other arts, namely a copy of the Ideas, but a *copy of the will itself*, the objectivity of which are the Ideas. For this reason the effect of music is so very much more powerful and penetrating than is that of the other arts, for these others speak only of the shadow, but music of the essence.

(SCHOPENHAUER, *The World as Will and Representation*, 52.257)

For Schopenhauer, music differed from other art forms, being not an image of the world as representation, but of the will. Independent of the world of representation, or appearance, it would exist if the world did not, 'which cannot be said of the other arts', because their existence is as part of the world of appearance. Music in this chapter is approached through two operas of the 1860s, Wagner's *Tristan und Isolde* (1865) and Verdi's *La forza del destino* (1862, revised 1869). Following Schopenhauer's argument means considering, in Wagner, how it is divided, and divides the subject who sings and who listens. With Verdi, it is to consider what is meant by conceptualisng 'the force of destiny' as music. For Wagner, I use Nietzsche; for Verdi – an example of middle-class but also popular theatre – I invoke Freud, whose 'A Difficulty in the Path of Psychoanalysis' (1917) said about 'the great thinker Schopenhauer' that his 'unconscious "Will" is equivalent to the mental instincts of psychoanalysis' (*SE*, 17.144–45).

So the will, the unconscious, and music, come together. Discussing the will in relation to music becomes necessary, since there, as perhaps nowhere else, we can speak about 'the will' in almost objective terms. While no-one can say what it is that music does when it is heard, or why 'unheard melodies' have as much force, or more sweetness as those heard, music acts directly and bodily, lending itself to thinking about the will while being an instance of it. In Schopenhauer, music expresses not specific states of mind or affect, but 'joy, pain, sorrow, horror, gaiety, merriment, peace of mind *themselves*, to a certain extent in the abstract' (52.261). These affectual states, part of the world as the will, are embodied: Schopenhauer says the world is 'embodied music as embodied will' (52.263). 'Instead of affirmation of the will, we can also say affirmation of the body' (60.327).

Like Nietzsche, who said 'I should not know how to get along without Rossini',[1] Schopenhauer likes Rossini (1792–1865), whose sense of the will's power echoes in those crescendos, which are his signature, as with the Overture to *Il barbiere di Siviglia* (1816). Rossini's music does not try to follow the words. It 'speaks its *own* language so distinctly and purely that it requires no words at all, and therefore produces its full effect even when rendered by instruments alone' (52.262). That fits the Overture to *Il barbiere di Siviglia*, which is so non-referential that it had already been used twice: for *Aureliano in Palmyra* (1813) an *opera seria*, and for *Elisabetta, Regina d'Inghilterra* (1815). And 'Una voce poco fa', Rosina's coquettish aria in *Il barbiere di Siviglia*, had already been sung by Elizabeth, the Queen in *Elisabetta*, who is not a coquette. Schopenhauer's point is made: the music is primary, it 'means' nothing; the words are secondary. The music is deceptive in relation to anyone who would fix a meaning to it.

Rossini's crescendos work powerfully in Don Basilio's aria 'Una calumnia', and in the last ensemble in Act 1, 'Fredda ed immobile', creating a world which, as Wilfrid Mellers wrote, is irrational, like the will, adding:

> the slip on the banana skin – the affront to human dignity – is a joke rooted deep in our tangled natures; and Rossini's buffoonery sometimes strikes home more disturbingly, more dangerously, than we like to think. The Rossini crescendo in the slander song from *The Barber* is frightening as well as funny; we cannot always dispel the suspicion that our hearts may be as hard as Rossini suggests.[2]

Mellers gives a sense of the will's anarchism and egoism, and how much it exists in comedy.[3] Music's persistence, whatever the situation, creates a gap between it and the attempt to give music words as in opera; for Schopenhauer, operatic music gives 'the most profound, ultimate, and secret information on the feeling expressed in the words, or the action presented in the opera' (2.39.448). It gives 'the ultimate and secret necessity' that controls incidents on the stage, showing 'its complete indifference to everything material in the incidents' while preserving 'its essential beauty, purity and sublimity' (2.39.449). There seems something of kitsch in this assessment of music as so pure, which must modify Schopenhauer's sense of it as the will. While heterogeneous to what is represented on the stage, anger or pathos, or comedy, it is superior to represented passion, and pure. Melody discloses the 'deepest secrets of human willing and feeling', yet always 'returns' to the keynote (1.52.260), as though always exhausting desire which starts from it.

Later comments on melody consider the soprano voice, which must be accompanied by a bass voice as suggesting 'inorganic . . . nature' beneath it. The bass, if required to sing a melody, requires 'a second fundamental bass for its accompaniment' (2.39.452). The bass is like a block of marble on which the human form has been impressed, and Schopenhauer sees it as appropriate to the Stone Guest in *Don Giovanni*. This suggests something interesting in Verdi, who uses, distinctively, the bass-baritone melodically, often playing on the point that it sounds strained, as if the will has been forced into a different register, made different.[4] The bass tones of Philip in Act 4 of *Don Carlos*, confronted by the more dominant bass of the Grand Inquisitor, imposing his non-human will on Philip, so that 'l'orgueil du Roi fléchit devant l'orgueil du prêtre' – the pride of the king yields before the pride of the priest – suggest the bass voice as the will, two powers of the will clashing against each other, one bass the exhausted will of Philip who knows that his wife does not love him, the other the inhuman will of the blind, aged Inquisitor.[5]

I *TRISTAN UND ISOLDE*

Schopenhauer's impact on Wagner, who adopted Schopenhauer's negation of the will, is familiar. It produces *Tristan und Isolde* (1865), the opera which more than any other, defined modernism in the mid-nineteenth century, and which is often taken as Wagner's affirmation of the power of love.[6] Before the action opens, Merold, Isolde's betrothed, was killed by Tristan in Cornwall, and his head returned to Ireland. But Tristan, wounded by Merold, and called Tantris, comes by boat to Ireland, blown by the wind, to be healed by Isolde. She draws out the fragment of sword left in Merold's skull, and by piecing it together with Tristan's sword, realised his identity – she has recomposed Tantris into Tristan – but has refrained from a revenge-killing. Tristan returns again to Ireland from Cornwall to claim Isolde for his uncle, King Mark. Act 1 shows the journey by ship from Ireland to Cornwall, and again, the winds are as the will. Isolde asks for music's engulfing power, when she evokes the breathing power within her, asking that it should be supplemented by winds which will produce sound which, sound and air together, will make the sea, another sonic emblem, drown them all:

> Erwache mir wieder,
> kühne Gewalt;
> herauf aus dem Busen,
> wo du dich bargst!
> Hört meinen Willen
> zagende Winde!
> [Awaken again in me, mighty power, emerge from my bosom where
> you lie hiding! Hear my will, half-hearted winds!]

Her will and the world as will, heard in the music, are identical, and both aimed at universal destruction. Brangaene is sent to Tristan to tell him that Isolde's will is that he should go to her. Isolde asserts her will, telling Kurwenal that she will not go with Tristran to meet King Mark; she wants to poison herself and Tristan. She tells Tristan she wants revenge. He, marked for death already, and impressed by guilt, asks for the poison which will 'heal' him, but Brangeane switches the drug – acting, as she sings in Act 2, against her lady's will – it is a love-potion, poison and medicine together, the *pharmakon*: the will, both killing and driving them to new life together. They fall in love, this being equivalent to mutual suicide, bringing out their death-drive. Sexual desire wants the night, and death: the libretto rejects the rational day, preferring night, as oblivion, death, the sphere of love, and of loss of identity.

In Act 2, Melot betrays Tristan and Isolde to King Mark, who says how he sought Isolde as a result of the people's will, and wants to know why he must suffer. Tristan replies that he cannot tell him that, but, as if allowing himself to be feminised, he accepts a wound given to him by Melot. In Act 3, he is at Kareol in Brittany, attended by Kurwenal. His longing (*Sehnsucht*) is for the completeness of death; he reflects how all his life has been that old solemn tune ('du alte ernste Weise') with its 'Klage Klang' (plaintive sound). It announced his father's death; and his mother's: 'he begot me and died; she, dying, gave me birth' ('er mich zeugt' und starb, / sie sterbend mich gebar'). That music must have sounded to them; that music which once asked him, and now again asks him, to what fate was he destined when he was born. 'Zu welchem Los'? – to what fate?'

The mood defines life as loss: Tristan sings that the music – the voice of the will – calls on him 'mich sehnen – und sterben' (to yearn ['sehen' is repeated some six times in this section] and die). Yearning, itself sexual, expressing the will, returns throughout, in an added repetition of one coincidence after another of the wound and poison. Tristan went with the poisoned wound in the boat to Ireland, and the old tune, virtually identified with the wind, sounded while he was silent. That wound Isolde healed and closed, but then opened up again with the sword, but then she let the sword drop. She healed; then she wounded him with the sword, perhaps metaphorically, but then failed to fulfil the implications of the wound she gave: she did not kill him. She gave him the poison draught ('Der Drank! Der Drank!'), which instead of killing him, as he had hoped, so ending the will's yearning, only intensified yearning, denying him Night, and oblivion.

That draught drunk and shared with Isolde in Act 1 he identifies with something he has prepared for himself, throughout his life. The yearning, the poison, the wound, the music, Isolde herself, are all the power of the will, whose character is feminine. Isolde's arrival makes him sing that as he fought against Merold with a bleeding wound, and Isolde healed him, so that will happen now: he tears off the bandages to expose the wound, to greet 'she who will close my wound for ever' ('Die mir die Wunde / auf ewig schliesse). At that moment he wants the world to pass away ('Vergeh' die Welt'). His act, self-infliction of a feminisation which has run through the work, gives himself death. Her arrival will close up the wound (i.e. killing him); she closes not the eyes, but the wound, his yearning, his will. He dies; Kurwenal kills Melot and is killed himself; the arrival of Mark, too late to give forgiveness to the lovers, leads to Isolde's dying as she 'hears' the music that for her represents Tristan, and as the audience hears it in the combination of her singing and the orchestral sound.

The self and the world are to be destroyed, in an expression of the will which annihilates both. The yearning is violent, sadistic and masochistic. It excites a music full of the power of the will, and unrefusable, as it exceeds everything, as Isolde's voice – expressive of individuality – is virtually drowned out by the repeated waves of orchestral sound which points to that music that she sings she hears. The image of sound-waves (a use for 'wave' that *OED* cites first from 1832) implies also waves of water, which are also 'the vast wave of the world's breath'. Like Wagner, who created for Bayreuth the sunken orchestra pit and the darkened auditorium to emphasise its power, as if sound issued from silence and so from everywhere, Isolde in her music of transformation (*Verklärung*), is fascinated: 'Höre ich nur / diese Weise' – do I alone hear this melody –sings that this music comes from the dead Tristan – 'aus ihm tönend' – sounding from him. Nietzsche calls this an instance of the 'vast Dionysian drive', 'swallow[ing] up the whole phenomenal world':

In dem wogenden Schwall,
In dem tönenden Schall,
In des Welt-Atems
wehendem All –
ertrinken,
versinken –
unbewusst –
höchste Lust!

In the heaving swell
Of the sea of bliss
In the ringing sound
Of the perfumed waves
In the wafting Whole
Of the world-breath –
To drown – to sink –
Unconscious – highest joy! (*BT*, 22.118–19)

Isolde has an auditory hallucination, which, like the desire for the dark in the love music of Act 2, is exclusionary: as the lovers sing, 'selbst dann

/ bin ich die Welt': I myself am the world. This final melody reprises the end of the love duet in Act 2, when they sang of themselves as having died ('So starben wir') in a fantasy of exchange of gendered identities: 'Tristan du, / ich Isolde, nicht mehr Tristan'. Isolde lets herself be taken over, as though acoustic events motivate actions.[7] A visual hallucination is also present: she sees Tristan with open eyes, and then sees/hears his breath stirring, which becomes melody which she alone hears. Sound, air and water coalesce synaesthetically, apocalyptically; sound waves drown in that 'oceanic state' Freud describes in *Civilization and its Discontents* which attempts 'the restoration of boundless narcissism'. Freud has been told the state can be accomplished by 'peculiar methods of breathing [which can] evoke new sensations and coaesthenias in oneself'.[8]

Isolde is held by that music-as-will which she takes as masculine, Tristan-like. Singing of it as overwhelming her with its 'ringing sound' and of drowning in it, she does not sing accompanying the orchestral music, which is prior to her, nor invoke it, but questions it, as she magnifies it with all she sings of it before sinking 'wie verklärt' – 'as if transfigured'. Obliteration of the principle of individuality associates with her desire for unconsciousness, with music as the unconscious. The fantasy is of the obliteration of the world: the apocalyptic desire, like Tristan's. Schopenhauer concludes that there is a positive knowledge which is derived from will-denial: he calls it 'ecstasy, rapture, illumination, union with God' (71.410). The contradiction is basic: sexual pleasure comes back with its denial; the will is most seen when refused, as was seen in 'Kant with Sade'. Freud comments on the thinking: referencing specifically this moment in *Tristan*, he links this sense of the 'end of the world', to paranoia. Isolde does not sing differently from what the overwhelming music sounds, and the music is identified, as Freud would say 'with the single love-object which absorbs all the cathexes directed upon the external world'.[9] Nor does Isolde lose her gender position: she confirms it. No disconfirming difference is allowed between what is without, and herself; her will establishes a narcissistic completeness.[10]

In the music-drama cycle *Der Ring des Nibelungen*, worked on through the 1850s and 1860s, and first performed complete in 1874, Wotan, patriarch among the gods, sees his will continually frustrated, and sings:

Auf geb ich mein Werk,
nur eines, will ich noch:

das Ende,
das Ende!
(I leave all my work;
but one thing I desire:
the ending,
that ending!)[11]

This desire anticipates the analysis concluding *The Genealogy of Morals*, and this end – the destruction of Valhalla and so of the world – happens in the last of the *Ring* cycle, *Götterdämmerung*. But whereas Schopenhauer sought a renunciation of the will, on account of the suffering it caused, and speaking as one suffering from the will, Wagner re-reads that, as if taking the side of the powerful whose sense is that the will must renounce everything. He speaks from the wrong position. It is the will which wills, not something which wants the end of the will. The point may be supplemented by Adorno, saying that in Wagner, suffering is trivialised by his 'accoutrements of grandeur', as indeed, suffering is filtered through the primitive and mythological world of *The Ring*, not seen as a reality in the present world. Suffering is:

diluted and reduced to the symbol of the unquenchable longing of the Will itself. Those wan, sickly heroes of Wagner – Tannhäuser, the Tristan of Act 3, Amfortas – are all such symbols and their pallor is more like the protective colouring of an infinite all-consuming passion than the mark of the finite torment of human misery.[12]

Wagner's heroes bear the weight of sexuality, making them the expression of the will, but they must deny it in others, like Parsifal with Kundry. That entails their own denial of the sexual, and the self-conflictual nature of the will, which seeks its own destruction.[13] And the desire for the end, as Schopenhauer indicates, is productive of sexual ecstasy, as Adorno noted: one commentator on Adorno comments:

Adorno detects a conventional happy ending lurking behind the Schopenhauerian facade of the world conflagration that engulfs the stage at the end of the *Ring*. The negation of the bourgeois world celebrated by Wagner, transfigured too quickly into the positive, forfeits its negativity and results in a false 'redemption' (*Erlösung*). The conclusion is unavoidable that for an authentic salvation, for a rigorously polemical *Rettung*, Wagner's catastrophe is *not catastrophic enough*. In the smooth roundedness of its construction, in the perfect arc with which it falls back upon its origin, the *Ring* lacks a caesura to rupture and complete it.[14]

If that is so, a triumphalism at the end of *Götterdämmerung* means that the idea of transcending the will becomes fake: it is not just that the will is divided, but that it colludes with the attempt to overcome it which is rhetorical, self-advertising. That evasiveness fits with Schopenhauer's preference for suffering, since 'happiness or satisfaction is of a *negative* nature, that is, simply the end of suffering, whereas pain is that which is positive' (*Parerga and Paralipomena*, 2.29.416). It is suffering which triumphs in Wagner. The masochistic nature of the music of *Tristan* gives voice to pain, enflaming it erotically.

Eric Chafe's recent study of *Tristan and Isolde* insists that Wagner amended Schopenhauer through writing (letter to Mathilde Wesendonck, Venice, 1 December 1858), that sexual love could produce:

> a complete pacification of the will through love, and not through any abstract human love but a love engendered on the basis of sexual love . . . in love there lies the possibility of raising oneself above the indi-vidual impulse of the will to a point where total mastery over the latter is achieved, and the generic will becomes fully conscious of itself, a consciousness which at this level, is necessarily synonymous with total pacification.[15]

The sexual will, expressed in sexual love, can drive out the will. This is having it both ways. In the same vein, Georges Liébert says Wagner negated 'the individual, egoistic, sterile will . . . not the universal will'.[16] Chafe glosses Wagner:

> through sexual love one might attain consciousness of the nature and universality of desire, or Will. This consciousness would lead to tran-scendence not only of one's own desire – the individual will – but also of the broader conception of desire, or will, that Schopenhauer described in terms of human enslavement to procreation of the species.[17]

179

Chafe underwrites Wagner's spiritualising of the operatic text: a desire to reject the will and yet have its benefits; it is a desire for a joy without pain, a kitsch-desire, which is what Blake's Urizen, and no doubt Schopenhauer wanted. Urizen attempted to legislate for this, creating laws which would govern impulses, with disastrous consequences.[18] In contrast, Nietzsche makes music the expression of 'original contradiction and pain' (BT, 5.35).

Chafe's argument virtually makes Tristan a Christ. He calls the deaths of the lovers:

> the goal of the Passion itself. Schopenhauer opened the door for such religious allegories in his describing the death of the tragic hero as atoning for the guilt of existence. (Chafe, 132–33)

That comment, licensing the ascetic ideal, shows Wagner criticism underwriting Schopenhauer. In contrast, The Birth of Tragedy relates the will to the affirmative Dionysian, just as it responds to Beethoven's Ninth Symphony, which Wagner had conducted in 1846. Wagner had discussed this, in his commemorative essay on Beethoven, as showing the limits of 'absolute music', since it drew forth the voice (and so words and meaning) to supplement the orchestra, with the setting of Schiller's 'An die Freude' (Ode to Joy).[19] Beethoven's music founds the dramatic, but the music is Schopenhauerian, as Wagner thought Beethoven was less concerned with the words' meaning than with their energy.[20] Yet Adorno thought that Beethoven 'forced music to speak' here; and finds the Ode to Joy a 'bourgeois Utopia', which includes the possibility of exclusion of the solitary; he finds it more 'questionable' than Nietzsche, and that criticism implies that The Birth of Tragedy cannot end a debate as to the value of the affirmativeness of the will in music.[21]

Schopenhauer cannot renew tragedy with his sense that it teaches resignation: he assumes the primacy of the individual, whose will must be negated. Wagner takes this from Schopenhauer, hence his music tends towards asserting the primacy of pain, but in contrast, Nietzsche refers to 'the Dionysian, with its original joy perceived even in pain' (BT, 24.128). There is no withdrawal from the will to live.[22] If Schopenhauer saw the world as embodied music, embodied will, Nietzsche says 'on the basis of the spirit of music . . . we can understand the joy experienced in the annihilation of the individual'. Nietzsche makes tragedy, born from music, say: 'Be that I am! Beneath the incessantly changing phenomena,

I am the eternally creative original mother, eternally compelling people to exist, eternally finding satisfaction in this changing world of phenomena' (*BT*, 16.90). So, too, discussing *Tristan*, music becomes the 'maternal womb' (*BT*, 21.113), which implies that Tristan and Isolde desire each other both as the mother.

Nietzsche continues by asking musicians to imagine:

> someone capable of experiencing the third act [of *Tristan*] . . . purely as a vast symphonic movement, with no help from word and image, without expiring under the convulsive beating of the wings of the entire soul? Imagine a man, who as here has laid his ear as it were on the heart chamber of the world-will, who feels the mad desire for existence flow outwards into all the veins of the world in the form of a thundering torrent or of the gentlest spraying brook, should such a man not suddenly shatter into pieces? How could such a man, enclosed in the miserable glass shell of human individuality, endure the echo of countless cries of pleasure and woe from the 'wide space of the nights of the world' [a quotation from Tristan] without miserably fleeing to his original home . . . ?

It could not be done; the third Act of *Tristan* cannot be experienced like Beethoven's Ninth. The Apollonian figures must give expression to the impersonality that sounds in the music, as allegories, speaking 'other' to what music speaks directly:

> Here the Apollonian power breaks out, directed towards the restoration of the almost shattered individual, with the curative balm of a blissful illusion: suddenly we believe that we still see nothing more than Tristan standing motionless, asking himself in muffled tones, 'The old melody, why does it wake me?' And what appeared to us earlier as a hollow sigh from the centre of being now only wants to say how 'desolate and empty is the sea'. (*BT*, 21.113–14)

The hollowness at the centre will recall discussion of Lacan on *das Ding*, on the lost object; that which launches desire. However much music speaks, it points to an absence in the will: this absence propels everything, so that music will always sound as dissonance (as with the Tristan chord), and man is 'dissonance in human form' (24.128, 25.130), which implies he is always incomplete, always needing resolution, which is what constitutes desire. Unlike Schopenhauer, by talking of the will 'playing', Nietzsche has no sense of denying the will; acceptance of it is Dionysian. The work of art involves looking and longing for something (beyond) looking, hearing, and longing for something beyond hearing, because both looking and hearing appeal to subjectivity. But art turns on the sense that these longings and subjectivity are substitutional, illusionistic, a point noted much earlier, at the end of the discussion of 'Kant with Sade' (see above, p. 26).

> That striving towards the infinite, the beating of the wings of longing, which accompanies the highest joy [this quotes from Isolde's last line] in clearly perceived reality, recall that we must recognise in both states [wanting to look and hear, and longing for something beyond both] a Dionysian phenomenon, which reveals to us again and again the playful construction and destruction of the individual world as the overflow of an original joy, in a similiar way to that in which Heraclitus the Obscure compares the world-forming force to a child at play, arranging and scattering stones here and there, building and then trampling sand-hills. (24.129)

To be caught in looking, and hearing, is to believe that personal subjectivity is all there is, and that means a dangerous entrapment in the personal will, such as has been described throughout the book. It is fascinating to see how Nietzsche takes Wagner's word 'longing', and turns it, not towards the absolute consummation in their absolute selves that happens with Tristan and Isolde, which makes everything at the end just slightly pompous (King Mark blessing the dead lovers!) but towards a sense of acceptance of desire and dissonance.

II *THE FORCE OF DESTINY*

I want to take another opera to illustrate the will, *La forza del destino*: a Verdian text with a Shakespeare-in-the-nineteenth-century plot. The will it is fascinated by includes the unwilled, the coincidental, that which entraps from the outside. As one of Verdi's 'opera of ideas' (*le opere a intenzione*), as he wrote in a letter to Cesare de Sanctis (May 21 1869),[23] it stresses a concept: 'destiny'. The title is – almost uniquely for Verdi – abstract, Schopenhauerian in its suggestibility.[24]

182

Verdi operas seem idealistic in relation to love or to the *patria*, or to patriarchy, or to revenge prompted by a curse, and read as constructed by the simple opposition of absolute values, reinforced along gender-lines and by voice-types which emphasise the hero, the tyrant, the heroine and the judge.[25] But these simplicities, which extend to the resolution of dissonances, are contradicted by plots whose complexity goes below rationality. *Macbeth* (1847 – revised 1865) is possessed by the slipperiness of choice and the persuasiveness of the inner dream-world. Complex narratives in *Il trovatore* (1853) or *Simon Boccanegra* (1857 – revised 1881), both from Antonio Garcia Gutiérrez (1813–84), complicate absolute values, since the difficulty of the plots introduces something uncanny into the narrative, making absolute yet virtually identifical forces oppose each other despite everything. *Il trovatore* and *La forza del destino*, by Gutiérrez's contemporary, Angel de Saavedra (1791–1865) put brothers, or quasi-brothers against each other with a hatred unmatched in Shakespeare, the relationship being either over a woman, or erotic in itself. Manrico, disguised as a troubadour, and a rebel against his brother, the Count of Luna – who believes his brother is dead but has been commanded by his dying father to search for him – is burned by his brother. Fire has the force of destiny: it claimed Azucena's mother and her son; it traumatised Azucena who destroyed her son, and avenges her mother's burning, which Luna's father ordered, on Luna, and implicitly, on Manrico, the other son, and a substitute for Azucena's own, burned, son. These are strange detours in plots which opera audiences often feel complacently superior to, but these plots respond to the force(s) of destiny. In *Un ballo in maschera* (1859), the strangeness is the process by which Gustavus is destroyed by Anckarstroem, as Mlle Arvidson has said would happen, against all likeliness. Destiny in these operas works by deviating or deferring – and *is* the force that deviates and defers.[26]

For Freud, *Oedipus* showed 'the force of destiny' (*SE*, 4.262), countermanding and carrying out the unconscious will. In *La forza del destino*, Oedipal, will-power shows itself in violence. In both the original play by Saavedra, and the opera, 'force' produces melancholia and a death-drive. Perhaps it is the force that Freud speculates on in 'Beyond the Pleasure Principle', that 'there *might* be such a thing as primary masochism' (*SE*, 18.55).[27] The colonial figure, Don Carlos, hates the heterogeneous Peruvian, whose compulsiveness is the opera's fascination. Heterogeneity recalls Georges Bataille, whose 'The Psychological

Structure of Fascism' distinguishes between the productive, 'useful' homogeneous aspect of society, and the heterogeneous, which contains elements the homogeneous cannot assimilate; the heterogeneous is other, incommensurate, and the homogeneous uses it to establish its rule.[28] So, in *Simon Boccanegra*, the hero is a corsair, a heterogeneous figure who after expelling the African pirates, more extreme figures of heterogeneity, is appointed to rule Genoa. This heterogeneous figure who has helped establish homogeneity, tries gaining acceptance from the homogeneous, the Genoan aristocrats, represented by Jacopo Fiesco, whose daughter and honour he has violated.

La forza del destino is equally fascinated by the heterogeneous figure, who desires his death: 'Lasciatemi morire', as he sings. But while self-punishing, heterogeneity shows in how he wipes out a whole family, unintentionally. His masochism shows when the Marchese challenges him red-handed, about to take off his daughter Leonora: he sings 'Io solo colpevole, colpevole son io' (I am guilty) baring his chest to be killed as if in colonial subordination. Then masochism turns violent: the pistol he throws down goes off, accidentally killing the Marchese. Throwing down the gun is ambivalent; and comments on the unconscious of the colonised will; which is virtually parricidal since Alvaro wants to be the Marchese's son in law; yet, in another way, he desires not a legal relationship, but, in abducting Leonora, something transgressive. Repeating this first ambiguity, he sings in his last duet with Carlo, 'qual nessun mi vide mai / io mi prostro al vostro piè' [as no one has ever seen me, I prostrate myself at your feet.] Having thrown himself down as a weapon, he is further self-abased. Yet a moment later, he fights after being slapped, beginning the *cabeletta*, 'Ah, segnasti la tua sorte' [you have signed your fate].

'The force of destiny' implies the will, and will-power, and willing, and resisting the will. Does Don Alvaro want the destiny he evokes, and the other he desires? He can only re-discover Leonora after killing her brother, so is his relationship to Don Carlo a substitute for his relation to Leonora, an apparent deviation which is, nonetheless, the main plot? Does he want the deaths of the male Calatravas? And Leonora? 'Beyond the Pleasure Principle', says of those who repeat, whether consciously or not, that 'the impression they give is of being pursued by a malignant fate or possessed by some "demonic" power' (*SE*, 18.21).[29] But Freud argues that 'their fate is for the most part arranged by themselves, and determined by early infantile influences'; i.e. by a family history. These intragenerational determinations explain the complex plot involving differing parents which, narrated in *Il trovatore*, returns in Azucena's call for vengeance; and explains the lapse of twenty-five years between the Prologue and first Act of *Simon Boccanegra*. The Freudian subject is unware of what constructs the will's autonomy. Freud returns to this in 'The Uncanny', perception of which involves a moment of doubling, when something frightening appears which 'leads back to what is known of old and long familiar'. This doubling-effect associates with repetition:

> it is possible to recognize the dominance in the unconscious mind of a 'compulsion to repeat' proceeding from the instinctual impulses, and probably inherent in the very nature of the instincts – a compulsion powerful enough to overrule the pleasure principle, lending to certain aspects of the mind their daemonic character.[30]

'Compulsion' compares with Verdi's *forza*, and the form this takes: repetition of motifs begun in the Overture.[31] Repetition means that it has two duels; it begins and ends in Spain. It starts with the father killed, concludes with the son killed. Don Carlo kills Leonora accidentally: though he meant to kill her, when he *does* so it is because he has misread the circumstances, and so does so out of a misconception, making her death also accidental. Beginning with a dead father (and Don Alvaro's offstage dead father), it ends with the Padre Guardiano, who makes rebellion against the father impossible. Repetition means that neither Don Alvaro nor Leonora can disguise themselves.

The opera's abstract idea is destiny, and its *force*. In the 1869 overture, does destiny or force sound in the force of the initial unison bars of the overture, which are repeated after a pause? The overture has many pauses and hesitancies, delays inside force: the chords reappear, capping the *allegro agitato e presto* string theme that follows, and is never sung. (They are back to open Act 1 – more thinly, more plaintively, more lingeringly. They begin Act 2.) To the slowness of this is opposed destiny, or its force, or the desire to escape either, in the *allegro*. But if to escape is also to move towards, it is unsurprising that destiny sounds again in the chords succeeding the *allegro*. This *allegro* theme, an abstract idea, voicing the abstract will, reappears when the Marchese intrudes on the lovers and dies in Act 1, and opens Act 2 scene 2 when Leonora hides at the convent, re-appearing last with Leonora, opening the last scene.[32]

The overture continues with music which is heard later as Alvaro's plaint, 'Le minaccie, i fieri accenti' – menaces, fiery tones (Act 4). First heard, 'con espressione' on flutes, oboes and clarinets, the *allegro* theme sounds between the phrases, almost interfering with them, personal subjectivity conflicting with itself, or something else. And the plaint does not resolve itself, but hesitates before a pause and is not quite finished. Leonora's 'Madre, pietosa Vergine' (Act 2 scene 2), an equivalent plaintive, slow melody, is also heard, softer than Alvaro, but also 'con espressione'. But when she sings it, towards the end, it is 'con più forza'. Then, her will colludes with the force of destiny: she wants to 'follow [her] own path to death' (*SE*, 18.39). In the overture, the music seems more serene, more contrastive with destiny. But the plaintiveness contrasts with the violence of music following, *'presto come prima'*. A duality is reasserted by the return to Alvaro's tune, twice punctuated by a pizzicato chord: the third time, left unresolved, exposed, as if marginal to the overture's ongoing drive.

Repetition has been made an abstract force, and destiny. For Freud, the repetition-compulsion overrides, contradicts the conservative pleasure principle, which aims to ensure that the organism will not be disturbed, that it will go to death in its own way. He comments on 'this perpetual recurrence of the same thing' (*SE*, 18. 22):

> we have unwittingly steered our course into the harbour of Schopenhauer's philosophy. For him death is 'the true result and to that extent the purpose of life' while the sexual instinct is the embodiment of the will to live. (*SE*, 18.49–50)

This quotes from 'Transcendent Speculation on the Apparent Deliberateness in the Fate of the Individual', in *Parerga and Paralipomena*. It cites Plotinus, that 'chance has no place in life' and speaks of destiny and of 'a secret and inexplicable power [which] guides all the turns and change) in our lives, indeed, often contrary to the intention we had at the time'. That power is the will, and as it turns away from life, so destiny happens to everyone 'in a manner that is quite individually suited to him and hence often in a long and roundabout way' (*PP*, 1.209, 218, 223). Freud's word 'unwittingly', quoted above, indicates that either un-willingly, or because of the will, he has coincided with Schopenhauer, bringing out a Schopenhauerian truth, while the harbour-image implies that the death drive is Schopenhauer's home. This 'destiny' is the opposite of what George Eliot means when commenting that anyone, 'watching keenly the stealthy convergence of human lots, sees a slow preparation of effects from one life on another', and adds that "Destiny stands by sarcastic with our *dramatis personae* folded in her hand' (*Middlemarch*, 11, 122). Eliot's interest is in character working against what hampers it, and creating opportunities. For, 'it always remains true that if we had been greater, cirumstance would have been less strong against us' (*Middlemarch*, 58.632). The novel's non-recognition of the uncanny contrasts strikingly with *La forza del destino*. 'Beyond the Pleasure Principle' makes repetition neurotic, trauma-seeking, undergone passively by the subject, experienced as a daemonic power. In 'The Uncanny' the repressed returns in repetition, in a series of substitutions: these repetitions with differences constitute the tortuous narrative effects in Verdi.

Freud relates these substitutions to the power of the castration-fear ('The Uncanny', *SE*, 17. 231). This, as a fantasised threat to masculinity, returns in multiple substitute narrative tropes and symbols, and each substitutive repetition acts doubly, in that it both attempts to ward off the castration fear, and recalls it. Derrida, commenting on Freud, says that he cannot argue that castration as a fantasy precedes substitution; rather, substitution, as though it was *more* originary than the castration-fear, 'relaunches' castration, which, while obviously not an 'originary' event, recurs again and again within substitutive forms. The primacy of repetition-as-substitution, which incorporates castration-anxieties, taken over into the interpretation of Verdi, would mean that the narrative, however definite sounding, starts from no single point of origin; its deferrals substituting for that non-origin.[33] Compulsion to repeat makes history or narrative substitutive acts which supplement an originary absence.

There is no chief victim in this combat of wills. In Act 3, preceded by a long clarinet solo, Don Alvaro's recitative and arioso reprises the narrative of his life appearing in Saavedra's play, but not quite. He sings that his father sought to free his native land from its foreign masters and by alliance with 'l'ultima degli' Incas' to win back his crown, but in vain. Born in prison, he is alive because his royal birth is known to no-one. His parents dreamed of a throne, and were awakened by the axe. The violence which killed his father is repeated when the Marchese is killed: unconscious revenge? He sings to Leonora, imagined dead, describing himself 'senza nome ed esule / in odio del destin / chiedo anelando, ahi, misero / la morte d'incontrar' [without name and exiled, in despite of destiny, a miserable man, yearning I call to meet with death]. A *destiny* to live as a colonial subject is crossed by *desire* for death, and repeats an earlier oppression, his parents' and his nation's. Don Carlo calls him a 'mulatto' in the last act, which in the 1860s, whether Verdi knew it or not, gains a new significance because of the American Civil War (1861–65). One neologism from that war was 'miscegenation'. Verdi's opera coincides with that war, and Don Carlo's racial insult unconsciously aligns the opera's subject-matter with the politics of race being then fought out in the United States, making the opera acquire meanings in the 1860s different from Saavedra's play of 1834. Yet Don Alvaro's father was, evidently, either an American Indian or a creole who identified with Peru against the Spanish. Carlo is more correct in calling Alvaro 'quell' Indo maledetto' in Act 3 scene 5, and 'l'Indiano' in Act 3 scene 6. So is Melitone, when reporting that he first called Raffaele a mulatto having seen him 'cotanto stralunato' [so staring, rolling his eyes] and then deciding he is like an 'Indian selvaggio' [a wild Indian].

Don Carlo's insult compares with the construction of race in the Civil War in William Faulkner's novel *Absalom, Absalom!* (1936). Henry Sutpen, son of the patriarch Thomas Sutpen, kills his half-brother Charles Bon, ostensibly because Bon, who may be a 'mulatto', is about to marry Henry's full sister, Judith. The act becomes the subject of speculative fantasy in subsequent attempts to narrativize it; it may be a response to Bon telling him 'I'm the nigger that's going to sleep with your sister'.[34] Bon's self-hating defiance is provoked by 'a mixture of despair and grief at his father's refusal to acknowledge him as his son.[35] This leaves open how much fear of incest, of miscegenation, and homosexuality account for Henry shooting Bon. All these parallels, contained in the rivalry between Charles Bon and Henry Sutpen over a sister, hold with the opera, especially when it is considered how the most developed duets are those between the men. But in Verdi, the black kills the white.

In Verdi's previous opera, *Un ballo in maschera*, originally set in Boston, and aware of colour since Ulrika is said to be 'dell' immondo / Sangue de' negri' [of filthy Negro blood], Riccardo is murdered by his Creole secretary, Renato, a character-type and a baritone similar to Simon Boccanegra, or Don Carlo in *La forza del destino*, and racially ambiguous.[36] In *Absalom, Absalom!* the destiny following the shooting of Charles Bon is the collapse of the 'house' that Thomas Sutpen wished to establish. Similarly, Don Alvaro destroys the Calatrava house. Perhaps that has its own oldness, and death-wish inscribed within Verdi's

Marchese, whose opening words, 'Buona notte' anticipate his imminent death: ostensibly protecting his daughter he goes to bed before her in a line foreshadowing his death ('Ti lascio').[37]

And his son, Don Carlo? Card-playing in Act 3, he nearly loses his life over a game and is saved by Alvaro. In his first Act 3 aria, he rejects opening the sealed package that Don Alvaro wants destroyed if he dies, but opens it to find Leonora's portrait. But Don Alvaro has already gambled in telling Carlo that he had a packet which was not to be opened. The packet means death: Don Carlo's words show melancholic awareness of that. Freud sees the gambler as unconsciously willing to lose.[38] Don Carlo gambles again when the surgeon says that Don Alvaro is healed – immediately *after* Don Carlo has discovered that he has reason enough to kill him. Don Alvaro revives to experience the father's death-sentence as implemented by the son's challenge. He defends himself: 'Non io, fu il destino, che il padre v'ha ucciso' [It was not I but destiny that killed your father] – destiny here meaning coincidence, or accident, or an impersonal will. Here, he asserts his difference. Involuntarily, near death, he had revolted from being associated with the Calatrava name (Act 3 scene 2). He had wanted to possess a member of the Calatrava and make that name adorn his 'crest' ('stemma') whose purity he insists on in Act 3 scene 3: it 'shines' ('splende') he sings, repeating it affirmatively. The crest evokes the father and plumes up his will. When he throws himself at Don Carlo's feet in Act 4, Don Carlo sees that as a proof of the stain ('la macchia') on his crest: that his paternity and masculinity are deficient, that the colonized subject lacks entitlement.

In Act 3, the past is re-opened, for he learns that Leonora is alive. The two men know that the mark of difference between them is Leonora, a Calatrava, part of a name attended by 'disonor'. Perception of dishonour which can never be avenged – especially as Don Alvaro refuses to fight when insulted – makes Don Carlo a victim of the force of destiny. Don Alvaro thinks of Leonora in the bosom of the angels, untouched by mortal sorrow. But in Act 3 scene 2, Don Carlo calls Don Alvaro the 'seduttore'.[39] He replies, 'non io che sedussi quell' angiol d'amore' [It was not I that seduced that angel of love], as if saying that Leonora was seduced, while repeatedly affirming her purity. So too, in Act 4, to Don Carlo: 'No, non fu disonorata. / Ve lo giura un sacerdote! / Sulla terra l'ho adorata / come in cielo amar si puote' [No, she was not dishonoured. A monk swears to you. I adored her on earth as one loves in heaven]. He affirms his own sexlessness, his lack of will, and sings of sacredness and idealization, as though he has been a monk throughout, albeit that in Act 1 he wanted to abduct Leonora. (Yet there, on his first entry, he says he has been delayed from getting to Leonora's home by a thousand things: she responds by asking for a day's postponement. Sexuality, part of the repetitions comprising 'the force of destiny', defers and delays. With both lovers vacillating, the action cannot start until precipitated by accidents, the father's return and his death.)

Don Carlo personalises the offence, hence his ill-will: he wants to think that his sister was dishonoured, because her dishonour besmirches him. Killing her will complete a work of self-hatred, like his hatred of the colonial other, who, when disguised, was loved: Preziosilla openly mocks his language of the ego. When Don Alvaro discovers in Act 3 that Leonora is alive he breaks into a warm, flowing *cantabile*, 'No, d'un imene il vincolo', asking for marriage to Leonora – being most lyrical at the moment of least realism. Don Carlo interrupts ('Stolto'), speeding the tempo, and, when he takes up the word again in a solo, ('Stolto! Stolto') going faster still. He, in that same solo had first called Alvaro 'brother' (fratello), in order to reject the relationship altogether. His unconscious has supplied him with the word and the thought: his abjection, inability to decide whether he is the same as the other, or radically different from him, makes him both use *and* refuse it, as if fascinated by it. In Act 4, Alvaro sings the plaint heard in the Overture, denying his feelings and expressing his forbearance; however non-sexual, ideal, it *is* sexual, being masochistic, unconsciously seductive, passive, feminine. Don Carlo responds with 'Ah! un suora mi lasciasti,' as the obsessional 'other' to Don Alvaro's music. The contest of wills culminates in Alvaro yielding to the colonial figure's superiority and throwing down the sword and resuming the plaintive tune ('No . . . no . . . l'inferno non trionfi'). But then Don Carlo slaps him, quickening the pace. Don Alvaro sings 'Ah segnasti la tua sorte' [you have sealed your destiny], initiating the *stretta*, and rushes off with Don Carlo, whose obsessionalism compels him towards dying on Don Alvaro's sword, yet the victor is not triumphant; he will not hear Carlo's confession, remaining the colonised subject.

These two operas come from composers who divide the nineteenth century between them. In them, the will is to be fought, yet it activates characters by destabilising their autonomy. The paradigm for nineteenth-century opera is music which contravenes conscious desire, and replaces it with a more urgent unconscious force: Schopenhauer's insights construct a century of music. Verdi's music engages actively with a history of the nineteenth-century, from an avowed national and at times cosmopolitan position. Wagner removes opera from history, mythicises the movements of the will, and may be criticised for it, as with Adorno, who said that 'no historical process is enacted in his music; in this lies his resemblance to the spirit of Schopenhauer's philosophy' (Adorno, 35): the will in both is essentialised, ahistorical. That is not quite true of Verdi, and a sign of it is how he makes opera a mixed genre, tragi-comedy, as if responding to uneven developments in the century, different times and different forms of the will.[40]

The comic mode, as with the Act 3 tarantella, praising madness which reigns in time of war, evokes the force of the will in another sense. Preziosilla, Trabuco, the *vivandières* and Melitone – who, anticipating *Falstaff*, hears Bacchus in the tarantella, and so anticipates the mood of *The Birth of Tragedy* – are agents of a heterogeneity which is placed in contrast with the dominant paranoid will and death-drive. Yet, that point made, they are less than the tragic obsessional moments, which evoke rather the spirit of the end of *The Genealogy of Morals*: man would rather will nothing, than not will. In that way, Verdi expresses what Wagner works out, and the death-drive in the operas is a similarity between them. Yet both are motivated by a strangeness which is more than their stated themes and plots, and it is no coincidence that to be discussed, they need the insights, equally, of Nietzsche and Freud.

8

NIETZSCHE'S 'WILL TO POWER'

I PRELUDE

For Heidegger, Nietzsche is the philosopher of the 'will to power', and of 'eternal return' saying that these may be thought together. This chapter's key text is *Thus Spoke Zarathustra* (1883–85) for its sense of the will, and ill-will, and the spirit of revenge, and for its attempt to break with that spirit of *ressentiment*, through the idea of 'eternal return'. A coda to the chapter looks briefly at Mahler and Delius, both composers wanting to draw out the Dionysian music within Nietzsche, and *Zarathustra*.

Discussing 'will to power' means discarding a book: no arguments about Nietzsche can or should be taken from *The Will to Power* (*Der Wille zur Macht*), published in 1901 by Nietzsche's sister, Elizabeth Förster-Nietzsche.[1] Not only is the title misleading, but the text is unreliable, having suffered from the sister's revisions.[2] Nor, even if Elizabeth Förster-Nietzsche, creating a thoroughly right-wing figure out of her brother and his writings, had been more accurate, or principled, would it be valid to build up any substantial thesis from Nietzsche's fragments and jottings (the *Nachlass*), as opposed to the writings which he completed. Certainly, *The Will to Power* is not the book which the first edition of *Beyond Good and Evil* announced as being 'in preparation': *The Will to Power: An Experiment in the Transvaluation of All Values. In Four Books*. Of that book, only *The Antichrist* appeared, and it seems that Nietzsche dropped plans for it. To discuss Nietzsche as the philosopher of 'will to power' may misrepresent him, though of course the phrase is his.[3]

Further, since Heidegger's commentary on Nietzsche, published in

1961 though taken from lectures given between 1936 and 1946, worked so much from *The Will to Power*, it is problematic to use him on will to power: it means working from and endorsing a text which cannot be validated as Nietzsche's. But the commentary is crucial for reading Heidegger.[4] Though his view of Nietzsche as the philosopher of 'will to power' has little to do with Heidegger's Fascism, which of course expresses exactly the 'will to nothingness' that Nietzsche diagnosed, it inevitably gives it some support: the associations of 'will to power' are with authoritarian rule.[5] Hence Georges Bataille's *On Nietzsche* (1945) has little favourable to say about 'will to power' as opposed to a 'will to chance'. Discussing 'The Three Transformations' at the beginning of the first part of *Thus Spoke Zarathustra* he says '*The will to power* is the lion: but isn't the child the *will to chance?*'[6] In Bataille, critique of 'the will' as a desire for self-assertion, 'to submit the world to its autonomy', is articulated as 'the will for autonomy'.[7]

In English translation, Heidegger's four volumes on Nietzsche become two books: 'The Will to Power as Art', and 'The Eternal Recurrence of the Same' in the first book. The German volume three has three parts: 'The Will to Power as Knowledge', 'The Eternal Recurrence of the Same and the Will to Power' and 'Nietzsche's Metaphysics'. Volume four is 'European Nihilism' and 'Nihilism as Determined by the History of Being'.[8] David Krell follows Hannah Arendt in arguing for a change in Heidegger's thought between the German volumes 1 and 2: Heidegger is sympathetic to 'the will to power' as it happens within art, and reads 'will to power' as a perpetual self-overcoming. Krell nonetheless notes, in the Heidegger of the first volume a stress on self-assertion (*Selbstbehauptung*) (*Nietzsche*, 1.60–61, compare *Nietzsche*, 4.273–74).

Even in this first volume, Heidegger works from a thesis making the will the central single thought of western metaphysics, giving as example Schelling's *On the Essence of Human Freedom* (1809): 'In the first and ultimate instance there is no other Being at all than Willing. Willing is Primal Being' (quoted, *Nietzsche*, 1.34). Certainly, willing is stamped on the Judaeo-Christian mentality, from the moment of '*Fiat lux*'. So, 'in [Nietzsche's] view will is nothing else than will to power, and power nothing less than the essence of will. Hence will to power is will to will, which is to say, willing is self-willing' (*N*, 1.37). The idea of the '*will-to-will*' persists, and Heidegger cites the close of *The Genealogy of Morals*, that man dare not will nothingness (*N*, 3.196). Discussion of 'will to power' makes Heidegger call Nietzsche a failed systematic thinker, the anatomist of 'European nihilism', whose sense of life as 'will to power' aims at the 'transvaluation of all values', in the face of 'the eternal recurrence of the same' and makes the 'Overman', 'the supreme configuration of the will to power' (*N*, 4.3–12).

Each stress here shows Heidegger making Nietzsche the end of the line from Plato, the last of those philosophers who are committed to 'presence', talking of 'values', as though these, visible and demonstrable, were evidences of a desire for presence, as if the values could be spoken about abstractly, and could be generalised from. Heidegger quotes from *The Will to Power* (no. 617): 'to *stamp* Becoming with the character of Being – that is the supreme *will to power*', and glosses this: 'one must shape Becoming as being in such a way that *as becoming* it is preserved' (*N*, 2.202). The 'eternal return' stamps things with permanence, because they return. The will to power, yearning for permanence, finds it in eternal return. So these thoughts, will to power and eternal recurrence of the same 'say the same' (*N*, 3.10). Nietzsche as the last philosopher, believing that the basic character of beings is will to power, which shows itself in 'the eternal return of the same', reveals himself as possessing a philosophy, discussed through *The Will to Power* and through *Thus Spoke Zarathustra*.[9]

II THE WILL TO POWER

We can begin with the section 'On Self-overcoming' (2.12), where Zarathustra questions what 'the wisest' call the 'will to truth'. Zarathustra denies that they have it; he says they have, rather, a 'will to the thinkability of all beings': desire for intelligibility and for interpretation, which is a will to control the other, to make the other thinkable in their terms, those of 'the wisest'. 'Truth' must mirror the identity of the wisest ones, expressing their narcissism; what motivates 'the wisest' is a 'will to power', as a desire for domination over others: but that concept exceeds what the 'wisest' think of, and believe they exercise.

It leads Zarathustra into saying something different: he has found out something, not by trying to make life thinkable, but by seeing it in a 'hundredfold mirror', which fragments and pluralises images, making impossible a one-to-one relationship between things and viewer. This mirror shows life's variousness. Its 'eye of life', shows three things: first, that 'all that is living is something that obeys'. The second: whoever cannot obey will be commanded. The third: commanding is harder than obeying, because commanding puts the self at risk, requiring going beyond rules and the 'thinkability of things', where these have become known, and knowledge of them is rule-bound: commanding means exceeding rule-bound behaviour (2.12.99).

But why does the living both obey *and* command, and in commanding, still practise obedience to its own commands? Nietzsche shifts from what people think they are doing in obeying or commanding, into what Life does, which differs from what happens in those who think they have control of the other, through reducing the other to 'thinkability'. Zarathustra says: 'where I found the living, there I found will to power, and even in the heart of one who serves I found a will to be master'. The weak serve to practise mastery over the weaker, and 'so does even the greatest yield, and risks for the sake of power – life itself. This is the yielding of the greatest, that it is risk and danger, and a dice-playing for death' (2.12.99). Those who sacrifice themselves, and seem subordinate, also have will to power. The great do not hold onto their power in so far as that is identifiable with life. Mastery is not simply holding onto domination. Rather, the great yield in being prepared to give up life. The power of commanding is inseparable from willingness to surrender life. The contrast is with the weak, who slink into the fortress and into the heart of the more powerful – and there steal power.

But Zarathustra goes further; Life, as a woman – as wisdom is a woman (1.7.36) – has spoken to him in the singular, giving him a secret in defining herself: 'I am *that which must always overcome itself*'. This is will to power, and it is feminine. Life's self-definition refuses definition: whatever can be said of life at one moment cannot be said in the next. Life overcomes itself; so must the self, as a fixed unity. Life 'goes under', to not renounce her overcoming; she sacrifices herself for power: and the imagery, of leaves falling, indicates that what is spoken of is not the power of the subject, but of life beyond the individual. Life's 'will to power' requires it to walk on '*crooked* ways', so that 'whatever I create and however much I love it – soon I must oppose both it and my love: thus my will wills it'. Life uses, but is not, the will to truth, and will hear nothing of a Darwinian 'will to existence':

> Only, where Life is, there too is will, though not will to life, but –
> thus I teach you – will to power!

195

Much is valued by the living more highly than life itself; but out of this very valuing, there speaks – will to power! (2.12.100)

At that point, Zarathustra ceases to say what Life said to him. His next words indicate that there can be no values – neither good, nor evil – which are not transitory. Any value is an expression of the will to power, which means it must always be displaced in favour of something else. Even the most highly valued is opposed by life in favour of something else; another way of putting this is that there can be no identity to anything; life's nature is to destroy identities (as things non-transitory), where these are thought to exist. Though the 'valuator', the creator of values, exercises 'force' to attempt to make the values created stick, yet:

a stronger force grows out of your values and a new overcoming, on which egg and eggshell shatter.

And whoever must be a creator in good and evil: verily he must first be an annihilator and shatter values. Thus does the highest evil belong to the highest good: but this latter is the creative. (2.12.100)

Enough emerges from here to indicate that – against Heidegger – there are no inherent values that can be brought about or named in Nietzsche's text; all are in movement, none permanent. Whereas there is a drive to conserve values, in the name of the thinkability of things, the risk to be taken by the 'creator in good and evil' is to allow creativity to increase at the expense of personal power. The will of the wisest, however, may be unable to acknowledge this. Will to power is not Darwinism, which relates to Malthusianism and Utilitarianism, and issues from a narrowed sense of life's spontaneity.[10] So 'Anti-Darwin', in *Twilight of the Idols* rejects the concept of 'the struggle for life', saying that 'Malthus should not be confused with nature':

Species do not grow in perfection: time and again the weak become the masters of the strong – for they are the great number, they are also cleverer . . . Darwin forgot intelligence (– that is English!), *the weak are more intelligent* . . . By intelligence it is clear that I mean caution, patience, cunning, disguise, great self-control and all that is mimicry (which last includes a large part of so-called virtue).[11]

This critiques the valuation given to any self-preservative drive, just as

'Beyond the Pleasure Principle' identifies a drive going beyond such self-preservation. The thought in Freud, which makes the will both the principle of excess and death-driven, is more conservative than in Nietzsche, who opposes the idea of self-preservation by will to power, which sacrifices the former in the name of risk. The former is an idea created by a teleological discourse, which thinks in terms of the species reaching completion. The point is made by Klossowski:

> Nietzsche does not admit the existence of a power *that would be unable to increase itself*. It is this incessant augmentation that makes him say that it is not simply 'power' but *will* to power.[12]

Power is neither objective or singular; it is not a question of knowing it if you have it; because consciousness is not something separate, super-intending the impulses and drives within the body; Nietzsche sees a fetishism involved in seeing a doer behind a deed, seeing 'the will as cause in general . . . the 'I' [*das Ich*] as Being . . . as substance'.[13] The energies implied in will to power are not willed, not the product of a subject, however they are misrepresented as the actions of a subject with a will.[14]

In *Beyond Good and Evil* (1886), section 19 criticises, as simplifying, the discourse which says that the human has a will, which can be called so, quasi-objectively.[15] (Schopenhauer's sense of the will's unitary character of the will is included here.) The will is rather a plurality of affects, 'a multiplicity of feelings', including involuntary movements in the body, and thought. 'What is called "freedom of the will" is essentially the affect of superiority felt towards the one who must obey: "I am free, 'he' must obey"'. So 'a person who *wills*: this person is commanding a Something in himself that obeys, or that he thinks is obeying'. Willing involves feelings (of attraction towards, or aversion), and thinking, and a desire to command or control. Willing is not a single action; its 'strangest thing' is that in any given case, we both command *and* obey, though the obeying part, which relates to the constraints placed upon the subject by feelings and thoughts, is forgotten; only the idea of command remains. Though the will's activity does not presume a single state, the rhetorical effect which is implied in using the word 'will' assumes just that:

> Because in the vast majority of cases, willing has only occurred when

there is also the *expectation* that the effect of the command . . . will follow, this *impression* has been translated into the feeling that there is a *necessary effect*; . . . the person willing thinks . . . that will and action are somehow one: he attributes his success in carrying out his willing to the will itself, and in this way enjoys an increase in that feeling of power that accompanies any kind of success.

The person who believes in their will upholds the relationship of cause to effect, thinking that what happens is the effect of their firm will:

Thus the person willing adds to his pleasurable feeling as commander the pleasurable feelings of the successful executing instrument, the serviceable 'underwill' or under-soul (our body after all is nothing but a social structure of many souls). *L'effet c'est moi*: what is occurring here occurs in every well-structured happy community where the ruling class identifies with the successes of the community as a whole.[16]

The ideology behind the word 'will' is of the possibility of command. Discarding categories which speak of 'laws of nature', which he calls only 'interpretation', Nietzsche posits an alternative interpretation: 'the universality and unconditionality in all "will to power"'. Seeing the course of the world as will to power 'is "necessary" and "predictable", *not* because laws are at work in it, but rather because these are absolutely *lacking*' (22.22–23). 'Laws' apply to what has been stabilised and fixed, but 'will to power' declares the unfinished nature of everything.

Beyond Good and Evil posits the 'mechanistic (or material) world' as one 'with the same level of reality that our affect has – that is, as a more rudimentary form of the world of affects'. It settles for the hypothesis that 'all mechanical events, in so far as energy is active in them, are really the energy of the will, the effect of the will', and that '*all* effective energy [is definable] unequivocally as: *the will to power*. The world as it is seen from the inside, the world defined and described by its "intelligible character" – would be simply "will to power" and that alone' (36.35–36). All affectual states, all organic functions, relate to a will to power, not to be differentiated in terms of separate wills, separate forms of subjectivity. My will acts because it has already been acted upon; it partakes of the drives and affects propelling the world. There is no outside perspective from which to view things, such as possible causes and effects; the subject who would say 'I think' in attempting to read this world is as much part of the will in its plurality as any mechanical, or material other part of the world.

In his *Nietzsche and Philosophy*, Deleuze agrees with this sense of will to power being a relationship between forces within and outside the body, and determined to the extent that 'each force is *affected* by other, inferior, or superior, forces. It follows that will to power is manifested as a capacity for being affected'. Deleuze continues that 'the more ways a body could be affected the more force it had'. This capacity for being affected is 'an affectivity, a sensibility, a sensation' and it is this which gives power. It is not that the will wants power, rather, 'power is the one that wills in the will', making the will 'essentially creative' (Deleuze, 62, 85).[17]

III ON PUNISHMENT

In *Zarathustra*, what we can see as the 'will to power' makes the will to be spoken of positively. A key text is 2.2, 'Upon the Isles of the Blest'. Here, where the recurrent idea is the impermanence of everything, Zarathustra tells his friends, 'let this be your will to truth': where 'everything [is] transformed into what is humanly thinkable, humanly visible, humanly feelable' (73). Zarathustra desires his friends to think the 'Overhuman', rather than thinking conjecturally, and therefore abstractly, of an abstract God whose existence as permanent ends the possibility of the 'creative will'. Belief in a God contrasts with thinking about the Overhuman, who is not more of the same as far as humanity is concerned, but goes beyond the human; the assumption which allows for the possibility of thinking of such a being is, that life comprises impermanence. Poets, too, especially Goethe, are said to 'lie too much', wishing for ideal permanence (compare 2.17, 'On the Poets').[18] So, while that realisation entails suffering, it is also the basis for creating. Indeed, 'creating' becomes 'the great redemption from suffering', which is the concomitant of impermanence. Creating requires 'much bitter dying'. Nonetheless 'such a fate does my will will':

All that is sentient suffers through me and is in prisons: but my willing always comes to me as my liberator and my joy-bringer. Willing liberates: that is the true teaching of will and freedom – thus does Zarathustra teach it to you.

> Willing-no-more and valuing-no-more and creating-no-more! Ah, that such great weariness might remain ever far from me!
>
> In understanding, too, I feel only my will's joy in begetting and becoming; and if there be innocence in my understanding, that is because the will to beget is in it.
>
> Away from God and Gods this will has lured me: what would there be to create if Gods – existed? (2.2.74–75)

The ego is where everything that feels suffers; but willing contrasts with the imprisonment that his ego produces; liberating, it enables creating. Knowledge is not a matter of accumulating details, but of 'begetting and becoming', both spontaneous and innocent, – and meaning that it has no vindictiveness towards the past, which is what is implied in revenge. Such willing moves the self away from any given knowledge, as, for example, centred around a God. And that 'willing liberates', reappears in 3.12, 'On Old and New Tablets', section 16: 'willing liberates, for willing is creating'. So the act of willing is the same as creation: willing is not so much a declaration of intent, but the act of creating, itself liberatory.

But that the human *can* accept impermanence and move forward is contested in 'On Redemption' (2.20), the chapter on revenge, which quotes from this. We move towards this section gradually: 'Upon the Isles of the Blest' is succeeded by attacks on Christianity, culminating with 'On the Virtuous', 'On the Rabble', and 'On the Tarantulas' (2.7), whose topic is revenge, which was prominent within the section on 'the virtuous', whose 'virtue' means justice, and justice revenge: 'with their virtue they want to claw out the eyes of their enemies' (2.5.82). 'On the Rabble' – which includes other writers – had introduced something different: Zarathustra's disgust at their existence, which makes him choke on the question, 'is the rabble, too, *needed* for life?' (2.6.84). Zarathustra's question is how he 'redeemed himself' from disgust, but it seems that the price of doing so can be only absolute separation from them. The nausea raises issues which become more pressing, especially in 'The Tarantulas'. These self-biters are 'hidden vengeance-seekers', 'preachers of equality', with a 'will to equality', which is the name for 'virtue'. Equality, which is the opposite to the argument that 'the human is something that shall be overcome' (Prologue, 3.11), associates with the rabble, which so disgusts Zarathustra. Virtue, then, becomes not an active heroic moving forward, but claws that spirit back, not being a virtue but rather the revenge that appears from behind the use of the word 'justice'.

Against that, Zarathustra desires *'that humanity might be redeemed from revenge'*: but we must read on, to 2.20, to see how revenge and the destructive will are linked. First, from 'The Tarantulas':

> You preachers of equality, the tyrants' madness of impotence cries out of you thus for 'equality': your most secret tyrants' desires disguise themselves thus in words of virtue.
>
> Soured arrogance, repressed envy, perhaps the arrogance and envy of your fathers: they burst forth from you as flames and the madness of revenge.
>
> What the father kept silent, that comes in the son to be spoken; and often I found the son to be the father's unveiled secret.
>
> Enthusiasts they resemble: yet it is not the heart that inspires them – but rather revenge. And if they become refined and cold, it is not the spirit, but rather envy, that makes them refined and cold. (2.7.86)

The will to equality desires to even up old scores. The son is the father's unveiled secret, as Harold Transome is with Matthew Jermyn, revealing what the father was like, showing that the past was no better than the present, as full of conceit and envy. So, either the patriarchs were impotent to act, but the sons are not, or, the idea is unsustainable that the patriarchs were men of honour or virtue, making their sons feel envious of their success, like Hamlet's reverence for his father. The fathers were also envious, consumed by *ressentiment* – like, perhaps, the Ghost in *Hamlet*. The son reveals the father, exposes what the past was, as a continuous structure of inequality. If the son tries taking revenge on what the father suffered, that raises questions about the relation of revenge to time past, which are resumed in 2.20. But the envy the son feels is also towards the father and that previous generation, not knowing that the father was as envious in his turn before him. This produces the 'compulsion to repeat', going over again what past generations have felt, and thinking that the will to equality will terminate that repetition of the past.

> From each of their complaints sounds revenge, in their every eulogy is an infliction of pain; and to be judges seems to them the highest bliss.

> Thus, however, I counsel you, my friends: Mistrust all in whom the drive to punish is powerful! (2.7.86)[19]

The 'drive to punish', as backward-looking, as ill-will, contrasts with the will to power. When Zarathustra says that the 'tarantulas' were formerly 'world-slanderers and heretic-burners' (2.7.87), that comments on the fathers. As ascetics they preached that life had to be rejected. They punished those whose deviancy might have implied that they were rejecting their will to truth with its asceticism. The justice of the Inquisition is in view here. Those who commanded unjustly now preach equality.

Insisting on equality shows its hatred of the past, when these 'tarantulas' suffered, like the 'fathers'. That hatred engenders the spirit of revenge. It also reacts badly to the present, where inequality is obvious; it shows a hatred of life since it is not likely ever to happen that equality will be manifest; and inequality appears between people who are objectively equal. And how could the idea that man must be overcome – which must make anyone respond by seeing themselves as subjects in process – relate to enforcing equality? Zarathustra, whose own implication in the argument is his nausea towards the 'rabble', which suggests his desire for revenge – a temptation acknowledged at the end of the chapter – says that justice tells him 'Human beings are not equal'. That statement is deliberately provocative; it rejects the ideology implied within the image of the scales of justice. Humans cannot be equal if they are considered as in process; 'justice' misdescribes how the singularity of the other can be accounted for.

Last in this chapter-cluster, 2.8, 'On the Famous Wise Men' addresses those who serve the people's superstitions: they play to those who believe in received truths, to get their reverence. Acting as a focus for the people and their superstition: their task is to guarantee the value of truth, hence Zarathustra listens to their refrain:

> 'For the truth is already here: for after all, the people is here! Woe, woe to those who seek!' – thus has it echoed through the ages.
>
> You wanted to justify your people in their revering: that you called 'will to truth' you famous wise men. (2.8.89)

To secure obedience, or reverence, and to prevent a spirit of 'seeking', these philosophers/religionists act as guardians of a truth already

202

unveiled. The will to truth implies their effort to justify that truth, to keep the people conforming in their reverence. They cannot afford to think that truth might not be single, graspable as such. Hence the 'will' is to control. The passage closes by saying that they are 'not driven by any strong wind and will' (2.8.91), these being synonymous for what Zarathustra calls 'Wild Wisdom', that which drives the 'free spirits' out into the deserts, meaning that they cannot be 'of the people'.

IV REVENGE

The crucial section on the will comes in section 20, beginning with one dialogue between Zarathustra and a hunchback, followed by another where Zarathustra turns to his disciples, saying that he walks among human beings 'as among many fragments and severed limbs of human beings' and that this is obvious when his eye 'flees from now to the past'. Zarathustra must be 'a seer, a willer, a creator, a future himself and a bridge to the future' as well as 'a cripple by this bridge'. But he says that he walks among the people as though they were 'fragments of the future', which implies that the future may be different, newly composed out of fragments. Creativity demands composing, as in music, and bringing together 'what is fragment and riddle and cruel coincidence'. So, 'to redeem that which has passed away and to recreate all 'It was' into a 'Thus I willed it!' – that alone should I call redemption'. 'Redemption' means not regarding the past as that from which people needed to be saved, the Christian understanding, a view which diminishes and criticises all worldly experience, but seeing it positively, not as a matter for regret but to be affirmed. Hence Zarathustra began the section declining to heal the hunchback, and the blind and the cripple, in answer to the hunchback, who wants him to do it for opportunistic reasons.

The 'redeemed' self says not merely that it accepts the point that time has taken things away, and that good things have now gone into the past; but adds 'thus I willed it' – gladly affirming that things have so slipped away. But in 'On Redemption', the will cannot make any such affirmation; the insight expressed in 2.2 about the creative will liberating (2.2.75) becomes inadequate in the face of the will's imprisonment:

Will – that is the liberator and joy-bringer: that is what I taught you, my friends! And now learn this as well: the will is still a prisoner.

203

Willing liberates: but what is it called that puts even the liberator in fetters?

'It was': that is the will's gnashing of teeth and loneliest sorrow. Powerless with respect to what has been done – it is an angry spectator of all that is past.

Backwards the will is unable to will; that it cannot break time and time's desire – that is the will's loneliest sorrow.

Willing liberates: what does the willing itself devise, that it may be free of its sorrow and mock at its dungeon?

Alas, every prisoner becomes a fool! Foolish too the way the imprisoned will redeems itself.

That time does not roll backwards, this rouses the will's fury; 'That which was' – that is the stone which it cannot roll away.

And so it rolls away in fury and ill-humour, and takes revenge on whatever does not, like itself, feel fury and ill-humour.

Thus did the will, the liberator, turn to hurting: and upon all that can suffer it takes revenge for its inability to go backwards.

The will liberates, and brings joy, but not here, because it is enchained; in contrast to 'will to power', it is 'powerless' in regard to the past, which it looks back on angrily, imprisoned because it cannot will backwards; it cannot relive the past, nor change what has happened. The phrase that quells it is 'It was'. This derives from the first chapter of 'On the Uses and Disadvantages of History for Life' (1874) as:

> the password which gives conflict, suffering and satiety access to man so as to remind him what his existence fundamentally is – an imperfect tense that can never become a perfect one [which makes] being only an uninterrupted has-been, a thing that lives by negating, consuming and contradicting itself.[20]

'It was' causes gnashing of teeth (the Biblical description of the damned, and of the angrily vindictive, see Acts, 7.54), and a 'loneliest sorrow'. The will cannot go backwards, nor break time nor 'time's desire', a different will, which moves forwards, away from the past, towards putting everything in the past. Zarathustra says again that willing liberates, asking how it can liberate itself from its sorrow and its prison. But there is no liberation; instead, the imprisoned will becomes a fool, marked by fury, and ill-temper towards 'that which was' which is called the stone which it cannot roll away, the stone which separates it from the past (as the women coming to the tomb of Jesus felt they would be separated from the body by the stone across the mouth of the tomb). So it rolls stones out of animosity and ill-humour and its *ressentiment* takes revenge on all whom it can make suffer, spoiling the innocence of what is in process of becoming. This liberator has become a torturer, and is for the second time said to take revenge 'because it cannot go back'.

The reaction defines revenge, as ill-will towards time, malevolence:

This, yes this alone, is what revenge itself is: the will's ill-will toward time and its 'It was'.

Verily, a great folly dwells in our will, and it has become a curse for all that is human that this folly has acquired spirit!

The spirit of revenge: that, my friends, has been up to now humanity's best reflection; and wherever there was suffering, there was always supposed to be punishment.

For 'punishment' is what revenge calls itself: with a hypocritical word it makes itself a good conscience.

And because there is suffering in whatever wills, from its inability to will backwards – thus willing itself and all life were supposed to be – punishment!

And then cloud upon cloud rolled across the spirit, until at last madness preached: 'Everything passes away, therefore everything deserves to pass away!'

'And this is itself justice, that law of time that time must devour its children': thus did madness preach.

'Morally things are ordered according to justice and punishment. Oh where is there redemption from the flux of things and the punishment "existence"?' Thus did madness preach.

'Can there be redemption where there is eternal justice? Alas, the stone, "it was" cannot be rolled away: eternal must all punishments be, too!' Thus did madness preach.

'No deed can be annihilated: so how could it be undone through punishment! This, this is what is eternal in the punishment 'existence': that existence itself must eternally be deed and guilt again!

'Unless the will should at last redeem itself and willing should become not-willing – ': but you know, my brothers, this fable-song of madness!

I led you from such fable-songs when I taught you, 'The will is a creator'.

All 'it was' is a fragment, a riddle, a cruel coincidence – until the creating will says to it, 'But thus I willed it!'

– Until the creating will says to it: 'But thus do I will it! Thus shall I will it!'

But has it ever spoken thus? And when will this happen? Has the will been unharnessed yet from its own folly?

Has the will yet become its own redeemer and joy-bringer? Has it unlearned the spirit of revenge and all gnashing of teeth?

And who has taught it reconciliation with time, and something higher than all reconciliation?

Something higher than any reconciliation the will that is will to power must will – yet how shall this happen? Who has yet taught it to will backwards and want back as well? (2.20.121–24).

The folly in the will is the impulse to compensate for time that has past. When 'revenge' is spoken of here, it is as the topic of a vast reflection in literature: as Zarathustra says, the folly in the will has gained spirit; revenge now has an entire philosophy (and politics!) justifying it. Hence there is now 'the spirit of revenge', as the secret name of philosophy from Anaximander to Schopenhauer. It gains strength from suffering, which it identifies with punishment, (someone suffering must be undergoing punishment!) and it calls revenge punishment, and so attains a good conscience, because punishment is *always* justifiable, because it always belongs to the discourse of justice. Whatever wills suffers, because of the folly with which the will has become identified, its frustration, which is its motivation, being that it cannot will backwards. So all willing, and life, as the expression of will, are thought of as punishment. The will's very ability to desire is to be seen as a punishment; desire is to be tabooed, as hopeless before it starts. Something new has happened: life is seen as punishment for something else. I am being revenged upon, my life is a punishment.

Another intensification follows in the history of the 'spirit' which this folly has acquired: cloud after cloud rolls across it, obscuring its vision, producing 'madness' which, as the angry will, makes six preachments. It first announces that everything perishes, therefore everything deserves to perish; words quoted from 2.14, 'On the Land of Culture'. That expresses the nihilism of an education undirected by any creativity

206

towards the future, or having a sense that the future is a product of creative signs – of 'prophetic dreams and astral signs', of an existing poetry which may be responded to. The mental attitude of people who do not think through this poetry is: 'Everything is worthy of perishing' (2.14.104).[21]

If everything perishes, that produces the demand to find a cause and effect in what happens, and to devalue everything that appears, but with the prejudice that what comes into being will not be worth it. The second preachment is that time (Kronos) must devour its children. As in *Untimely Meditations*, the condition of life is that it lives by 'negating, consuming, and contradicting itself'. The first and last terms imply a rejection of Hegel, but 'consume' recalls Saturn (Kronos) who indeed comes into existence by the action of castrating his father (*WWR*, 1.31), so that Time comes into being on the basis of an originary violence committed against what has produced it. That Saturn devours his children is thinkable in two ways. The past devours the present in the form of the fathers' 'soured arrogance, repressed envy' which spoils the children, as commented on with 'The Tarantulas' (2.7.86), as if passing on its own castration; second, the present spoils the future from happening. The statement implies that the present, and the future, condemns everything in the past to nothing, sees it as valueless, as Zeus castrates his father. This law of time is called 'justice', as if past, present and future were all anxious not to let any of the others be better than it; cutting the others down to size, in a will to equality, and called a 'law of time', as though time, the impersonal agency, took vengeance on all that happened, and that which could become.

These two utterances receive support from a fragment from Anaximander of Miletus (c.610 – 546 BCE), previously cited in the unpublished lectures *Philosophy in the Tragic Age of the Greeks* (*Die Philosophie im tragischen Zeitalter der Griechen*):

> Where the source of things is, to that place they must also pass away, according to necessity, for they must pay penance and be judged for their injustices in accordance with the ordinance of time.[22]

This implies that everything is marked out by incompleteness, and contains negativity within it; those who are alive have an inherent sense of guilt, and know that only death can expiate that. Separate existence, identity, is an 'illegitimate emancipation from eternal being, a wrong

for which destruction is the only penance' . . . wherever definite qualities are perceivable, we can prophesy . . . the passing away of these
qualities' (*Philosophy in the Tragic Age*, 46–47). It is as if the appearance
of no single character or entity or quality can be justified; it must represent something imperfect whose existence must be regarded as an
injustice. Eternal being, primal being, 'that which truly *is*', as Nietzsche
calls it, from which qualities emerge, has no definite characteristics;
these, as imperfect, must be destroyed as they appear. What comes into
being has a definite being, while primal being as indefinite contains
nothing specific; Nietzsche compares it to the Kantian *Ding an sich*,
which is equivalent to aligning it with Schopenhauer's will. Any specific
existence, in being less than that, is 'unjust'; Nietzsche imagines
Anaximander saying:

> What is your existence worth? And if it is worthless, why are you
> here? Your guilt, I see, causes you to tarry in your existence. With
> your death you will have to expiate it. (*Philosophy in the Tragic Age*,
> 48)

Everything should pass away; the best thing is to be free of existence as
a punishment, but going out of life is also a punishment. Everything is
justice and punishment, these two being equated. A desire to take
revenge on the past, impossible because the past is in the past, has
devalued all life to the extent that life itself, inherently incomplete –
otherwise it could not pass away – is considered to be punishment. Its
disappearance is part of the 'flux of things', which is then disliked as that
which brings things into play and then removes them as if to introduce
something different which will be no better. Time and the flux of things
are made essential qualities, with the power of agency.

Nietzsche's lecture continues with Heraclitus:

> As Heraclitus sees time, so does Schopenhauer. He repeatedly said of
> it that every moment in it exists only insofar as it has just consumed
> the preceding one, its father, and is them immediately consumed
> likewise. And that past and future are as perishable as any dream, but
> that the present is but the dimensionless and durationless borderline
> between the two. (*Philosophy in the Tragic Age*, 52–53)[23]

Here, the conditions of existence are seen as intolerable at any moment of history; a desire to destroy the past is a secret agenda within historical thinking. But that anger is constructed by the sense of the nothingness of the present.

The third question asked how there could be redemption from the 'flux of things' – that Heraclitean concept, here applied to time – out of the sense of life as like Ixion's wheel. Fourth, with the question 'Can there be redemption . . . ', madness asks if there can be any end to punishment. Must it not last as long as justice does? Justice is eternal; so no finite action can deal with it. As the stone 'it was' can never be rolled away – that is, however hard you try, you can never forget that something happened in the past, and any present punishment can never negate that – so all punishment must be eternal too. The voice of madness sounds as if it is Christian, hence the allusion to the unmoveable stone at the mouth of the tomb where the dead Christ was placed.[24] The logic is that eternal justice means eternal punishment (all your life is seen as a form of suffering) and justice cannot satisfy vengeance, because 'it was' remains to torment the revenger, its ineradicability making all revenge futile.

This produces madness's fifth voice. If punishment cannot undo the deed, there is nothing left but the repetition of crime and punishment, eternally recurring, but not in the sense that Nietzsche wishes to give to the eternal return. What is the nature of the punishment called 'existence', save that it must be these two things over and over again? But they are not two things, but one, since every crime is also a punishment of something deemed to have gone before. Any different future is already wiped out by this eternal recurrence; the Overman becomes an impossible concept. Existence as meaning punishment, taken from madness's fourth preachment of madness, opens the door for Schopenhauer, the sixth mad voice.

This suggests that the will should at last deliver itself, and willing become non-willing. This Buddhism within Schopenhauer is called a 'fable-song', attractive, like the Sirens, and productive of Wagnerianism. Schopenhauer was anticipated in two earlier sections of *Zarathustra*, the first, wittily called 'On Immaculate Perception' (2.15), which compares the traditionally chaste moon, separate from the earth, observing it merely, to the philosopher who observes beauty 'disinterestedly', i.e. in Kantian fashion. Immaculate perception slanders desire, and says 'I want nothing from things, except that I may lie there before them like a mirror with a hundred eyes'.[25] In contrast, creation and innocence and 'becoming' wants no separation from what it sees: 'Where is there beauty? Wherever I *must will* with all my will; where I want to love and go under, that an image might not remain mere image' (2.15.106). This approach, which risks death, is unSchopenhauerian, and opposite to an 'emasculated leering'.[26] Schopenhauer returns as 'The Soothsayer' (2.19), after two more sections, first on the poets, then on 'great events', dealing with the fire-hound as the figure of revolution. The Soothsayer's mantra is 'All is empty, all is the same, all has been', words which Zarathustra listens to, before sleeping and dreaming that 'all life I had renounced' and that he had become the guardian of death, confronted by the past figured as glass coffins containing 'life which had been overcome' (2.19.117). In the dream Zarathustra has keys, but cannot use them, and is suddenly confronted with a wind casting a black coffin before him, which opens, revealing laughter and 'a thousand masks of children, angels, owls, fools, and child-sized butterflies' (2.19.118). Zarathustra tells the dream, but falls silent, for he does not know its interpretation; which suggests his self-division, the extent to which he secretly sides with the Schopenhauerian philosophy of negation, and does not want the return of that 'other' life with its potential to mock. He must repress knowledge of his failure from himself.

The Schopenhaurian preaching of madness is seductive, producing the nauseated reaction to, and withdrawal from, the 'rabble'. But withdrawal of the will means a cessation of everything, for it is the only possibility of moving forward; to say 'the will is a creator', reverting to 'Upon the Isles of the Blest' (2.2.74), means critiquing Schopenhauer, seeing him as productive of, and inspired by, revenge. Zarathustra returns to a definition of what 'it was' means: it is only a fragment, or riddle, or cruel coincidence, teasing the person who looks on it to find in it a meaning, unless the will can say three things: 'But thus I willed it', 'But thus do I will it' and 'Thus shall I will it', all anti-Schopenhauerian statements. What would saying the first mean? It would sound like a Stoical rationalisation, accepting the point that what was done could not be undone; it would be an act of bravado which was meaningless, because there can be no choice except to accept the past as past. The same would apply to the statement 'thus do I will it': the statement can only imply something voluntary if it relates to the future: 'Thus shall I will it', which means that the 'I' as formed by the past accepts that past by wanting to repeat it.

This triple statement leaves Zarathustra with eight question-marks.

Has the will spoken like that? Is there any chance that it ever will, that it will be unharnessed from its folly? At present, it speaks otherwise, in its madness: since Anaximander, since Christianity, and since Schopenhauer, it has never ceased to 'gnash its teeth', in anger towards itself in its impotence, and revenge towards others. It has not 'unlearned' revenge, and this prompts the sixth question: 'And who has taught it reconciliation with time' – that theme of Levinas for whom time is 'the other', and what cannot be possessed, nor opposed – 'and something higher than any reconciliation?'

This seventh question is reiterated: 'Something higher than any reconciliation the will that is will to power must will – yet how shall this happen?' What goes beyond reconciliation, except willing the way that time exists, so altering a relationship to it, could only be part of the will to power, the way life continually overcomes itself. The question is how the will in the subject could become this more impersonal will to power. How can it happen? Who can teach such a thing, so that – the eighth question goes – the will which is the will to power should will backwards and to want back as well? There are two questions there, the first being, how could there be a teacher who could make the will to power will the past, not to deal with it, but to repeat it, want it back as it was? There can be no such teacher, if not Zarathustra. No outside will can supplement the will to power in the subject, whose will is, however, frozen, trapped in a prison which makes it a subject. Zarathustra has asked a question but must fall silent, because of the contradiction in his speech, which he has unconsciously revealed, though his disciples do not see it. He says 'It is hard to live with human beings because keeping silent is so hard. Especially for one who is garrulous', repeating words from 'On those that Pity' (2.3.77). Keeping silent there meant not patronising others; here, it means not betraying the self, as he has done, not giving rein to the unconscious. But the hunchback has heard, and has kept his face covered, like Socrates in the *Phaedrus* when he was ashamed of the power of rhetoric, which betrays love. His point is that Zarathustra speaks differently to him, than to his disciples, but more, that Zarathustra speaks differently to his students (all those listening to him) than to himself. The hunchback has the last word: there is no concluding 'Thus spoke Zarathustra', because he has noticed that Zarathustra's talk outruns what he can say. He has been caught by the point that if will to power needed to be taught, it would be non-existent; a fiction to counter a sense of despair. A teacher would imply that an outside agency was needed to supplement the will. Zarathustra has presented himself as recomposing 'what is fragment and riddle and cruel coincidence' but has also shown the will as imprisoned, and needing something outside it to deliver it. The 'creative will' of 2.2 fails, leaving only impotent madness, resembling the preachings of madness already rehearsed.

But the second question which is implicit in asking who has taught the will to will backwards and want backwards as well implies a new sense of the will to power, that this must be able not only to overcome itself continually, but also to take up what has past, and want it back. This is what has already been implied in the idea of eternal return. That is also implicit in this chapter, in the idea of existence being eternally deed and guilt again, and in the desire to be able to say 'Thus I willed it . . . Thus shall I will it'; and even more in 'willing backwards'. That would do more than make the past acceptable to the self, it would confront the past as fragment, as riddle, and as accident. Can the eternal return be seen as the will to power? But it is not possible for an individual to affirm eternal return as an act of will; such voluntarism, which poses the will as an entity driving the subject, misreads the nature of the subject, because the will is not an entity, and the idea of eternal return would make impossible any expression of the will.

V HEIDEGGER

Before continuing with eternal return, Heidegger's discussion of this passage, in *What is Called Thinking?* needs examination.[27] We remember that Heidegger's Nietzsche is a metaphysician, imposing permanency (Being) upon a world of flux; this being the 'will to power'. Heidegger's reading of 'On Deliverance' (2.20) varies subtly from the reading already given. He starts with Schelling, 'there is no being other than willing. Willing is primal being' and Schelling saying that the will has 'independence of time' (90–91). The idea, then, is that the will is what makes being, identity; it is the essence of *Dasein*. Heidegger writes: 'we have since noted that "will", in the language of modern metaphysics does not mean only human willing, but that "will" and "willing" are the name of the Being of beings as a whole' (95). And the will stands free of time; that is part of its permanency. If that is so, it becomes definitional that the will can only be bitter towards time, which takes away the will's autonomy. Time, thought of on the basis of presence, as we talk about 'the present', is that which is also of the essence of being, but if time is represented as the present which passes away, which takes away all thought of permanence, then time contradicts the will.

So Heidegger says 'Revenge is *the will's* revulsion'; rendering revenge as 'revulsion', more than 'ill-will' (95, emphasis added). Without the will, there could be no thought of revenge. But if revenge is the will's revulsion, then revenge is not directed specifically against others, but against time, and life, and the self. If the will's revulsion is against time and its 'It was', that defines time as that which is 'passing away' (96). The 'rigor mortis' (103) of 'it was' cuts away at the will's permanence: 'To be properly things in their Being means to be independent of time in the sense of a passing away' (102). So 'the revulsion of revenge is not against the mere passing of time, but against the time that makes the passing pass away in the past, against the "It was"' (103). The result is that since the will cannot will the going away of time, so it must will 'the constant recurrence of every "It was"' (104). By doing so, the will is secured in its position, so that 'the eternal recurrence of the same is the supreme triumph of the metaphysics of the will that eternally wills its own willing' (104). So the will wills itself. 'The nature of revenge as will, and as revulsion against the passing away, is conceived in the light of will as primal being – the will which wills itself eternally as the eternal recurrence of the same' (107).

Heidegger insists that, to date, and in philosophic thought, the spirit of revenge has always characterised the will, as man's best reflection: it must do, not only because, as we have seen, the will loses its being because of time passing, but also because 'it was' 'becomes the sorrow and despair of all willing which, being what it is, always wills forward [the point was discussed with relation to Hannah Arendt, in the Introduction], and is always foiled by the bygones that life fixed firmly in the past' (92). So the will must wish everything to pass away, it must say that everything is worthy to pass away, in the name of 'punishment' (95). To be delivered from revenge, which is desirable, means willing future recurrence. The will remains; it cannot do otherwise. Zarathustra cannot let the will go; in that sense Nietzsche remains a metaphysician. That carries the further implication: that the will is only delivered from revenge because it wills eternal return, which means that it remains a structure of revenge: eternal return is a strategy to avoid revulsion. In Heidegger's reading, the eternal return does not eliminate the will, and therefore does not eliminate revenge. The only way to eliminate revenge would be to eliminate the will.

VI ETERNAL RETURN

So does eternal return confirm the will, as Heidegger thinks, or threaten its identity? The crisis of eternal return is at the heart of 'On the Vision and Riddle' (3.2), where Zarathustra speaks to the sailors, those whose lives are both exploratory and adventurous, and who are committed to difficulty, but are unlike Theseus, since, when in the labyrinth of difficulty, they do not grope at a thread with cowardly hand. He announces a riddle, which is also a vision of the loneliest, and a look into the 'abyss'.

Zarathustra describes climbing upward carrying the spirit of heaviness, half dwarf, half blind mole, the subterranean animal now out of its sphere. His wisdom whispers that there can be no becoming, or overcoming; everything must revert to what it was before. Zarathustra's reaction is summarised in the words he says that 'Courage' speaks – 'Was *that* life? Well then! One more time!', willing eternal return, in the spirit of *The Gay Science* 341. He says that the name of the gateway is inscribed above it: 'Moment' (*Augenblick*), and its two faces look out on two roads, one the long lane back, and the other which goes outwards; past and future. These roads 'contradict' each other at the meeting point of the Moment, which contains them both; the Moment being then full (a moment of presence) and being both inside time and yet outside it too: as the moment the time when everything comes to a standstill, with the possibility of a complete reversal of everything.

Zarathustra's question to the dwarf is whether the roads contradict themselves eternally. The dwarf makes a general reply that 'time itself is a circle', which means it is neither linear nor progressive, but that the two roads Zarathustra has described meet, so locking the self into time. Zarathustra reponds that the dwarf is making things too easy for himself: he is denying contradiction, a plurality in time:

'Behold . . . this moment! From this gateway Moment a long eternal lane runs *backward*: behind us lies an eternity.

'Must not whatever among all things *can* walk have walked this lane already? Must not whatever among all things *can* happen have happened, and been done, and passed by already?

214

'And if everything has already been, what do you think, dwarf, of this moment? Must this gateway too not already – have been?

'And are not all things knotted together so tightly that this moment draws after it *all* things that are to come? Thus – itself as well?

'For whatever among all things can walk: in this long lane out too – it must walk once more! –

'And this slow-moving spider, crawling in the moonlight, and this moonlight itself, and I and you in the gateway, whispering together, whispering of eternal things – must we not all have been here before?

'– and come again and walk in that other lane, out there, before us, in this long and dreadful lane – must we not eternally come back again? –' (3.2.136–37)

The 'moment' stands as the instant outside time, and meaning that eternal return is there, but, it would seem – though this is more a point associated with Walter Benjamin – having also the potential to bring about 'a Messianic cessation of happening, or, put differently, a revolutionary chance in the fight for the oppressed past'.[28] Perhaps the point that the 'Moment' is *written* implies that only writing can claim it; writing that looks to the power of the instant. Zarathustra does not give an explanation or justification of eternal return, but only a riddle which combines repetition and contradicton. The spirit of gravity who makes things too easy for himself, because he thinks that he has mastered life, and understands it, cannot follow it: he soon vanishes.

Everything comes back exactly as before; that is what the dwarf had failed to see. All of them, including the slow spider and the moonlight, both referred to in the earliest formulation of this passage in *The Gay Science*, have been on the lane before, and will come back, on the other lane. Things may recur but without awareness of it. What is happening now is already a repetition, to be repeated. The Moment has been before; and since everything is in repetition, it draws after it all things that are to come, so that it draws itself along as well. Yet the Moment perhaps contains that other potentiality in it, which would make it unique, outside the flow of repetition, the moment which, in Benjamin's terms, 'makes thinking suddenly stop in a configuration pregnant with tensions', which means also 'the Messianic cessation of happening'. As reversing, changing a chronology defined as 'homogeneous, empty time' (*Illuminations*, 266), it would certainly also be the end of the will as ill-will, which is what the dwarf represents. Yet it is a question whether Nietzsche could take Benjamin's reading, making the moment both inside and outside.

At that point, Zarathustra suddenly hears a dog howling, and remembers a time in childhood when a dog was howling 'bristling, with his head stretched up' as if traumatised, at a moment when the full moon was passing over the house. The moon suggests the deathly power of Schopenhauerian teaching, as discussed in 'Immaculate Perceptions' (2.15), and the episode is a *memoire involontaire*, where a crisis evokes a childhood trauma. Such a memory is a form of eternal recurrence; it suggests that Zarathustra is 'in' the moment.[29] Now he sees the man on the ground with the black snake which has crawled into his mouth, choking him, and sees the dog again, which howls and cries for help. It is another moment of death, like seeing the moon. Zarathustra shouts that the man must bite the snake, and 'my horror, my hate, my disgust, my compassion, all my good and bad cried out of me with a single cry'. Zarathustra asks for the riddle and vision to be interpreted, his question being '*Who* is the shepherd into whose throat the snake thus crawled? *Who* is the man into whose throat all that is heaviest and blackest will crawl?' The shepherd bites, and springs up laughing, no longer a shepherd, leaving a yearning for that laughter which makes Zarathustra conclude 'how can I bear to go on living! And how could I bear to die right now! –' (3.2.138).

A riddle has neither single answer, nor one not overladen with an irony which relativises all answers. There may be hope; or nothing of hope, if the Moment is an empty space where the two paths meet. If the latter, that would imply it was a traumatic moment. If the gateway is nothing, it is also a fetish, covering over nothing.[30] If everything returns exactly as it was, then, as Freud suggests about the double, no unique identity can be claimed; plurality destroys all singular being. Freud recalls the idea of the 'double' as 'a preservation against extinction', and then immediately unsettles the point, saying: 'this invention of doubling as a preservation against extinction has its counterpart in the language of dreams, which is fond of representing castration by a doubling or multiplication of a genital symbol'. So the double becomes 'the uncanny harbinger of death'.[31] Repetition has castrating force, and the Moment either confirms that, acts like a fetish against it, or checks it. Eternal return becomes a way of obliterating, not perpetuating, identity. Here Klossowski's point, which is *his* answer to the riddle, is essential:

the 'death of God' [announced at the beginning of *Zarathustra*, Prologue 2.11] (the God who guarantees the identity of the responsible self) opens up the soul to all its possible identities, already apprehended in the various *Stimmungen* [moods] of the Nitzschean soul. The revelation of the Eternal Return brings about, as necessity, the successive realisations of all possible identities: 'at bottom every name every name of history is I' [quoting a letter from Nietzsche to Burkhardt].[32]

Klossowski takes the death of God to mean the end of all stable identity; nothing grounds such identity. Thus if 'I' return, that means the return of everything other to me; eternal return cannot mean the return of the same, but the dissolution of the same. If everything returns, it is as a plurality; all identities are momentary combinations of possibilities.

That is implicit in the 'vision' and 'riddle'. Both are double, the vision of the Moment being one, and the vision of the shepherd another, the latter emerging from another vision, that of Zarathustra's past, and doubling that. Perhaps these two visions – the gateway and the shepherd – also double each other. The second vision doubles everything; the dog, both in the past and in the present, and Zarathustra as dog, shepherd, Zarathustra and snake all at once.

In 3.13, 'The Convalescent', Zarathustra suffers a violent reaction of disgust which recalls to the reader 'The Vision and the Riddle', which it seems to repeat, save that here the 'monster' is not specifically called a snake, and Zarathustra shows no signs of noticing the connection with 3.2, which should prevent *necessarily* identifying 3. 2 and 3.13 for interpretive purposes. 'The Convalescent' speaks of the 'small human being, and especially the poet' who 'accuses life in words', adding a comment on the moral masochist, whose will is present in its denial:

> The human being is the cruellest beast toward itself; and in all that calls itself 'sinner' and 'cross-bearer' and 'penitent', do not fail to hear the lust that lurks in this lamenting and accusing [. . .]

> The great loathing for the human being – *that* is what choked me and had crawled into my throat, and what the soothsayer foretold: 'All is the same, nothing is worthwhile, knowing chokes'.

> A long twilight limped ahead of me, a death-weary, death drunken mournfulness that was talking with a yawning mouth.

'Eternally it recurs, the human being you are so weary of, the small
human being' – thus yawned my mournfulness and dragged its feet
and could not go to sleep. . . . (3.13.191)

The 'eternal recurrence of the smallest' is for Zarathustra his 'disgust'
(3.13.192). The Soothsayer suggests Schopenhauer, who, it will be
recalled, was heard in 2.19, and reappears in 3.12.16, which reports on
people dismissing the will as liberating and creating. In 3.13, what
crawls into the throat represents disgust for the 'human, all too human',
and the awareness that this must eternally return, as choking knowledge
itself, giving Schopenhauerian pessimism, a killing knowledge. The
disgust is part of an inward affectual state, and is symbolised in
Zarathustra's animals, who are manifestations of Zarathustra,
suggesting that the horror has to do with being the same as the small
man; and it is part of an outward state since it reacts to a knowledge
which is felt to be destructive. But perhaps Schopenhauer's teaching is
a part of Zarathustra that he cannot want to recognise in himself, the
small man's philosophy, productive of complaint which is also accusation. Eternal return seems not to be will to power, neither in Heidegger's
nor in Nietzsche's sense, since it does not show life overcoming itself.
Yet its 'repetition of the same' is a source of horror *and* liberation,
requiring, for the latter, the will to bite through the snake; a will itself
wholly ambiguous, not a single reified thing, rather, the combined
impulse of horror, hatred and loathing, pity, goodness and badness.

'The Vision and the Riddle' moves from mole to spider to dog to
snake; the dog being perhaps an image of the ego, and attached to the
shepherd, inseparable from him, and making him dependent on it as
representative of the ego.[33] Perhaps what chokes the shepherd, is what
terrified the dog, sensitive to thieves and ghosts. Perhaps the eternal
return is terrifying because of its destruction of the individual ego (that
would not be inconsistent with Benjamin's sense of the moment).
Perhaps the snake suggests the tenacious power of the ego. That makes
the snake ambiguous, as both the idea of the ego which resists eternal
return, and the figure of return. Traditionally, the snake as the *ourobos*,
the serpent with its tail in its mouth, suggests eternity, time as a circle.
Its head in the shepherd's throat suggests that the past (the tail) creates
the present, so that eternal return becomes both the expression of eternal
return and so of difference, *and* that the continuance of time, and its
return, perpetuates the ego, in the sense that it perpetuates the rule of

the Same. Then biting the snake breaks the hegemony by which time dictates subjectivity, severing present from past.

This makes the mouth of the shepherd analogous to the Moment. Both bite, the latter with the power to shut, like the eye, and to destroy, as with the force of castration; that idea would receive support from the phallicism symbolised in the snake; but then the snake, as a phallic double, would also suggest the power of castration at work within shepherd and Zarathustra, like Medusa's head. Eternal return must be seen in a double form; as that which returns as with the force of the same, suggestive of identity, and as the power of the Moment, which dissolves identity because it is empty space, and because it has such castrating power, and because it is not empty, but the meeting point of contradictions, hence changing everything, including everything of identity. The Moment to which things come back is always the moment of difference, which constitutes it as the will to power, overcoming all that is past. The undecidability between these interpretations makes the eternal return both real, and empty: a fetishistic thought analogous to Freud's description of the subtlety of the fetish where 'both the disavowal and the affirmation of the castration have found their way into the construction of the fetish itself'.[34]

I do not interpret the vision of the snake as being an intellectual fear, or think of such intellectualism producing the loaded, physical image of it penetrating the mouth, unable to go further or be retracted. The nausea is physical, not intellectual, disgust; an affront to the body. The image registers a crisis coming from outside and taking over the inside, and expressive of something inside; it indicates a biform identity unable to spit out what is other within it: a sexuality and a sexual nausea together which constitute the castration fear. Perhaps the figure laughing at the end, no longer shepherd, and with neither the dog as ego nor snake, suggests the liberated will, but if so, what was the meaning of the act whereby the snake, as embodying time which devours its children, has lost its potency? And if he is the will, then Nietzsche is not free – as Klossowski indicates – from an ambiguity which sees the will as no thing, but part of the impulses of the body, and as something like the 'I', a structure described as fetishistic. I will complete the quotation of paragraph from Klossowski, the first half of which was given earlier:

The term *'Wille ZUR Macht'* . . . indicates an intention – a tendency *towards* – something he has already declared to be a fiction of language' [that is, Nietzsche has disallowed thinking of power as something discrete]. A perpetual equivocity ensues, despite all his efforts to distinguish his own use of the term from the traditional concept of the will. (*Nietzsche and the Vicious Circle*, 46)

In which case, the equivocity cannot quite rule out Heidegger's reading: that the eternal return establishes the will. The riddle remains a riddle, ambiguous. If the reward for bisecting the snake, as both the figure of eternal return of the same, and as the ego (these things are not ultimately distinct) is to create this new figure, he, however Dionysian – there is no Dionysus in *Zarathustra* – seems like a single figure, the will. Klossowski speculates whether 'in Nietzsche's thought, the Return is simply a pure *metaphor* for the *will to power*' (*Nietzsche and the Vicious Circle*, 104), and it must remain a speculation. For to be a metaphor, the will would have to disappear entirely, and be replaced by the return of the different.

It is time to reconsider the Nietzschean will through music, briefly, through Mahler and Delius.

VII   MAHLER AND DELIUS

Mahler writes in July 1896 about his Third Symphony, written that year and first performed in 1903; 'imagine such a *great work*, in which in fact the *whole world* is mirrored – one is, so to speak, no more than an instrument on which the Universe plays, I tell you, in some places it strikes even me as uncanny; it seems as if I hadn't written it at all.'[35] Rather than writing, composing may be conceptualised as listening, as if the text is already written and the music repeats an earlier music. And the sounds of nature may be turned to, as the voice of the other, as opposed to the voice of art, of artistic illusion and taste.[36] The apocalyptic implications in the whole world being mirrored will be noted. There is a fascination with multi-directional sound. So Donald Mitchell argues, also saying that Mahler's shift of orchestral sound from strings to wind responds to two different perceptions of how sound sounds within air.[37] Mahler abolishes divisions between art and life, and sound and music.

Despite Constantine Floros saying Mahler was not Nietzschean in the Third Symphony, Mahler's work seems resonant of Nietzsche, down to its subtitle, *Die Fröhliche Wissenschaft*. The first movement was subtitled in 1896 'Bacchic Procession', recalling *The Birth of Tragedy* – as Mahler described the last movement, the Adagio, 'the highest level of the structure: God!, or, if you like, the *Übermensch*'.[38] The fourth movement, 'What Night Tells Me', an alto solo, is most relevant for the will: coming from *Thus Spake Zarathustra* (3.15 – 'The Second Dance-Song'). This, once entitled 'Vita Feminina', and following another once called 'Ariadne', leads into the 'The Seven Seals' which concluded *Zarathustra*'s third part, and its end.[39]

The section 'Ariadne', renamed 'On the Great Yearning', comprises twenty-two addresses by Zarathustra to his soul. One says she will have to sing with passionate song:

> till all seas become quite still, that they may hearken to your yearning
> – till over quiet and yearning seas the bark floats, the golden wonder,
> around whose gold all good and bad and wonderful things now frolic.
> (3.14.195)

It is the boat of Dionysos; the mood contrasts with Tristan waiting for Isolde's boat. In the following section, 'The Other Dance-Song', Zarathustra looks into the eye of Life, and sees 'a golden-hued boat . . . glinting on nocturnal waters' (3.15.196). The appearance of Dionysos' boat, if it is that, associates with the feminine. Life plays castanets, like Carmen, and the dance, described in 21 measures, begins, with Zarathustra's 'My heels started pulsing, my toes began listening for what you would propose: for the dancer has his ear – deep down in his toes'. After the dance-section, Life replies, with her delicate ears closed, telling him not to crack his whip so terribly; since 'noise murders thoughts'. The point relates to the power of rhythm, and Zarathustra's desire for sense to be punctual, immediate, filled with presence. Speaking of 'our island and our own green meadow', Life is both Ariadne and Dionysos, but she further accuses Zarathustra of thinking, at the hour of midnight, of leaving her, like a Theseus. The midnight hour is a moment for thinking of mortality, and for thinking, because life leads to death, that life cannot be justified; giving a preference for Wisdom, as abstract, over Life. Zarathustra's reply to this accusation is to say that Life knows not only that, but something else too, and whispers it into her ear: she replies 'You *know* that, O Zarathustra? No one knows that –' (3.15.198).

Whatever secret he tells, it is not told, but it produces the song, requiring imaginary music, where the singer is unattributable, and the time midnight, the Dionysiac hour, deeper than the noonday, as the moment of the shortest shadow, can know. The midnight has the poten-tiality of being the 'moment' discussed with the eternal return: the moment which contains its other, and which reverses everything. The song repeats 'deep' seven times. The stroke of one is heard, and each hour is named, 'Twelve' being the last line, after which comes a pause, with no response.[40] 'Twelve' resonates, or echoes, response coming in another form, in the next section, 'The Seven Seals'. But the song returns in 4.19.12: Zarathustra calls it 'One more time', saying that signifies 'Unto all eternity'.

The song, a dialogue, turns the sound of bells into a meaning by enumerating the numbers, so that they speak to the subject after *'One'* 'O man! Take care' producing a response after *'Two'*, 'What does Deep Midnight now declare?' Midnight begins speaking after *'Three'*: 'I sleep, I sleep / From deepest dream I rise for air / The world is deep, / Deeper than the day had been aware. / Deep is its woe – / Joy – deeper still than misery: / Woe says: Now go! / Yet all joy wants Eternity – / – wants deepest, deep Eternity!' Midnight is absolute transition; do we go on, or not? There is a contradiction there. The pain says 'Go', but while Joy (*Lust*) does not speak, nonetheless as deeper than pain, Joy is said to will eternity. Life does not appear: she has been replaced by the desire for eternity, which is not separate from life, but within it, the deep inten-sity of the Moment in life. It is the Moment within the eternal return, now affirmed, now willed. So the refrain of the last section, 'The Seven Seals' is *'For I love you, O Eternity.'*

Mahler's setting adds 'O Mensch' to make up two six-line stanzas:

O Mensch! Gieb Acht!
Was spricht die tiefe Mitternacht?
– Ich schlief, ich schlief –
Aus tiefem Traum bin ich erwacht: –
Die Welt ist tief,
Und tiefer als der Tag gedacht.

O Mensch, O Mensch
Tief ist ihr Weh
Lust – tiefer noch als Herzeleid;
Weh spricht; Vergeh! –

Doch alles Lust will Ewigkeit –
– will tiefe, tiefe Ewigkeit!"
[O man, take heed! / What does the deep midnight say? I slept! I
slept! I have awoken from deep dreaming! The world is deep! / And
deeper than the day conceives!

O man! O man! / Deep! Deep is its woe! Joy, joy deeper still than
heart-ache! / Woe says: be lost / But all joy wills eternity! – Wills
deep, deep eternity!][41]

Music gives voice, as in Beethoven's Ninth Symphony, and as such
embodies midnight, and dream, and dream-interpretation. While there
is no dialogue for two voices, the music, with the oboe responding as if
to a call after the question of the second line, and with the solo violin
after the eighth line, makes the attribution of a single subject speaking
impossible. The Dionysiac, which sings in soft tones, for small ears, is
feminine, not masculine power: there is no percussion, no Zarathustran
whips, and trumpets, muted, are only heard in two bars (97, 99). The
music calls, like Brangene calling the lovers in *Tristan*, but calls as an
other, addressing an other outside its scope, called 'Man', but neither
created nor named within it. The call has neither destination nor punctual aim. The musical setting responds to what has already been created
in the symphony, producing a resonance, not a definable meaning.

Delius's *A Mass of Life* (1905, an oratorio in two parts first conducted
by Thomas Beecham in 1909) also responds to *Zarathustra*. Much of the
material derives from both the form and the content of 'The Drunken
Song' (4.19), which is built up on fragments of 'O Mensch! Giebt Acht',
which must be sung by all 'higher humans' as 'Zarathustra's roundelay'
(*Zarathustras Rundgesang*).[42] The first part of *A Mass of Life* opens with a
setting of 3.12, section 30: Zarathustra's address to his will; as a double
chorus, this is both plural – a collective will – and a single will, heard
together. It asks that the 'I' may be 'ready and ripe in the Great Midday',
and so defines one of the axial points of *A Mass of Life*, the other being
midnight.

A second section, from 4.13, for baritone, encourages laughter and
dance, as equivalents to the power of the will. A third, from 'The Other
Dance-Song' (3.15), is like a nocturne in pairing Life and Night.
Wordless voices sound over the water at night. All soloists – soprano,
mezzo-soprano, tenor and baritone, appear, alongside the chorus, and

under the shadow of midnight; leading to the first setting of 'O Mensch! Giebt Acht!' for the basses of the chorus, making it as different as possible from Mahler's setting. There is no setting of the bells, nor of the numbering that comes between each statement. The fourth section, derived from 4.19.4, part of the 'Drunken Song', is more self-questioning, and leads to the question 'Was sprecht die tiefe Mittenacht?', taking the midnight as though it, like death, provided the greatest challenge to life; but then, Midnight – the 'moment' – is also life. The fifth part (2.9), also for baritone and chorus, repeats as a refrain 'Nacht ist es' (it is night), with a preference for the night over the day.

The second part, after an orchestral prelude, is subtitled 'On the Mountains', and moves towards evocation of the noon-tide: it draws material from 2.6, 3.12, 2.1, and from the end of 2.20: 'Rise up now, rise up, you Great Midday', with which it starts and returns at the end. Its second section taken from 'The Drunken Song'(4.19.6), is affirmative of joy, and of death together, evoking 'drunken midnight-dying happiness, which sings, the world is deep, *deeper than day had been aware*', quoting, of course, from 'O Mensch! Giebt Ach'. In the word 'tief' (deep), a musical significance may be heard. Its third is from 'The Dance Song' (2.9), and it concludes with the questioning and melancholia that evening brings. The fourth, from 4.10, with the pastoral of shepherds' pipes, celebrates the midday sleeping, so answering the prayer to the Will in Part 1 section 1. Just as midnight is drunken, so the midday is the moment not for masculine self-assertion, the expression of the sun as symbol of nature, but for sleep; both these axial points show the relaxation of the will.[43] The fifth returns to 'The Drunken Song' (4.19.8), so that it finishes with a quotation from 'O Mensch': now the lyre of Part 2 section 2, which was evoked, comes back again, but drunken itself, and so, developing that earlier part, as midnight's lyre.

The last section, written in 1898 as 'Mittersnachtschied', returns to an earlier section in 'The Drunken Song', to 4.19.2 and 3, so that it starts with 'Kommt' ('Come'). So it suggests openness to experience, the relaxation of the personal will, openness to the other. It then adds the whole of 'O Mensch' again from 4.19.12, and reverts to the statements about joy (4.19.11), concluding with the words that joy wills eternity: 'Will tiefe, tiefe Ewigkeit'. These words, which finish the last three sections of 'The Drunken Song' do, indeed, make it a 'Rundgesang', quoted, then enlarged on, then repeated, then led up to again through the progress of 'O Mensch'. They suggest that in some ways, it is not only Life, and

Midnight, but Joy herself, as evoked in the Ninth Symphony – though here Joy is 'Lust', not 'Freude' – who speaks in the poem, and guarantees both midday and midnight.

More than Mahler, Delius emphasises *Thus Spoke Zarathustra* as music, and, with its first movement in mind, brings it back to the Schopenhaurian will. But it is not so in a dominating and annihilating sense, but as on the side of that which represents an avoidance of the personal will, music expressing itself like drunken song, Dionysiac in character, and returning again and again as aware of midnight – that which must be heard, as music itself – as the potential for all experience. Adorno's reading of Mahler brings out the Nietzschean quality within him which exceeds questions of 'influence' and says that affirmation is ambiguous: 'Mahler was a poor yea-sayer'.[44] Delius brings out less of the pressure-points in Nietzsche's text, which weigh on Zarathustra, so its affirmation of the will to eternity, not the subject's will, but that of joy, is less complex, or contradictory than either Nietzsche or Mahler; but it does not make *Zarathustra* a magnification of the personal will.

9

CONCLUSION
Foucault's vouloir-savoir

Here, at present I felt afresh – for I had felt it again and again – how my equilibrium depended on the success of rigid will, the will to shut my eyes as tight as possible to the truth that what I had to deal with was, revoltingly, against nature. I could only get on at all by taking 'nature' into my confidence and my account, by treating my monstrous ordeal as a push in a direction unusual, of course, and unpleasant, but demanding after all, for a fair front, only another turn of the screw of ordinary human virtue.

(HENRY JAMES, The Turn of the Screw)[1]

Every unlimited condition of the will leads to evil. Ambition and lust are unlimited expressions of will. As the theologians have always perceived, the natural totality of the will must be destroyed. The will must shatter into a thousand pieces. The elements of the will that have proliferated so greatly limit one another. This gives rise to the limited, terrestrial will. Whatever goes beyond them and calls for the (supreme) unity of intention is not the object of the will; it does not require the intention of the *will*. Prayer, however, can be unlimited.

(WALTER BENJAMIN)[2]

I begin by summarising. Reading the will means tracing an historical process wherein the will becomes more and more integral to the person, even identifiable with him, as with Will in Langland, where 'Will' is both allegorical and his own name, as with the subject who says 'my name is Will' in Shakespeare. If the self-divided will becomes a precise entity in Augustine, giving or withholding assent to desire, its insistence in Shakespeare is as synonymous with appetite, or affect, or desire, and with the sexual, as both the body and its members and that which moves, or fails to move, the body. That equivalence of the will to the self accounts for the epigraph from Walter Benjamin: here, hostility to the will relates to his repudiation of individual subjectivity.

A recurring duality exists within perceptions of the will: between having a passionate belief in its power, and withdrawing from it. There seems a recurrent strain between seeing the will as imperious, wilful, ill-willed, directed outside itself in paranoid form, as perhaps is the case with the governess in *The Turn of the Screw*, a title which is synomymous with the action of the will, or marked by lack of will. Independent of the conscious self, it becomes the unconscious 'drive' in Freud, and what moves the drive. There is a discursive move towards thinking of the will as impossible to control, or a desire to stand outside its impersonal force; so with Schopenhauer, whose reading was rejected by Nietzsche, who nonetheless sees the personal will as a fetish, giving a sense of individual subjectivity. The discourse which makes music the embodiment of the will is so persuasive an argument expressed in such persuasive music – Beethoven, Wagner – that it is hard to stand outside it.

For Augustine, following Paul, the will comes into being by the law, reacting through desire to the interdicted. Yet the law is a will, calling forth a contestatory will; or the law is a desire which awakens conflict-ual desire. The question is not simply whether there can be desire outside the law; because if the law is desire, then that will is already instantiated; and is conflictual, reactive, as law; and active, though cast as reactive, as desire. The law as the will relates to the will as law, which is a constant within the texts discussed. To say 'I will' with regard to the body and to 'my' property, no longer mine because of my death, is complex because it involves the desire to assert an individual identity beyond what lim-its identity and declares its fictional status. In that sense the last will and testament is self-assertive. Yet it also seems that people shrink from mak-ing a will because of the implications of death that it carries: a will is for the death-bed, and acknowledges limitations. The will expresses then both an imperious demand and a recognition of its failure.

Nietzsche distinguishes between the will as an assertive power by which the ego believes that it is constituted as complete, and will to power as outside the power of the subject, and working by its self-over-coming. The first term used includes the 'will to truth', and 'truth' assumes that there is a depth beyond appearances; 'a will to truth' assumes subjectivity in the knower and in what is to be known; perhaps this is the very meaning of the word 'will' in the discourse we have traced throughout the book. Yet even in Nietzsche, it is not clear that willing the eternal return, as part of self-overcoming, is not to be thought of as an act of will, with its attendant dangers.

The will as constitutive of the ego is in the service of the 'ascetic ideal'. But in *The Genealogy of Morals*, 3.24, Nietzsche puts it the other way: the will to truth, which begets asceticism, is nothing other than a belief in the ascetic ideal, and it is belief in 'the absolute value of "the true" which stems from the ascetic ideal and stands or falls with it'. At this point, Nietzsche quotes from Book 5 (section 344) of *The Gay Science* where the 'will to truth' means 'I will not deceive, not even myself' because *'with that we stand on moral ground'*:

> For you only have to ask yourself carefully, 'Why do you not want to deceive?', especially if it should seem . . . as if life aimed at semblance, meaning error, deception, simulation, delusion, self-delusion, and when the great sweep of life has actually always shown itself to be on the side of the most unscrupulous *polytropoi*. Charitably interpreted, such a resolve might perhaps be a quixotism, a minor slightly mad enthusiasm, but it might also be something more serious, namely a principle that is hostile to life and destructive. – 'Will to truth' – that might be a concealed will to death.
>
> [. . .] those who are truthful . . . thus *affirm another world* than the world of life, nature, and history; and insofar as they affirm this 'other world' – look, must they not by the same token negate its counterpart, this world, our world? But . . . it is still a *metaphysical faith* upon which our faith in science rests – that even we seekers after knowledge today, we godless anti-metaphysicians still take our fire, too, from the flame lit by a faith that is thousands of years old, that Christian faith which was also the faith of Plato, that God is the truth, that truth is divine. – But what if this should become more and more incredible, if nothing should prove to be divine any more unless it were error, blindness, the lie – if God himself should prove to be our most enduring lie?[3]

The will to power has nothing to do with seeking 'the truth', it exists polytropically, producing trope after trope, image after image, none laying claim to 'truth'. It makes everything more labyrinthine. The person who says he will not be deceived is at best a Don Quixote – the reverse of an Odysseus, Homer's polytropic man, someone whose madness is that he believes the world is a deception, but that he can see the truth of it, and has the will to right it. To watch someone at work who had a will to truth could be as pleasant as to watch Don Quixote with his touching innocence, producing always unexpected results. But at worst the person with the will to truth has a 'will to death', because death fixes everything of 'the other'; death is necessary because what is dead does not argue with the investigator, and gives the appearance that there is a unified, single truth.

If the will to truth is the will to death, that only brings out the strangeness of the idea that the truth is that which must be willed, commanded, made to come to heel. It recalls Heidegger's emphasis on the 'enframing' power of technology, which itself is seen as a mode of 'revealing' and 'challenging' (*Herausfordern*). Heidegger writes: 'we now name that challenging claim which gathers man thither to order the self-revealing as standing reserve: *Ge-stell* (Enframing)'.[4] So, within this 'enframing', the human has been created and is forced, challenged, to yield itself up as raw material; the human is not the master of technology, but mastered by it. If 'enframing' demands that the self has to reveal itself, that enforces the sense that I am now compelled to speak of myself confessionally. 'Truth' is extracted from that which has been compelled to reveal itself, and to see itself as standing forth, as a reserve to be used. Everything that has been made to stand forth, the human and the object-world alike, is made into material that has been stockpiled, ready to be used, ready for the 'developers'. Yet Heidegger, thinking of the triumph of 'enframing' says that 'the essence of freedom is *originally* not connected with the will or even with the causality of human willing' ('The Question Concerning Technology', 25). The work of technology produces the will.

The modernising, developing industrialist is the subject of D.H. Lawrence, in *Women in Love* (1920), in the portrait of Gerald Crich, the mine-owner, highly erotic and attractive to both men and women. His every action turns out to be death-driven, while he is also suicidal. Ursula Brangwen early on comments that Gerald has 'got *go*', and Gudrun Brangwen asks 'where does his *go* go to, what becomes of it?' Ursula answers, 'It goes in applying the latest appliances'.[5] Gerald has what Heidegger calls 'the will to will'. It is at that point that Ursula tells Gudrun that Gerald 'accidentally' shot his brother, and the discussion this could engender about intention should certainly recall the terms of *La forza del destino*, and even my discussion of Gwendolen Harleth as an unconscious murderess. Lawrence's fascination with Gerald is at the heart of *Women in Love*, and of Leavis' analysis of it in terms of the 'will'.

Lawrence's will seems to differ from Nietzsche's, in its humanism, as being linked to a perception of the ego as always problematic, attempting to dominate, and as opposed to the body. The latter, in Lawrence, is the seat of 'life', and of energies which countermand the will. Here, perhaps, Lawrence simplifies, and his disparagement of Freud associates with his unifying of 'life' as against the will, and setting aside the death-drive, which it may be simplistic in him to associate solely with the will. Lawrence seems to think that the will can be suspended so that 'that which is perfectly ourselves can take place in us', as Birkin says in a crucial dialogue with Ursula where he speaks of 'a final me which is stark and impersonal and beyond responsibility' (*Women in Love*, 146, 147).

Where the human has been wholly framed by technology, by 'the latest appliances', as Heidegger's assessment suggests, Lawrentian humanism loses something of its authority. The will to will, of which Heidegger speaks, works through technology.[6] Technology is defined here as, in essence, not in its empirical detail, 'completed metaphysics'. It is the name given to that which sets things into a position of permanence, giving them completed being and meaning. As if with Gerald Crich in mind, Heidegger writes:

> In virtue of the fact that the will is sometimes personified in individual 'men of will', it looks as if the will to will were the radiation of these persons. The opinion arises that the human will is the origin of the will to will, *whereas man is willed by the will to will* without experiencing the essence of this willing.
>
> In that man is what is thus willed, and what is posited in the will to will, 'the will' is also of necessity addressed in its essence and released as the instance of truth. The question is whether the individuals and communities are in virtue of this will . . . without knowing that they are already outwitted by it. The uniqueness of Being shows itself in the will to will, too, which only admits one direction in which to will. The uniformity of the world of the will to will stems from this. ('Overcoming Metaphysics', 81–82, my emphasis.)

230

This gives Heidegger's sense that the will within technology has created and defined the human (with no room for a Nietzschean going beyond the human), and that it has defined the human as essentially marked by will, and therefore condemned to live with it. Heidegger and Lawrence are both analysts of what Lawrence calls 'the plausible ethics of productivity' (*Women in Love*, 56), but neither attribute agency to the will, as Marxism would and could, but both attribute it to essential qualities in being (Heidegger) or in the will (Lawrence). The lack of agency in Heidegger is more problematic, because it is impossible to separate it from his support for the Nazis: at best, the critique of technology wilfully lacks agency driving the technological, at worst, he seems to have been deliberately blind.[7] Or did an acceptance of the power of the will give an excuse to Heidegger to endorse Nazism?

Heidegger contrasts to this compelling of the truth to stand forth within the enframing of technology: *Gelassenheit*, 'releasement', or 'letting be', surrendering voluntarism in a new passivity; the term comes from Meister Eckhart (c.1260–1328), where it refers to letting go of the will in a releasement to God's will. Or, as Piccarda frames it in Dante's *Paradiso* 3.85: 'E'n la sua volontade e nostra pace': in his will is our peace. But, it will be noted, that as with *Measure for Measure*, that contentment still depends on another will, that of God, and the 'twisting free' of the will that Heidegger considers still requires a certain voluntarism, *Gelassenheit* still being a manifestation of the will; the desire to let go is also a part of the will.[8] The question concerning technology presents enframing as complete, but nonetheless argues for a 'saving power' within it too (28); the statement has the power to make it not apparent what the problem is; if technology is both the problem and the solution, Heidegger seems to minimise his argument's political importance.

The 'will to truth', as part of a will to technology, demands the assumption that there is a truthful world which can be brought into representation. No 'seeker after knowledge', as Nietzsche used the term, however avowedly secular, can escape thinking there is a truth somewhere to be discerned. But, argues *The Genealogy of Morals*, why place a value on truth? Asking that means questioning the ascetic ideal, which posits the truth as an ideal. This questioning carries into the work of Michel Foucault (1926–84), which meditates on it, and in its own stylishness, answers it in ways outside the expectations raised in Nietzsche: that is, Foucault is not a commentator on Nietzsche, but his work, because it is not that of a disciple, brings out so much more that is in

231

Nietzsche.[9] His interest is in the will to knowledge (*la volonté de savoir*), a will to increase knowledge, and knowledge as a will which exerts itself upon others.

La volonté de savoir was the title of a series of historical investigations that Foucault conducted in the 1970s, with the object of forming 'a morphology of the will to knowledge'.[10] *La volonté de savoir* is also the French title of *The History of Sexuality* (1976). Before that, Foucault was the philosopher of *The Archaeology of Knowledge* (*L'archéologie du savoir*, 1969); 'archaeology' being 'an approach to the history of thought that eliminates the fundamental role of the human subject'.[11] 'Archaeology' as a mode of discussing history in terms of different discursive formations does not depend on the primacy of man as originating history, assuring its continuity, by being its author and guaranteeing its continuity by his own. And so it is not essentially different from 'genealogy', the method of Foucault's books of the 1970s, though Gutting suggests that genealogy goes further 'by explaining (through the connections with power) changes in the history of discourse that are merely described by archaeology' (Gutting, 7). The first of those works of genealogy, *Discipline and Punish*, connects Benthamism, and the planning of the Panopticon, to Heidegger's ideas in an historical mode: it gives an historical example of enframing by studying the prison, and its ability to make the prisoner stand forth, and to be revealed, in that drive which brings everything into representation.[12] The title *La volonté de savoir* suggests that desire, appetite, affects which are covertly sexual, produce knowledge, whose content is the antithesis of the ascetic ideal, save that – as with Angelo in *Measure for Measure*- the ascetic ideal is sexual. If knowledge is a will, then the impulse within knowing produces sexuality within a will to truth, or a will to death. Knowledge and will become inseparable, to know is to will, to will is to know.

But why does Foucault speak more of the will to knowledge, not the will to truth? He speaks of the latter in his inaugural lecture at the Collège de France, 'The Order of Discourse' (1970), saying that academic discourse creates an inside and outside, to exclude certain forms of discourse:

> what this will to truth has been . . . which has crossed so many centuries of our history; what it is, in its general form, the type of division which governs our will to know [*notre volonté de savoir*], then what we

see taking shape is perhaps something like a system of exclusion, a historical, modifiable, and institutionally constraining system. (54)[13]

A statement has to be 'in the true' (60). Whether true or false, the statement must belong within the conventions established which allow for a particular discourse to be articulated, or which disallow it. In that way 'power' and 'knowledge' have to be thought together; the will to knowledge always operates on lines which enforce power-relations. The University is committed to knowledge, rather than to truth, because being in the truth is a precondition to the will to knowledge. 'Nietzsche, Genealogy, History' (1971), the essay where Foucault sets out his debt to Nietzsche, discusses how knowledge is not neutral, 'devoid of passions and committed solely to truth'. Each successive form of scientific consciousness (to be laid bare by 'genealogy'), shows that there has been no calm Platonic succession of ideas running through history; the 'will to knowledge' contains 'instinct, passion, the inquisitor's devotion, cruel subtlety and malice'. This position:

> encourages the dangers of research and delights in disturbing discoveries. The historical analysis of this rancorous will to knowledge [*vouloir-savoir*] reveals that all knowledge rests upon injustice (that there is no right, not even in the act of knowing, to truth or a foundation for truth) and that the instinct for knowledge is malicious [. . .]. It does not achieve a universal truth; man is not given an exact and serene mastery of nature. On the contrary, it ceaselessly multiplies the risks, creates dangers in every area; it breaks down illusory defences; it dissolves the unity of the subject; it releases those elements of itself that are devoted to its subversion and destruction. [. . .] Its development is not tied to the constitution and affirmation of a free subject; rather, it creates a progressive enslavement to its instinctive violence. Where religions once demanded the sacrifice of bodies, knowledge now calls for experimentation on ourselves . . .[14]

The 'analysis' Foucault speaks of is 'genealogy', and the claim is that *vouloir-savoir* is inseparable from *ressentiment*, which would identify the will to know with the will to revenge. This implies a fixed, and paranoid approach to the object, but more, in Foucault's 'rancorous will to knowledge', the will is impelled by ill-will. Knowledge as willed is alien, objectified; what is to be known, and from a position of domination, is what is to be taken revenge upon. The will to knowledge perpetuates injustice. *Surveiller et punir* – 'Supervise and Punish' better than *Discipline and Punish* – catches the identification that Foucault makes; the drive to be the supervisor – to be in charge of knowledge – is Zarathustra's 'drive to punish'. For 'surveiller', recalling a discussion from chapter 2, we may consider Othello believing that Desdemona and Cassio are in bed together:

> OTHELLO: I'll not endure it. Would I were satisfied!
> IAGO: I see, sir, you are eaten up with passion.
> I do repent me that I put it to you.
> You would be satisfied?
> OTHELLO: Would? Nay, and I will.
> IAGO: And may. But how, how satisfied, my lord?
> Would you, the supervisor, grossly gape on,
> Behold her topped?
> OTHELLO: Death and damnation! O!
> (Othello, 3.3.395–401)

Everything is relevant here: Othello 'gaping', as an 'O', a nothing, in contrast to his emphatic 'and I will'; and satisfaction as complete knowledge, knowledge of his wife's supposed adultery, only to be had by becoming 'the supervisor', possessed of the scopic drive which proclaims not mastery but two other things, the desire to see – as constituting complete knowledge – and the desire to harm himself, so that the emphasis in 'I will' is also the impotence of his 'O'. The point compares with the lament of Lucrece, that she has been 'overseen' (*The Rape of Lucrece*, 1206), looked on in a way which combines the wilfulness of the eye and the power of rape. Foucault's analysis of how knowledge is malicious, how it enchains the free subject, forces subjectivity constantly to analyse itself, which is the topic of *The History of Sexuality*, aligns the word 'malice' to the idea of 'ill-will' and answers the question: why 'will to knowledge' and not 'will to truth'? Because the will to knowledge is a passion which pluralises itself endlessly, and which has the power to hurt.

This may be seen from the central section of *La volonté de savoir*. 'Scientia Sexualis' asks, as a problem: why has there been no *ars erotica* within western discourse? Why, instead of the erotic being seen as pleasure – as having no truth which may be gleaned from it, being so singular that no generalisation could be formed from it – has it become part of a scientific discourse, so that from its every aspect some 'truth' can be learned? If the erotic is the will to power, as Nietzsche understands that term, the will to knowledge tames that will. Foucault begins answering the question by reference to Christian confessional practices, beginning with the Papal requirement for annual confession made in 1215.[15] He points out the absolute 'exorbitance' of the demand to confess: a will to knowledge which required 'immense labour' (60). That was equally true of Charcot's clinic for studying hysteria; the 'enormous apparatus' for observing was a 'machinery for incitement' (55), for 'continuous incitement to discourse and to truth' (56). The 'immense apparatus for producing truth' (56) – 'immense' appears twice on pages 55 and 56 – suggests Kafka's machine in 'In the Penal Colony'. Foucault's writing shows a baroque structure coming into force to extract the truth of the confessional, and to turn the subject who confesses into an introspective being, and inciting in the subject the 'hysteria' which a will to knowledge has created: this pathologising being an example of the 'malice' Foucault spoke of before. The subject is forced into self-analysis. The word *avowal*, for instance, moves from meaning 'a guarantee of the status, identity, and value granted by one person to another' to 'someone's acknowledgement of his own actions and thoughts' (58). But since 'that immense will to knowledge . . . has sustained the establishment of scientific discourse in the West' (55), the baton has now passed from Christian confession to science, so that 'the rituals of confession [now] function within the norms of scientific regularity' (65). Foucault uses Nietzsche's point that secular science is as metaphysical as Christianity in believing that there is a truth to be extracted from any investigation. Confession becomes clinically encoded, belief in causality is strengthened, enforcing belief in the power of anyone being able to give a narrative of the self. Sexuality is argued to have a 'latency' behind it which can be brought out. Confessional statements needed interpretation, and sexuality was pronounced as a morbid state (65–67). Elements of this control, it has already been suggested, are even found in Daniel Deronda's treatment of Gwendolen, marking a will to truth within him.

Foucault argues that 'sexuality' came into play as a discourse which must speak its truth and the nineteenth century 'did not confront sex with a fundamental refusal of recognition' but 'put into operation an entire machinery for producing true discourses concerning it' (69).

That discourse is made to seem 'that which divides [the subject] . . . causes him to be ignorant of himself' (70). The subject is not in charge of his/her own discourse; what he or she is can only be known by another. Foucault sees this production of knowledge as a new, and truly perverse, *ars erotica*, 'pleasure in the truth of pleasure, the pleasure of knowing that truth, of discovering and exposing it, the fascination of seeing it and telling it,' (71). The fascination is for the subject 'recognising' and bringing into apparently spontaneous representation his or her own constructed sexuality.

At the heart of the will to knowledge is its connection to power. Foucault says we would have to have an 'inverted image of power' to believe that the voices which convey the 'formidable injunction to tell what one is and what one does' speak of freedom. Rather the 'immense labour' to which 'the West has submitted generations' produces 'men's subjection: their constitution as subjects in both senses of the word' (60). The passage in Foucault is famous: to be constituted as a subject means becoming subjected to a discourse, such as that of law (85). But it also means the opposite: feeling that the self is the subject with the power of discourse, able to own the discourse of sexuality, feeling 'yes, that is me'. The confessional requirement makes me turn the discourse onto myself in a will to knowledge both sexual and Socratic (know thyself). The ascetic ideal is powerful in the drive towards a sexual knowledge, because it is a will to truth, i.e. a desire that the sexual should be seen neither as play nor illusion, but as real, and serious. The effect of power is most truly felt, that is, most truly inverted, when the subject speaks his/her own language of the ascetic ideal in a mode which sees that as expansionist and an access to power. The section 'Scientia Sexualis' gives way to another discussing power; Foucault asks if we should say that 'one is always "inside" power, there is no "escaping" it, there is no absolute outside where it is concerned' (95).

That statement must be qualified, because there is no essential power to be spoken of, yet it makes a point: the 'will to knowledge' does not presuppose a model of the outside and the inside – i.e. the subject marked by interiority – it works by creating the individual subject who continues that creation. There the difference between knowledge and truth becomes apparent; knowledge does not assume a point of rest; since it will always be the function of institutions and subjects to produce knowledge, never with the sense that truth has been attained.

And 'knowledge' pluralises over a void. Discussing Raymond Roussel, Foucault says that his writing emerges:

> not where the canonical figures of speech originate, but that neutral
> space within language where the hollowness of the word is shown as
> an insidious void, arid and a trap. Roussel considers this game, which
> rhetoric exploited to extend its meaning, as a gap which is stretched
> open as wide as possible and meticulously measured. He felt there is,
> beyond the quasi-liberties of expression, an absolute emptiness of
> being that he felt he must surround, dominate, and overwhelm with
> pure invention: that is what he calls, in opposition to reality, thought.
> [. . .] He doesn't want to duplicate the reality of another world, but,
> in the spontaneous duality of language, he wants to discover an unex-
> pected space, and to cover it with things never said before.[16]

The postmodern produces knowledge within the awareness of a void, because there is no privileged truth to be discovered, which means that there can be no end in view, no completeness. Perhaps that makes the will to knowledge masculine, as the desire for the fetish, what covers over phallic nothingness. And the will seems to be the fear of being no thing, and in its anxiety, it seems to be the will to will as well. Yet the playfulness which is implied in the creation of language in Roussel also implies an interest in Foucault throughout, particularly in his last work, in self-fashioning, in styling an existence which escapes the dictatorial power of the will. Foucault's interest in 'arts of existence' and 'techniques of the self' contrast with the techniques for observing and seeing which he describes in the wake of Heidegger's will to technology.[17] This creating of a style perhaps offers a way of thinking escaping the rule of the will. We are left asking whether the subject can exist with a spon-taneous, and poetic will which escapes the charge of being reactive, rancorous, self-assertive, a way of being, and living, not constructed by the will as anxious and ill-willed.

The voices in this chapter, significantly masculine, non-Freudian non-Marxist, pose the question what they leave out in making 'the will' the problem of modernity, already demonstrated in genocides in Europe, Asia and Africa in the twentieth century. One Marxist analysis, working from the problem of the 'ascetic ideal' and the will this manifests, relates its contemporary form to a fundamentalism activating revolutionary Islam and, more so, the empire-building of the USA and NATO, whose excuse is globalisation, and those Western values which conceal the will to nothingness. It paraphrases the analysis of *The Genealogy of Morals* as follows:

> Why is it that human beings, faced with the cruelty and disappoint-
> ment of the present, seem drawn ineluctably to one or another version
> of the warrior ideal (or the warrior crossed with the flagellant): to a
> dedication to hardness, ruthlessness, fierce bonding, closure against
> the mereness of the everyday; to a dedication finally to Death – to the
> making, the forcing of history, and the re-writing of the future
> according to the script of some dismal Messiah?[18]

This book has tried to explain what network of ideas and affects around willing and the power of the will have had such effect, but the end of an analysis can only repeat the problem, in the words which have activated so much of this book, Nietzsche's verdict on the ascetic ideal and its will to truth: 'man would rather will *nothingness* than *not* will at all'.

NOTES

INTRODUCTION

1 Christopher Marlowe, *Tamburlaine the Great* Part 1. 2.7.18–29, in *The Complete Plays*, ed. J.B. Steane (Harmondsworth: Penguin, 1969), 132–33. See Harry Levin, *The Overreacher: A Study of Christopher Marlowe* (Cambridge, Mass.: Harvard University Press, 1952), 38–40, and Michael Black, *Poetic Drama as Mirror of the Will* (London: Vision, 1977).

2 Leo Tolstoy, *War and Peace* (1869) 3.2.28, trans. Rosemary Edmonds (Harmondsworth: Penguin, 1957), 2 vols, vol. 2, 931.

3 Nietzsche, *On the Genealogy of Morals* 3.28 trans. Douglas Smith (Oxford: Oxford University Press, 1996), 136. Walter Kaufmann, in *On the Genealogy of Morals and Ecce Homo* (New York: Vintage, 1967), 163 notes the pun in what is translated as 'an aversion to life' – *Widerwillen*.

4 Judith N. Shklar, *Men and Citizens: A Study of Rousseau's Social Theory* (Cambridge: Cambridge University Press, 1969), 72.

5 See John H. Smith, *Dialectics of the Will: Freedom, Power and Understanding in Modern French and German Thought* (Detroit: Wayne State University Press, 2000).

6 'Tripos: in Three Discourses' in *The English Works of Thomas Hobbes of Malmsebury* (London: John Bohn, 1840), vol. 4, 68–70.

7 Judith N. Shklar, *Men and Citizens: A Study of Rousseau's Social Theory*, 193, quoting Montesquieu, *The Spirit of the Laws* 1.8, Shklar, 193. See also Patrick Riley, *The General Will Before Rousseau: The Transformation of the Divine into the Civic* (Princeton: Princeton University Press, 1986) for Montesquieu, who used the 'general will' to suggest public opinion, like Rousseau, 168–69.

8 Hegel, *The Phenomenology of Spirit*, trans. A.V. Miller (Oxford: Oxford University Press, 1977), sections 584, pp. 356–57, and 590, 360.

9 Barry Nicholas, *An Introduction to Roman Law* (Oxford: Clarendon Press, 1962), 252.

10 Daniel Sperling, *Posthumous Interests: Legal and Ethical Perspectives* (Cambridge: Cambridge University Press, 2008), 149, quoting Abigail J. Sykes, in *Vermont Law Review*, 2001, 936; see also Sperling, 40–47.

11 Tony Hunt, *Villon's Last Will: Language and Authority in the Testament* (Oxford: Clarendon, 1996).

12 Robert Henryson, *Poems* ed. Charles Elliott (Oxford: Oxford University Press, 1974), 106–7.

13 On *Summer's Last Will and Testament*, see C.L. Barber, *Shakespeare's Festive Comedy: A Study of Dramatic Form and its Relation to Social Custom* (Princeton: Princeton University Press, 1959), 58–86.

14 Jacques Derrida, *Of Grammatology*, trans. Gayatri Chakravorty Spivak (Baltimore: Johns Hopkins University Press, 1976), 69.

15 Michael Millgate, *Testamentary Acts: Browning, Tennyson, James, Hardy* (Oxford: Clarendon Press, 1992), 175–205.

16 Hannah Arendt, *The Life of the Mind: 1: Thinking; 2: Willing* (New York: Harcourt Brace and Co., 1978, two volumes in one), 2.14.

17 Translation by Francis Golffing, in Nietzsche, *The Birth of Tragedy and The Genealogy of Morals* (New York: Doubleday, Anchor 1956), 299.

18 Georg Simmel, *Schopenhauer and Nietzsche*, trans. Helmut Loiskandl, Deena Weinstein, and Michael Weindtein (Amherst: University of Massachusetts Press, 1986), 27, 30.

19 Schopenhauer, *The World as Will and Representation*, trans. E.J. Payne (New York: Dover, 1969, reprint from 1958), 2 vols, by chapter and page-number, and volume number where necessary. The second volume was added to the second edition of 1844. For Nietzsche and Schopenhauer see Christopher Janaway (ed.), *Willing and Nothingness: Schopenhauer as Nietzsche's Educator* (Oxford: Clarendon Press, 1998).

20 Kant, *Critique of Pure Reason*, trans. Norman Kemp Smith (London: Macmillan, 1929), 354 (A.383); quoted Schopenhauer 1.435.

21 Peter Szondi, *An Essay on the Tragic*, trans. Paul Fleming (Stanford: Stanford University Press, 2002), 29–30.

22 Nietzsche quotes this in *The Birth of Tragedy*, trans. Douglas Smith (Oxford: Oxford University Press, 2000), 1.21 (henceforth *BT* plus chapter and page-number), as expressive of the Apollonian state, as opposed to the Dionysiac, an anarchic and imageless art-form, fragmenting images, and expressed in music. Nietzsche cites Schopenhauer on the 'strangeness' felt by the Apollonian, because he is aware of something other, apart from what he represents: 'from that presentiment arises that ineradicable *dread*, common to all human beings . . . [as when] some change has occurred without a cause, or a deceased person exists again; or when in any other way the past or the future is present, or the distant is near' (63.353).

23 See John E. Atwell, *Schopenhauer on the Character of the World: The Metaphysics of Will* (Berkeley: University of California Press, 1995), 154–72. Atwell identifies the intellect with the will: 28, 153, 211–12. The will is wit and will together, that which acts, and that which allows itself – as the will – to gain mastery over itself, as Atwell suggests (153). Compare Freud on the superego, as formed by the ego to police it, 'The Ego and the Id' (1923),

Standard Edition of the Works of Sigmund Freud, trans. James Strachey (London: Hogarth Press, 24 vols, 1953–1961), 19.34–39, 51–58. (Henceforth, *SE* for Freud).

24 The scream in Wagner is the expression of the will for Philip Friedheim, 'Wagner and the Aesthetics of the Scream', *Nineteenth-Century Music* 7 (1983), 63–70.

25 Nietzsche, *Twilight of the Idols*, trans. Duncan Large (Oxford: Oxford University Press, 1998), see 3.5.18, and 6.3 (28), and 6.7 (31).

26 Leander E. Keck, *Romans: Abingdon New Testament Commentaries* (Nashville: Abingdon Press, 2005), 182.

27 For James D.G. Dunn, *Romans 1–8: Word Biblical Commentary vol. 38* (Dallas: Texas, 1988), 380, 'the commandment in view is "You shall not covet" taken as characterising the commandment broken by Adam'. He sees the primary reference of the law in Romans 7 to be to the commandment in Genesis 2.17, and reads the chapter as applying to humanity (Adam) after the Fall.

28 John Ziesler, *Paul's Letter to the Romans* (London: SCM Press, 1989), 189.

29 Alain Badiou, *Saint Paul: The Foundation of Universalism*, trans. Ray Brassier (Stanford: Stanford University Press, 2003), 55–56.

30 Jacques Lacan, *The Ethics of Psychoanalysis 1959–1960: The Seminar of Jacques Lacan*, ed. Jacques-Alain Miller, trans. Dennis Porter (London: Routledge, 1992), 20. Further references as Lacan plus page-number.

31 Freud, 'Project for a Scientific Psychology', *SE* 1, 331.

32 Freud, 'Negation', *SE* 19, 237–38.

33 'Kant with Sade' in Jacques Lacan, *Ecrits*, trans. Bruce Fink (New York: W.W. Norton, 2006), 646. (An earlier translation by James B. Swenson appeared in *October* 51 (1984), 55–104.) Henceforth KS plus page-number. See Jacques Alain-Miller, in Richard Feldstein, Bruce Fink and Maire Janus (eds.), *Reading Seminars I and II: Lacan's Return to Freud* (Albany: SUNY, 1996), 212–37, and Ruth Sample, 'Lacan, Kant and Sade', *Journal of the British Society of Phenomenology*, 26 (1995), 5–16, explaining Kant by contrast with Hume, who conflates the will with the passions, reason being unable to control the will: 'reason alone can never be a motive to any action of the will, and secondly, it can never oppose passion in the direction of the will'; 'reason is, and ought to be, only the slave of the passions, and can never pretend to any other office than to serve and obey them'. Hume follows Malebranche, who cites Romans 7.23; see *The Search After Truth*, quoted, Hume, *Treatise of Human Nature*, 2 vols, ed. David Fate Norton and Mary J. Norton (Oxford: Oxford University Press, 2007), 2.870; quotations, 1.265, 266, in section 2.3 'Of the Will and Direct Passions'. Kant's will is rational, a 'kind of causality belonging to living beings insofar as they are rational . . . what else . . . can freedom of the will be but

autonomy, i.e. the property that the will has of being a law to itself? The proposition that the will is in every action a law to itself expresses, however, nothing but the principle of acting according to no other maxim than that which can at the same time have itself as a universal law for its object. Now this is precisely the formula of the categorical imperative and is the principle of morality. Thus a free will and a will subject to moral laws are one and the same', Kant, *Grounding for the Metaphysics of Morals*, trans. Jame W. Ellington (Indiana: Hackett, 1981), sections 446, 447, 49. Kant concludes this because a free will and a will under moral laws are the same, because the will is a cause, and a cause is identified by its effects, so it must be regular (a cause does not have random effects). This identifies the will with practical reason. It is only necessary to will in such a way that it can be the basis of universal law.

34 Immanuel Kant, *Critique of Practical Reason*, trans. Werner S. Pluhar (Indianapolis: Hackett, 2002), 104.

35 Kant was criticised by Theodor Adorno and Max Horkheimer in *Dialectic of Enlightenment*, trans. John Cumming (London: Verso, 1979), 81–119; they paired Kant with Sade for sadism inside the moral law. Gilbert D. Chaitin, *Rhetoric and Culture in Lacan* (Cambridge: Cambridge University Press, 1996), 193, discusses the accusations that Kant's ethic has a relation to Nazism, and says that Lacan's analysis of Kant's practical reason is 'a psychoanalytic explanation of Horkheimer's remark in 'The End of Reason' (1941) that 'sacrifice can be rational when it becomes necessary to defend the state's power which is alone capable of guaranteeing the existence of those whose sacrifice it demands. The idea of reason, even in its nominalistic and purified form, has always justified sacrifice' (quoted from Andrew Arato and Eike Gebhardt (eds.), *The Essential Frankfurt School Reader* (Oxford: Blackwell, 1978), 32–33.

36 Kant, *Critique of Practical Reason*, 45

37 Kant, *Critique of Practical Reason*, 95–96: 'Consequently we can see, a priori, that the moral law as determining basis of the will, by infringing all our inclinations, must bring about a feeling that can be called pain'.

38 See Slavoj Žižek, *The Ticklish Subject: The Absent Centre of Political Ontology* (London: Verso, 1999), 152–53. He concludes that '"there *is* a way of discovering the relationship to *das Ding* somewhere beyond the Law" Lacan: *Ethics* 84] – the whole point of the ethics of psychoanalysis is to formulate the possibility of a relationship that avoids the pitfalls of the superego inculpation that accounts for the "morbid" enjoyment of sin', (153).

39 Lacan, *The Four Fundamental Concepts of Psychoanalysis: The Seminar of Jacques Lacan Book XI*, ed. Jacques Alain-Miller, trans. Alan Sheridan (New York: W.W. Norton, 1977), 275–76.

40 Freud, 'Repression', *SE* 14. 146.

41 John Rajchman, *Truth and Eros: Foucault, Lacan, and the Question of Ethics* (London: Routledge, 1991), 81–82.

42 See Kant, *Critique of Practical Reason*, 44.

43 Alenka Zupančič, *Ethics of the Real: Kant, Lacan* (London: Verso, 2000) 100. I have changed her word 'want' into 'will' in the quotation, for emphasis. The case is taken up again in 'Kant with Sade': see KS, 659–60, making Lacan say 'law and repressed desire are one and the same thing' (KS, 660).

44 Philippe Van Haute, 'Death and Sublimation in Lacan's reading of Antigone', in Sarah Harasym (ed.), *Levinas and Lacan: The Missed Encounter* (Albany: SUNY, 1998), 115–16.

45 The analytic philosopher for whom the will underlies physical actions, as a synonym for 'trying', making each physical act, such as walking, both the act and volitional, a matter of trying, is Brian O'Shaughnessy, *The Will: A Dual Aspect Theory*, 2 vols (Cambridge: Cambridge University Press, 1980, second edition 2008). See H.D. Lewis, 'O'Shaughnessy on Mind and Body', *Religious Studies* 18 (1982), 379–97, and O'Shaughnessy's presentation of his work, including a defence of Schopenhauer, 'Theories of the Bodily Will' in Thomas Pink and M.W.F. Stone (eds.), *The Will and Human Action: From Antiquity to the Present Day* (London: Routledge, 2004), 197–211. This book is valuable for earlier essays, e.g. Richard Sorabji, on 'The Concept of the Will from Plato to Maximus the Confessor', 6–28. I am less concerned with the will as a defensible entity, or as actual, or as attached to concepts of personal freedom; rather as part of how subjectivity has been historically constructed.

46 Michel Foucault, *Language, Counter-Memory, Practice*, ed. Donald F. Bouchard (Ithaca: Cornell University Press, 1977), 199.

1 THE WILL: THREE INSTANCES

1 Discussed in *Nicomachean Ethics* 3.4. 111b 21 and 7.3.1145b 25–26.

2 See 'Intimations of the Will in Greek Tragedy', Jean-Pierre Vernant and Pierre Vidal-Naquet, *Tragedy and Myth in Ancient Greece*, trans. Janet Lloyd (Brighton, Sussex: Harvester Press, 1981), 28–62.

3 See Albrecht Dihle, *The Theory of Will in Classical Antiquity* (Berkeley: University of California Press, 1982), 123. Dihle argues that even Saint Paul does not coin an unequivocal term to denote the notion of will (88). Modern philosophy explains evil in terms of a theodicy; see Susan Neiman, *Evil in Modern Thought: An Alternative History of Philosophy* (Princeton: Princeton University Press, 2002).

4 On the classical history of the will, and for Augustine, see Richard Sorabji, *Emotion and Peace of Mind: From Stoic Agitation to Christian Temptation* (Oxford: Oxford University Press, 2000), 303–417.

5 Augustine, *Confessions* 7.3, trans. R.S. Pine-Coffin (Harmondworth: Penguin, 1961), 136.

6 Emile Benveniste, *Problems in General Linguistics*, trans. Mary Elizabeth Meek (Coral Gables, Florida: University of Miami Press, 1971), 223–30.

7 James O'Donnell, *Augustine: Confessions: Commentary*, 2 vols (Oxford: Clarendon Press, 1992), 2.30. See also John M. Rist, *Augustine: Ancient Thought Baptised* (Cambridge: Cambridge University Press 1994), 148–202; Peter Brown, *Augustine of Hippo* (1967, London: Faber, 2000), 141ff.

8 Augustine, *Concerning the City of God Against the Pagans*, trans. Henry Bettenson (Harmondsworth: Penguin, 1972), 14.3.551.

9 Cp. *City of God* 14.13: '[Adam and Eve] could not have arrived at the evil act if an evil will had not preceded it. Now, could anything but pride have been the start of the evil will? For "pride is the start of every kind of sin". And what is pride except a longing for a perverse kind of exultation?' (571).

10 John Wilmot, Earl of Rochester, *The Complete Works*, ed. Frank H. Ellis (Harmondsworth: Penguin, 1994), 68.

11 Quotations from *Piers Plowman: the C Text*, ed. Derek Pearsall (Exeter: University of Exeter Press, 1994); here, C.5.88; the prayer in the Paternoster has been changed from 'Fiat voluntas tua'.

12 See Risto Saarinen, *Weakness of the Will in Medieval Thought: From Augustine to Buridan* (Leiden: E.J. Brill 1994), 87, 91. For the absence of free will in early modern Protestantism, see John Stachniewski, *The Persecutory Imagination: English Puritanism and the Literature of Religious Despair* (Oxford: Clarendon Press, 1991).

13 Quoted, Gordon Leff, *Medieval Thought* (Harmondsworth: Penguin, 1958), 270.

14 John M. Bowers, *The Crisis of Will in Piers Plowman* (Washington: Catholic University of America, 1986).

15 Janet Coleman, *Piers Plowman and the Moderni* (Roma: Edizioni di Storia e Letturatura, 1981), 31–33

16 See Gordon Leff, *Bradwardine and the Pelagians: A Study of the* De Causa Dei *and its Opponents* (Cambridge: Cambridge University Press, 1957) and Heiko Augustinus Oberman, *Archbishop Thomas Bradwardine: A Fourteenth-Century Augustinian* (Utrecht: Kemink & Zoon, 1957).

17 See David Lawton, 'The Subject of *Piers Plowman*', *Yearbook of Langland Studies* 1 (1987), 1–30.

18 See Anne M. Scott, 'Voluntary Poverty and Involuntary need: Will's Experience of being a Poor Man', in *Piers Plowman and the Poor* (Dublin: Four Courts Press, 2004), 156–92. Scott notes that merchants made wills before going on voyages (137).

19 James Simpson, *Piers Plowman: An Introduction*, 2nd edition (Exeter: University of Exeter Press, 2007), 86–90.

20 In the B text, the Dreamer says, "'I have lyved in londe", quod I, "my name is Longe Wille" (B.15.152); *The Vision of Piers Plowman: A Complete Version of the B-Text*, ed. A.V.C. Schmidt (London: Everyman, 1987), 181. This seems to be a line which establishes the name, signing the poem. See discussion by Anne Middleton, 'William Langland's "Kynde Name": Authorial Signature and Social Identity in Late Fourteenth-Century England', in Lee Patterson (ed.), *Literary Practice and Social Change in Britain, 1380–1530* (Berkeley: University of California Press, 1990), 15–82. She notes that 'longe wille' may imply 'long-sufferance' (43), and links 'longe' to the idea of longing, another form of willing; that the line relates to the 'Lond of Longyng' (B.11.7–9), which itself implies desire, or the will, and is itself 'an authorial signature' (44). John Burrow, in *Langland's Fictions* (Oxford: Clarendon Press, 1993), 82–108, supports the view of Passus 5 in the C text as corresponding to something in Langland, and also draws attention to the end of the confession of Wrath in B.5.183–85, which concludes with Repantance bidding Wrath to amend, and then, 'And bad me wilne to wepe my wikkednesse to amende', noting the auto-biographical and confessional moment there (88–89). See also Burrow, 'Words, Works and Will: Theme and Structure in *Piers Plowman*, in S.S. Hussey (ed.), *Piers Plowman: Critical Approaches* (London: Methuen, 1969), 111–24

21 See Bowers, 177, and Simpson, 90–91 for Thought as here 'a superficial state of rational reflection'.

22 See my treatment of melancholia in *Allegory and the Work of Melancholy: The Late Medieval and Shakespeare* (Amsterdam: Rodopi, 2004), in relation to *Piers Plowman*, and to a reading which suggests that Will becomes more and more an isolated figure of folly throughout the text: this for me consti-tutes much of its interest, as an early chapter in the history of madness. See also Scott, 180–92, and my discussions on *acedia* in *Dante in Purgatory: States of Affect* (Turnhout: Brepols, 2010).

23 Nicolette Zeeman, *Piers Plowman and the Medieval Discourse of Desire* (Cambridge: Cambridge University Press, 2006), 78. See her discussion of the will, 64–108.

24 Zeeman, 10. She quotes James Simpson, 65, that ME 'wil' translates 'both *sensualitas* and *voluntas* – both wayward desire and a rational appetite' (65).

25 Zeeman, 69. See Pearsall's note in his edition, 'Free Will is the highest gift of God to man: it is the whole intellectual and spiritual faculty of man divinely illumined'; Bowers' discussion (42) quotes E.T Donaldson, that free will is 'that part of man which bears the impress of the image of God to which man was created'.

26 Zeeman, 73. She quotes Louise Fradenburg, *Sacrifice Your Love: Psycho-analysis, Historicism, Chaucer* (Minneapolis: University of Minnesota Press, 2002), 200: on the will as 'a point of intersection between desire and intention, between the dissolution of resolution into sensuality and the gathering of the appetites around a deliberate decision to make something happen' (71).

27 Quotations from Kenneth Palmer's Arden edition (1982), and that of David Bevington (1998), and the Oxford, by Kenneth Muir (1982), and the Cambridge editions: Alice Walker (1957), Anthony Dawson (2003). All discussions of Shakespeare must take account of Quarto and Folio differences and difficulties of dating (here, Q and F): there is not space to treat these here, but see editions cited, and, for instance, Gary Taylor and Stanley Wells, with John Jowett and William Montgomery (eds.), *William Shakespeare: A Textual Companion* (New York: W.W. Norton, 1997). Where editions of the plays and poems are not cited, I use the Norton edition, ed. Stephen Greenblatt (New York: W.W. Norton, 1997). For the view that *Troilus* was written for the Inns of Court, see W.R. Elton, *Shakespeare's Troilus and Cressida and the Inns of Court* (Aldershot: Ashgate, 2000). For Achilles as Robert Devereux, Earl of Essex, executed 25 February 1601, see Eric S. Mallin, 'Emulous Factions and the Collapse of Chivalry: *Troilus and Cressida*', *Representations* 29 (1990), 145–79. The Armed Prologue may evoke Jonson's *Poetaster*, perhaps mid-1601.

28 See John D. Cox, 'The Error of our Eye in *Troilus and Cressida*', *Comparative Drama* 10 (1976), 147–71. Other exceptions are in *Henry VI part 2*, and *Titus Andronicus*. On the play, see G. Wilson Knight, *The Wheel of Fire* (Oxford: Oxford University Press, 1965), Derek Traversi, *An Approach to Shakespeare, vol. 2: Troilus and Cressida to The Tempest* (London: Hollis and Carter, 1969), 26–42; Jonathan Dollimore, *Radical Tragedy* (Chicago: Chicago University Press, 1984); Janet Adelman, *Suffocating Mothers: Fantasies of Maternal Origin in Shakespeare's Plays, Hamlet to The Tempest* (New York: Routledge, 1992), 38–65; Barbara Bowen, *Gender in the Theatre of War: Shakespeare's Troilus and Cressida* (New York: Garland, 1993).

29 Palmer annotates 'will' as 'self-will', adding: 'will is of course an ambiguous term and embodies already the sliding from egotism to lust'. He adds that 'appetite' includes all the passions, drawing attention to the line 'he that is proud eats up himself' (2.3.156). Thersites adds that 'lechery eats itself' (5.4.35).

30 Alison Findlay, *Illegitimate Power: Bastards in Renaissance Drama* (Manchester: Manchester University Press, 1994), 233. This comments on Thersites, but I do not agree that 'the text persistently encourages [the audience] to identify with the bastard's sceptical viewpoint' (235), even if this covers only on his Act 5 appearances.

31 The point is made by Muir (30) and by Palmer, not by Bevington.

32 See René Girard, 'The Politics of Desire in *Troilus and Cressida*', in Patricia Parker and Geoffrey Hartman (eds.), *Shakespeare and the Question of Theory* (London: Methuen, 1985), 188–209.

33 For 'ambivalence', making the subject both active and passive, masculine and feminine, sadistic and masochistic, see Freud's 'Instincts and their Vicissitudes', *SE* 14, 109–40. This discusses 'the phase of incorporating or devouring – a type of love which is consistent with abolishing the object's separate existence and which may therefore be described as ambivalent' (138).

34 Jane Adamson examines Achilles's reaction to seeing Hector, 4.5.241–45, that this 'woman's longing' has suddenly changed: 'there is no question in Achilles's mind about whether or not he will kill Hector; the only question is *where*' . . . .Achilles's "will" seems involuntary or prevoluntary. It rears up from some primitive substratum of his self, from somewhere way below the roots of "reasons". He wants to destroy Hector because the prospect of doing so is irresistibly desirable. He has a sudden "stomach" or hunger for those meaty limbs. None other will satisfy' – Jane Adamson, *Troilus and Cressida* (Brighton: Harvester, 1987), 131–32.

35 L.C. Knights, *Some Shakespearian Themes and an Approach to Hamlet* (Harmondsworth: Penguin 1966), 70.

36 Joel Fineman, 'Fratricide and Cuckoldry: Shakespeare's Doubles', in Murray Schwartz and Coppélia Kahn (eds.), *Representing Shakespeare: New Psychoanalytic Essays* (Baltimore: Johns Hopkins University Press, 1980), 95.

2 'I'LL BE REVENGED ON THE WHOLE PACK OF YOU': SHAKESPEARE AND MARSTON

1 Quotations from *The Merchant of Venice*, ed. M.M. Mahood (Cambridge: Cambridge University Press, 1987). *The Merchant of Venice* is usually dated to 1597–98, being entered in the Stationers' Register on 22 July 1598, which indicates that it had an alternative title, *The Jew of Venice*. Acted before James the First on 10 February 1605. Joan Ozark Holmer, *The Merchant of Venice: Choice, Hazard and Consequence* (London: Macmillan, 1995) gives a Christian reading, which seems idealising; see Janet Adelman, *Blood Relations: Christian and Jew in The Merchant of Venice* (Chicago: University of Chicago Press, 2008) stressing anti-semitism from the Christians; see also Lisa Freinkel, *Reading Shakespeare's Will* (New York: Columbia University Press, 2002), 237–91, and James Shapiro, *Shakespeare and the Jews* (New York: Columbia University Press, 1996), 187–89.

2 On Shakespeare's will, and inheritance in Shakespeare's plays, see Richard Wilson, 'A Constant Will to Publish: Shakespeare's Dead Hand' in *Will Power: Essays on Shakespearian Authority* (Hemel Hempstead: Harvester Wheatsheaf, 1993), 197–237. See also Joyce Rogers, *The Second Best Bed: Shakespeare's Will in a New Light* (Westport, Connecticut: Greenwood Press, 1993), on religious implications within the term 'second best bed' left to Shakespeare's wife; see also B.J. Sokol and Mary Sokol, *Shakespeare's Legal Language: A Dictionary* (London: Athlone, 2000).

3 For the father's will and the daughter's, see Deborah G. Burks, '"I'll Want my Will Else"': *The Changeling* and Women's Complicity with their Rapists', *ELH* 62.4 (1995), 759–90.

4 *As You Like It*, ed. Alan Brissenden (Oxford: Oxford University Press, 1993). Juliet Dusinberre, editing for the New Arden, believes it was performed on Shrove Tuesday, 1599. She compares the forest to the abbey of Thelema in Rabelais' *Gargantua*, as a place for discovering a new will and freedom: see her 'As *Who* Liked It?' *Shakespeare Survey* 46, 1993, 9–21.

5 See B.J. and Mary Sokol, *Shakespeare, Law and Marriage* (Cambridge: Cambridge University Press, 2003), 170–76, and 164–71.

6 Freud, 'The Theme of the Three Caskets', *SE* 12.291–301. See Sarah Kofman, 'Conversions: *The Merchant of Venice under the Sign of Saturn*', trans. Shaun Whiteside in Peter Collier and Helga Geyer-Ryan (eds.), *Literary Theory Today* (Cambridge: Polity Press, 1990), 142–66. There is another psychoanalytic reading of the play in Lyn Stephens, 'A Wilderness of Monkeys; A Psychodynamic Study of *The Merchant of Venice*' in B.J. Sokol (ed.), *The Undiscover'd Country: New Essays on Psychoanalysis and Shakespeare* (London: Free Association Books, 1993), 91–129. See also Leonard Tennenhouse, 'The Counterfeit Order of *The Merchant of Venice*' in Murray M. Schwartz and Coppélia Khan (eds.), *Representing Shakespeare: New Psychoanalytic Essays* (Baltimore: Johns Hopkins University Press, 1980), 54–69.

7 Mahood notes, though critically, the suggestion that the song 'Tell me where is Fancy bred' contains rhymes with 'lead'. That the song constructs Bassanio's thinking is persuasively discussed by Peter J. Seng, *The Vocal Songs in the Plays of Shakespeare: A Critical History* (Cambridge, Mass.: Harvard University Press, 1967), 36–43, and Harry Berger jr, 'Mercy and Mercifixion', *Making Trifles out of Terrors: Redistributing Complicities in Shakespeare* ed. Peter Erickson (Stanford: Stanford University Press, 1997), 1–9.

8 See Steve Patterson, 'The Bankruptcy of Homoerotic Amity in Shakespeare's *The Merchant of Venice*', *Shakespeare Quarterly* 50 (1999), 9–32.

9 Karen Newman, 'Portia's Ring: Unruly Women and Structures of Exchange', *Shakespeare Quarterly* 38 (1985), 19–33, quotation p. 31.

248

10 See Robert S. Bennett, 'The Reform of a Malcontent: Jaques and the Meaning of *As You Like It*', *Shakespeare Studies* 9 (1976), 183–204. For Jaques as parodying the traveller in Italy, see Z.S. Fink, 'Jaques and the Malcontent Traveler', *Philological Quarterly* 14 (1935), 237–52; this discusses 'malcontent' as a new word of the beginning of the 1580s, linking it from the start with political discontent (247).

11 Quotations from John Marston, *What You Will*, ed. M.R. Woodhead (Nottingham: Nottingham Drama Texts, 1980). First printed 1607, assumed to have been performed around 1601–2 as a play for the boys at St Paul's; soon after *Hamlet*, to which its plot, as often in Marston, refers (the husband, Albano has come back from being drowned, but his widow, Celia, has forgotten him). It is thought to contain a parody of Jonson's *Cynthia's Revels* (late 1600) as part of the 'War of the theatres', – from Jonson's *Every Man Out of his Humour* (Globe, late 1599) which referred to Marston's *Histriomastix*, probably performed at the Inns of Court in 1599, or else written for the re-opening of the St Paul's boys' theatre, September 1599, before Jonson's play. *Jack Drum's Entertainment* (perhaps by Marston) followed mid 1600, and *What You Will* in early 1601; followed by Jonson's attack on Marston and Dekker in *Poetaster*, perhaps late 1601, alongside Dekker's *Satiromastix*, perhaps written with Marston. See Philip J. Finkelpearl, *John Marston of the Middle Temple: An Elizabethan Dramatist in his Social Setting* (Cambride, Mass.: Harvard University Press, 1969), 162–77 and 178–94; George L. Geckle, *John Marston's Drama: Themes, Images, Sources* (Rutherford: Associated University Presses, 1980); T.F. Wharton (ed.), *The Drama of John Marston: Critical Revisions* (Cambridge: Cambridge University Press, 2000); essay on *What You Will* by Matthew Steggle (45–49), and for *The Malcontent*, Kiernan Ryan (145–61) and T.F. Wharton (181–93). On the war of the theatres, see Tom Cain (ed.), *Ben Jonson: Poetaster* (Manchester: Manchester University Press, 1995), 30–36.

12 Ben Jonson, *Every Man Out of his Humour*, ed. Helen Ostovich (Manchester: Manchester University Press, 2001), under 'Characters', 102. See Ann Barton, *Ben Jonson, Dramatist* (Cambridge: Cambridge University Press, 1984), 58–73.

13 See David Farley-Hills, *Shakespeare and the Rival Playwrights, 1600–1606* (London: Routledge, 1990), comparing *Troilus and Cressida* with *What You Will*.

14 See Lisa Jardine, 'Twins and Travesties: Gender, Dependency and Sexual Availability in *Twelfth Night*', in Susan Zimmerman (ed.), *Erotic Politics: Desire on the Renaissance Stage* (London: Routledge, 1992), 27–38. Here, 'dependent youths and dependent women are expected to "submit", under the order of familial authority, to those above them' (28).

15 *Twelfth Night*, first printed in the Folio, perhaps dates from 1601, with a

record of a performance at the Middle Temple in February 1602. Perhaps part of the 'war of the theatres', and satirical against Jonson: see Arden edition, ed. J.M. Lothian and T.W. Craik (London: Methuen, 1975), xxxii–xxxiv, suggesting the play was aware of *Satiromastix*. Cain's edition of *Poetaster* places *Twelfth Night* earlier, following *What You Will* by a few months (Cain, 36–38). Quotations from the Oxford edition, of Roger Warren and Stanley Wells (1994). See Barbara Everett, 'Or What You Will', *Essays in Criticism*, 35 (1985), 294–314, and J.L. Simmons, 'A Source for Shakespeare's Malvolio: The Elizabethan Controversy with the Puritans', *Huntington Library Quarterly* 36.3 (1973), 181–201, and Stephen Greenblatt, 'Fiction and Friction' in *Shakespearean Negotiations* (Berkeley: University of California Press, 1988), 66–93.

16 The name Fabian is used by Marston's friend Everard Guilpin, in his satires, *Skialetheia* (1598), succeeding Marston's *The Scourge of Villainy*, see Finkelpearl, 88. The link suggests the satirical nature of the trick played on Malvolio, and asks about the 'ill-will' of the satirist.

17 *The Malcontent* was performed by the children at Blackfriars' theatre *c.* 1603, printed 1604. Quotations from the Revels edition ed. G.K. Hunter (Manchester: Manchester University Press, 1975); also useful are the old New Mermaid editions of Bernard Harris (1967), and W. David Kay (London: A.C. Black, 1998) and the Cambridge edition of *The Selected Plays of John Marston*, ed. MacDonald P. Jackson and Michael Neill (1986). See Ira Clark, 'Character and Cosmos in Marston's *Malcontent*', *Modern Language Studies* 13.2 (1983), 80–86 and John Greenwood, 'The Mannerist Marston', *Modern Language Review* 82.4 (1987), 817–29; Douglas Lanier, 'Satire, Self-Concealment and Statecraft: The Game of Identity in John Marston's *The Malcontent*', *Pacific Coast Philology* 22 (1987), 35–45; T.F. Wharton, '*The Malcontent*: Dreams, Visions, Fantasies', *Essays in Criticism* 24 (1974), 261–74. R.A. Foakes, *Shakespeare: The Dark Comedies to the Last Plays: From Satire to Celebration* (London: Routledge and Kegan Paul, 1971), 31–81 is useful.

18 Walter Benjamin, *The Origin of German Tragic Drama*, trans. John Osborne (London: Verso, 1977), 88. See James R. Keller, *Princes, Soldiers and Rogues: The Politic Malcontent of Renaissance Drama* (New York: Peter Lang, 1993).

19 For sexual images associated with the malcontent, e.g. of castration and homosexuality (the malcontent is 'male-content'), see Mark Thornton Burnett, 'Staging the Malcontent in Early Modern England', in Arthur F. Kinney (ed.), *A Companion to Renaissance Drama* (Oxford: Blackwell, 2002), 336–52.

20 On tragi-comedy, see David L. Hirst, *Tragicomedy* (London: Methuen, 1984), and Larry S. Champion, '*The Malcontent* and the Shape of Elizabethan-Jacobean Comedy', *Studies in English Literature 1500–1900* 25.2 (1985), 361–79.

21 Quotations from the old Arden *Much Ado About Nothing*, ed. A.R. Humphreys (1981). The play appeared as a Quarto in 1600. See Jean E. Howard, 'Renaissance Antitheatricality and the Politics of Gender and Rank in *Much Ado About Nothing*' in Jean E. Howard and Marion E. O'Connor, *Shakespeare Reproduced: The Text in History and Ideology* (London: Methuen, 1987), 163–87.

22 I assume Thomas Middleton's authorship, the date, late 1606: see MacDonald P. Jackson in Gary Taylor and John Lavignino (eds.), *Thomas Middleton and Early Modern Textual Culture: A Companion to the Collected Works* (Oxford: Clarendon Press, 2007), 360–63.

23 On melancholy and the malcontent, see L.C. Knights, *Drama and Society in the Age of Jonson* (Harmondsworth: Penguin, 1962), 261–74.

24 The quotation, from Coleridge's notes, comes from his *Lectures 1809–1819: On Literature*, ed. R.A. Foakes (Princeton: Princeton University Press, 1987), vol. 2, 315.

25 *Othello*, Oxford edition, ed. Michael Neill (2006). I also use the Arden, ed. E.A.J. Honigmann (1997). M.J. Ridley's Arden (1958) works with the Quarto (1622). Performed before James 1 on November 1 1604, Neill dates its writing to 1602–3, associating it with *Hamlet*, and *Troilus and Cressida* (399–404); Honigmann more with *Twelfth Night*, 1601–2. The *Textual Companion*, 126, puts the play in 1603–4, after *Measure for Measure*.

26 See Hugh Grady, 'Iago and the Dialectic of Enlightenment: Reason, Will, and Desire in *Othello*', *Criticism* 37.4 (1995), 537–58, the basis of Grady's *Shakespeare's Universal Wolf: Studies in Early Modern Reification* (Oxford: Clarendon Press, 1996). For Adorno and Horkheimer, see *Dialectic of Enlightenment*, 89.

27 Joel Fineman, 'The Sound of O in *Othello*: The Real of the Tragedy of Desire' in *The Subjectivity Effect in Western Literary Tradition: Essays towards the Release of Shakespeare's Will* (Cambridge, Mass.: MIT Press, 1991), 143–64. Fineman relates the *thel* of Othello to Greek *thelema*, Greek for 'will'; cp. footnote 4 above.

28 Freud, 'Some Neurotic Mechanisms in Jealousy, Paranoia and Homosexuality' (1922), *SE* 18.224.

29 T.G.A. Nelson and Charles Haines, 'Othello's Unconsummated Marriage', *Essays in Criticism* 33 (1983), 1–18.

3 LAW AND WILL IN *MEASURE FOR MEASURE*

1 Quotations from *Measure for Measure*, ed. N.W. Bawcutt (Oxford: Oxford University Press, 1991). Also used: the Arden edition ed. J.W. Lever (London: Methuen, 1965), the Penguin, ed. J.M. Nosworthy (Harmondsworth, 1969) and the New Cambridge, ed. Brian Gibbons

(Cambridge, 1991). The play appears in Gary Taylor and John Lavagnino (eds.), *Thomas Middleton: The Collected Works*, 2 vols (Oxford: Oxford University Press, 2008), vol 1. 1542–85, ed. John Jowett, arguing that it was revised by Middleton perhaps 'several years after Shakespeare's death', but before the Folio (1623). See also Stanley Wells and Gary Taylor (eds.), *William Shakespeare: A Textual Companion* (New York: W.W. Norton, 1997), 468–75, and Gary Taylor and John Jowett, *Shakespeare Reshaped 1606–1623* (Oxford: Oxford University Press, 1993), 107–236. 'Revisions' are especially to 1.2.1–82, seen as added material, some additions to Escalus's speeches in 2.1. (especially 37–40, 263–73), the transposition of the Duke's soliloquies in 3.1.515–36 and 4.1.58–63, and additional material in 4.1.1–25, and 4.3.1–18. I do not discuss the Shakespeare/Middleton relationship, but assume that it does not materially affect a reading of the play which assumes single authorship.

2 'Mercy' appears fifteen times, after 'mortality and mercy' (1.1.45). Escalus says 'mercy is not itself that oft looks so, / Pardon is still the nurse of second woe' (2.1.270–71). Isabella makes it a synonym for pardon (2.2.49–50; 2.4.113). She speaks of the value of mercy (2.2.63, 2.2.79), and of Angelo's 'devilish mercy' (3.1.66). To Claudio, she says 'Mercy to thee would prove itself a bawd' (3.1.152). Lucio speaks of the Duke's mercy (3.1.382); Escalus says of Mistress Overdone's continuance in bawdiness, 'This would make mercy swear and play the tyrant' (3.1.451). Mariana says to the Duke 'I cry you mercy, sir' (4.1.10), and the Duke comments on Angelo's supposed 'pardon' (4.2.112–13). For 'mercy' in 5.1.479, and 5.1.487, see below.

3 For the disguised Duke, and other disguised rulers, see Rosalind Miles, *The Problem of Measure for Measure* (London: Vision 1976), 125–96, and Thomas A. Pendleton, 'Shakespeare's Disguised Duke Play: Middleton, Marston, and the Sources of *Measure for Measure*', in John W. Mahon and Thomas A. Pendleton (eds.), *'Fanned and Winnowed Opinions': Shakespearian Essays Presented to Harold Jenkins* (London: Methuen, 1987), 79–98, discussing *The Phoenix* and *The Malcontent*. Amongst other material on the play not otherwise referenced, see William Empson, 'Sense in *Measure for Measure*', *The Structure of Complex Words* (London: Chatto and Windus, 1951), 270–88.

4 Gibbons, 116, gives three readings of this: 'referring to Angelo's corrupt hope of seducing her, and so "crossing" the pious hope for his honour that she has just uttered', and 'Angelo means that he is going towards evil where his daily prayers ask that he may *not* be led' and 'where prayers *thwart* and *impede* will'.

5 'If the will is wrongly directed, the emotions will be wrong; if the will is right, the emotions will be not only blameless, but praiseworthy. The will is engaged in all of them; in fact they are all essentially acts of will' –

Augustine, *City of God* 14.6, trans. Henry Bettenson (Harmondsworth: Penguin 1972), 555.

6　The Folio reads 'all-building law'; Johnson proposed the emendation.

7　L.C. Knights, 'The Ambiguity of "Measure for Measure"', *Scrutiny* 10 (1942), 223. The essay by F.R. Leavis, 'The Greatness of "Measure for Measure"', *Scrutiny* 10 (1942), 234–47, and that by D. A. Traversi, '"Measure for Measure"', *Scrutiny* 11 (1942), 40–58, are part of a crucial debate about the play, partly deriving from G. Wilson Knight, '*Measure for Measure* and the Gospels', *The Wheel of Fire*, 73–96. The theological reading is most emphasised in R.W. Battenhouse, '*Measure for Measure* and the Christian Doctrine of the Atonement,' *PMLA* 61 (1946), 1029–59.

8　Bawcutt and Gibbons (124) reject the emendation 'that long I have been sick for'; Gibbons saying of 'longing' that 'omission of the personal pronoun possibly gives extra emphasis to this word, with its erotic connotation'.

9　For 'brakes of ice', see *Textual Companion* 471 (Bawcutt amends to 'brakes of vice'), and see the discussions by Lever, who, taking 'brakes' as 'constrictions' suggests that 'brakes of ice' means 'hell-pains'; he also refers to James Winny's defence of 'brake' as 'thicket', by comparison with *Henry the Eighth* 1.2.75–77: 'the rough brake / That virtue must go through'. For 'brakes' as 'breaks' see R.V. Holdsworth, '*Measure for Measure*, Middleton and "Brakes of Ice"' *Notes and Queries* 236 (1991), 64–67. Gibbons (101) agrees, citing *The Revenger's Tragedy* 4.4.79–81 on women's falsity: 'Why she first begins with one / Who afterwards to a thousand proves a whore: "Break ice in one place, it will crack in more"' (Middleton edition, see note 1). See also Pendleton (note 3, 92–93) comparing the lines with the Epilogue to *The Malcontent* lines 5–9.

10　The pun on 'fault' and 'false' is discussed by Stephen Booth, *Shakespeare's Sonnets* (New Haven 1977), 480–81. Perhaps 'fall' is also heard in 'fault'. See John H. Ashington, '"Fault" in Shakespeare', *Shakespeare Quarterly* 36 (1985), 330–34.

11　See, for example, David Craig, 'Love and Society: *Measure for Measure* and our own Times' in Arnold Kettle (ed.), *Shakespeare in a Changing World* (London: Lawrence and Wishart, 1964), 195–216. For the sexual implications of Isabella's chastity, see William Empson, *Seven Types of Ambiguity* (1930) (Harmondsworth: Penguin, 1961), 202–3. See the double meanings in 'art' and 'play' in Claudio's description: 'she hath prosperous art /When she will play with reason and discourse' (1.2.182–83).

12　Jacques Derrida, 'Force of Law: The "Mystical Foundation of Authority"', *Acts of Religion*, ed. Gil Anidjar (London: Routledge, 2002), 277.

13　See David Lindley, 'The Stubbornness of Barnardine: Justice and Mercy in *Measure for Measure*', *Shakespeare Yearbook* 7 (1996), 333–51.

14 The point is emphasised by James Smith, *Shakespearian and Other Essays* (Cambridge: Cambridge University Press, 1974), 112.

15 So Darryl J. Gless, *Measure for Measure: The Law and the Convent* (Princeton, 1979), 195–96, comparing Isabella's desire for 'justice' with *The Spanish Tragedy*'s drive towards revenge.

16 Mary Lascelles, *Shakespeare's Measure for Measure* (London: Athlone, 1953): 'he is pardoned for the sake of Isabel's dead brother to intimate that, after the experience he has undergone, he is indeed as one returned from the dead' (130, with emphasis in original).

17 Jacques Derrida, *On Cosmopolitanism and Forgiveness*, trans. Mark Dooley and Michael Hughes (London: Routledge, 2001), 27. Derrida's emphasis.

4 THE 'CRAFT OF WILL' IN SHAKESPEARE'S POETRY

1 Francis Meres had already referred to Shakespeare's 'sugred Sonnets among his private friends' in *Palladis Tamia, Wit's Treasury*, 1598, as well as *Venus and Adonis* and *The Rape of Lucrece*. See Norton edition 3324–25 for Meres on Shakespeare. It is not essential to assume that the Sonnets Meres refers to are those of *Shakespeare's Sonnets*. Sonnets 138 and 144 appeared in William Jaggard's publication of *The Passionate Pilgrim. By W. Shakespeare* in 1599. This comprised twenty poems, including three sonnets from the 1598 Quarto of *Love's Labour's Lost*. Editions of the poems, including *The Rape of Lucrece* and *A Lover's Complaint* which I have used, include: F.T. Prince (Arden, 1960), J.C. Maxwell (Cambridge, 1969), John Roe (Cambridge, 2006), and Katherine Duncan-Jones and H.R. Woudhuysen (Arden, 2007). Maxwell, while negative about *A Lover's Complaint*, dates it to the 1600s, associating it most with *Troilus and Cressida*. For a minority view that *A Lover's Complaint* is not by Shakespeare, see Brian Vickers, *Shakespeare, A Lover's Complaint and John Davies of Hereford* (Cambridge: Cambridge University Press, 2007); see Roe, 59–61, 78–79.

2 The Quarto version appears in Stephen Booth, *Shakespeare's Sonnets* (New Haven: Yale University Press, 1977); see 466 for Booth on the Quarto's printing of 'will'. Other editions of the Sonnets: John Kerrigan for Penguin (1986), G. Blakemore Evans for Cambridge, introduction by Anthony Hecht (1996), Katherine Duncan-Jones for Arden (London: Thomson, 1997); and Helen Vendler, *The Art of Shakespeare's Sonnets* (Cambridge, Mass.: Harvard University Press, 1997) and Colin Burrow, *The Complete Sonnets and Poems* (Oxford, 2002).

3 See Michael Hattaway, 'Fleshing his will in the Spoil of her Honour: Desire, Misogyny and the Perils of Chivalry', *Shakespeare Survey* 46 (1984), 121–35.

4 *Venus and Adonis* appeared in a Quarto of 1593, and *The Rape of Lucrece* in

1594, being entered in the Stationers' Register 9 May 1594, as called 'the Ravyshement of Lucrece'; and called 'Lucrece' simply on the title-page. On the 'sick-thoughted' (*Venus and Adonis*, 5), i.e. lovesick Venus' desires, see Catherine Belsey, 'Love as *trompe l'oeil*: Taxonomies of Desire in *Venus and Adonis*', *Shakespeare Quarterly* 46 (1995), 252–76.

5 On *The Rape of Lucrece*, see Coppélia Kahn, 'The Rape in Shakespeare's *Lucrece*', *Shakespeare Studies* 9 (1976), 45–72 (an early feminist analysis); Sarah E. Quay, '"Lucrece the Chaste": The Construction of Rape in Shakespeare's "The Rape of Lucrece"', *Modern Language Studies* 25 (1995), 3–17; Catherine Belsey, 'Tarquin Dispossessed: Expropriation and Consent in "The Rape of Lucrece"; *Shakespeare Quarterly* 52 (2001), 315–35, which reads the text in the light of Augustine's comments on Lucrece, and gives a full bibliography; '"Read it in me": The Author's Will in *Lucrece*', *Shakespeare Quarterly* 57 (2006), 45–70. See Joel Fineman, 'Shakespeare's Will: The Temporality of Rape', *Representations* 20 (1987), 25–76; page-references come from this, but it is reprinted in *The Subjectivity Effect in Western Literary Tradition: Essays towards the Release of Shakespeare's Will* (Cambridge, Mass.: MIT Press, 1991), with an introduction by Stephen Greenblatt.

6 Duncan-Jones and Woudhuysen note at 1299 oppositions between wit and will in Shakespeare, and in Sidney's *Apologie for Poetry*: 'our erected wit maketh us know what perfection is, and yet our infected will keepeth us from reaching unto it'. See also Maxwell's conjectural reading of 'A Lover's Complaint', 161; 'By blunting us, to make our wits more keen' to 'make our wills more keen'; note Roe's comment on this. *Lucrece* 1299 suggests that the will not only cancels out the wit, but also, if wit and will associate with each other rather than contrast, reinforces it, makes the testamentary will more forceful.

7 Reviewing Brian Vickers, *Shakespeare, A Lover's Complaint, and John Davies of Hereford* by David Bevington, *Renaissance Quarterly*, 60 (2007), 1463–66 (see 1465).

8 Duncan-Jones follows the Quarto, 'Consent's bewitched' (and see Burrow's note): consent is bewitched before he has granted the desire of the consenting person to be seduced.

9 For this group of sonnets addressed to the woman, see Michael J. B. Allen, 'Shakespeare's Man Descending a Staircase: Sonnets 126 to 154', *Shakespeare Survey* 31 (1978), 127–38. He quotes Philip Edwards on these poems as 'describing a certain kind of hopelessness'.

10 For a brief account of the state of knowledge about the Sonnets, see Paul Edmondson and Stanley Wells, *Shakespeare's Sonnets* (Oxford: Oxford University Press, 2004), and Josephine A. Roberts, '"Thou maist have thy *Will*": The Sonnets of Shakespeare and his Stepsisters', *Shakespeare Quarterly*

47 (1996), 407–23; this quotes the proverb 'Women must have their wills while they live because they make none when they die' (417). For their dating, see A. Kent Hieatt, Charles W. Hieatt and Anne Lake Prescott, 'When Did Shakespeare Write Sonnets 1609?' *Studies in Philology* 88 (1991), 69–109. On Shakespeare as aware of being both writer for the theatre and poet, especially in poems addressed to the young man, see Patrick Cheney on Shakespeare's poetry, *Shakespeare: National Poet-Playwright* (Cambridge: Cambridge University Press, 2004), giving informative readings of the poems.

11 Joel Fineman, *Shakespeare's Perjured Eye: The Invention of Poetic Subjectivity in the Sonnets* (Berkeley: University of California Press, 1986), 289–96. Fineman died in 1989; drafts towards his book on the will appeared in *The Subjectivity Effect in Western Literary Tradition: Essays towards the Release of Shakespeare's Will.*

12 Fineman, 'Shakespeare's Will: The Temporality of Rape', *Representations* 20 (1987), 29.

13 See 'Shakespeare's Ear': 'Shakespeare's sonnets, because they explicitly put the difference *of* language into words, thereby invent and motivate the poetics of heterosexuality, by which I . . . specify a necessarily misogynist desire, on the part of a necessarily male subject, whom the sonnets call "Will" for the true-false Woman who exists as a peculiar and paradoxical but still necessary "hetero-" or other, to the essential sameness of a familiar and profoundly orthodox "homo-" (*The Subjectivity Effect*, 224).

14 Syneciosis, as oxymoronic, produces a 'strange harmony by linking together an adjective and noun of opposing meanings. But the label also applies to a statement that uncovers similarities in two seemingly dissimilar things', one example being where opposites have the same etymology' – Heather Dubrow, *Captive Victors: Shakespeare's Narrative Poems and Sonnets* (Ithaca: Cornell University Press, 1987), 80–82. Dubrow analyses *Lucrece* through a distinction between antithesis and syneciosis, the first relating to Lucrece, the second to the world of rape: she sees a 'confrontation between a sensibility predicated on the clarities of antithesis and a world based on the complexities of syneciosis' (101).

15 The Lacanian expression appears in the 'Seminar on *The Purloined Letter*', *Ecrits*, trans. Bruce Fink (New York: W.W. Norton, 2006), 30.

16 See Fineman's footnote 35, quoting from Lacan on 'The Purloined Letter', saying it is a 'shorthand way of summarising his understanding of how it happens a subject comes to be a desiring subject when he accedes to speech'. In Fineman, Collatine has passed from 'true vision to false language' ('The Temporality of Rape', 75), the condition of the 'will'.

17 See comments on Fineman by Colin Burrow in his edition of *The Complete Sonnets and Poems* (Oxford, 2002), 13–15. He considers that the sonnets to

the woman were written earlier. Fineman's argument, however, is not a chronological one, nor to do with poetic sophistication, but with the unity presented by the book's publication in 1609. It is in the book's effect that there appears a 'modern consciousness', a concept Burrow overly plays down. The various Ardens make no mention of Fineman, nor does Cheney, but he attracts a strong reaction from Lisa Freinkel, *Reading Shakespeare's Will* (New York: Columbia University Press, 2002), which includes chapters on the Sonnets, and on 135 and 136 in particular, and on *The Merchant of Venice*. She calls him a 'formalist' (xix) presumably on the basis of his close readings, saying that the chiastic structures he discovers in the poems mean that there is no movement forward in them, such as she wants to find through an Augustinian figural interpretation. But she neglects his argument about sexual difference. See also, against Fineman, Marion Trousdale, 'Reading the Early Modern Text', *Shakespeare Survey* 50 (1997), 135–45.

18 See discussion of the relationship of melancholia to complaint, and to exaggeration in Freud's 'Mourning and Melancholia', *SE* 14.248.

19 Compare 112.3: 'For what care I who calls me well or ill', and see Booth's comments, 362–63. See Vendler on sonnet 58, on a complex of puns on will, ill, hell, well, with other words: kill (sonnet 40), evil (119), vile, will and evil in 121, and ill, evil, devil and hell in 144, plus the Quarto spelling of evill, which gives ill; devil includes evil, and evil and vile form an anagram.

20 Vendler (389) calls these 'attainder poems', and adds no. 87; she thinks the group turns on 'the young man's repudiation of the speaker' (391).

21 Peter L. Rudnytsky, '"The Darke and Vicious Place": The Dread of the Vagina in *King Lear*', *Modern Philology* 96.3 (1999), 291–311.

22 Vendler paraphrases the first three lines, assuming that the lady has refused, saying: 'Come not so near – my soul rebuffs thy will'. The 'I' answers: '"If thy soul check thee that I come so near, thy soul is blind. Will is a faculty of the soul, along with intellect, and thy soul knows (not having lost its other faculty, intellect), that *will* belongs in the soul too"' (578).

23 Fineman, *Shakespeare's Perjured Eye*, 285.

24 See Cheney, 84, quoting Richard Halpern, and 94

25 Burrow, 130, discusses Stephen Orgel's reading, in *Impersonations: The Performance of Gender in Shakespeare's England* (Cambridge: Cambridge University Press, 1996), 57, which allows the reading of 'Mine be thy love, and thy love's use their treasure' as 'let my love be yours, and let your loves make use of their treasure'.

26 See Richard P. Wheeler, '"And my loud crying still" – The Sonnets, *The Merchant of Venice* and *Othello*', in *Shakespeare's 'Rough Magic': Renaissance Essays in Honour of C.L. Barber*, ed. Peter Erickson and Coppélia Kahn (Newark: University of Delaware Press, 1982), 193–209.

27 David Schalkwyk, *Speech and Performance in Shakespeare's Sonnets and Plays* (Cambridge: Cambridge University Press, 2002), 187

28 One of the poems included in *The Passsionate Pilgrim*, with slight differences; see Booth, 496.

5 DICKENS AND TROLLOPE

1 Tobias Smollett, *Roderick Random* (1748), ch. 4, ed. Paul-Gabriel Boucé (Oxford: Oxford University Press, 1979), 14.

2 Walter Scott, *Guy Mannering* (1815) 2.17, ed. Peter Garside and Jane Millgate (Harmondsworth: Penguin, 2003), 220.

3 T.S. Eliot, *The Waste Land*, 409–10, in *The Complete Poems and Plays* (London: Faber and Faber, 1969), 74.

4 See Arthur S. Marks, 'Wilkie, Hogarth & Hazlitt: "The Reading of a Will": Its Origins and Legacy', *Studies in Romanticism* 48.4 (2009), 583–640; Nicholas Tromans, *David Wilkie: The People's Painter* (Edinburgh: Edinburgh University Press, 2007), 48–51.

5 James Boswell, *Boswell's Life of Johnson*, ed. Mowbray Morris (London: Macmillan, 1894), 270.

6 See Cathrine O. Frank, *Law, Literature and the Transmission of Culture in England, 1837–1925* (Farnham: Ashgate, 2010).

7 See Nicholas Powell, in Evelyn Joll, Martin Butlin and Luke Herrmann, *The Oxford Companion to Turner* (Oxford: Oxford University Press, 2001), 382–84.

8 See R. D. McMaster, *Trollope and the Law* (London: Macmillan, 1986), and Richard C. Buke, 'Accommodation and Transcendence: Last Wills in Trollope's Novels', *Dickens Studies Annual* 15 (1986), 291–307. For Trollope's conservatism, see Asa Briggs, 'Trollope, Bagehot, and the English Constitution', *Victorian People* (Harmondsworth: Penguin, 1965), 95–124,

9 Quotations from *Orley Farm*, ed. David Skilton, 2 vols in 1 (Oxford: Oxford University Press, 1985). See Glynn-Ellen Fisichelli, 'The Language of Law and Love: Anthony Trollope's *Orley Farm*', *ELH* 61 (1994), 635–53.

10 Quoted, Kieran Dolin, *Fiction and the Law: Legal Discourse in Victorian and Modernist Literature* (Cambridge: Cambridge University Press, 1999), 117.

11 Coral Lansbury, *The Reasonable Man: Trollope's Legal Fiction* (Princeton: Princeton University Press, 1981), 166.

12 Anthony Trollope, *The Eustace Diamonds*, ch. 25, ed. Stephen Gill and John Sutherland (Harmondsworth: Penguin, 1969), 261–66. See Alan Roth, 'He Thought he was Right (But Wasn't)': Property Law in *The Eustace Diamonds*', *Stamford Law Review* 44 (1992), 897–97.

13 Anthony Trollope, *Cousin Henry*, ed. Julian Thompson (Oxford: Oxford University Press, 1987), 250

14 Wilkie Collins, *The Moonstone*, ed. John Sutherland (Oxford: World's Classics, 1999), 424.

15 See Alexander Welsh, *Strong Representations: Narrative and Circumstantial Evidence in England* (Baltimore: Johns Hopkins University Press, 1992): for *The Moonstone*, 215–36.

16 George Eliot, *Adam Bede*, ch. 17, ed. Stephen Gill (Harmondsworth: Penguin, 1980), 177

17 Wilkie Collins, *The Woman in White*, ed. John Sutherland (Oxford: Oxford University Press, 1996), 5, 6.

18 See John R. Reed, *Victorian Will* (Athens: Ohio University Press, 1989), 245–74 (Dickens), 277–308 (Eliot). Reed's subject is free will.

19 Charles Dickens, *David Copperfield*, ed. Jeremy Tambling (Harmondsworth: Penguin, 2004), 941. Further references in the text.

20 Quotation, Nina Burgis, ed., *David Copperfield* (Oxford: Oxford University Press, 1981), xxiii.

21 Dickens, *Bleak House*, ch. 8, ed. Norman Page, with introduction by J. Hillis Miller (Harmondsworth: Penguin, 1971), 145. See Timothy Peltason, 'Esther's Will' in my *Bleak House: New Casebooks* (London: Macmillan, 1998), 205–27.

22 On Chancery, see Susan Shatto, *The Companion to Bleak House* (London: Unwin Hyam, 1988), 28–30.

23 On Eldon as Lord Chancellor, see Rose A. Melikan, *John Scott, Lord Eldon, 1751–1838: The Duty of Loyalty* (Cambridge: Cambridge University Press, 1999), 295–325.

24 See Marjorie Stone, 'Dickens, Bentham, and the Fictions of the Law: A Victorian Controversy and Its Consequences', *Victorian Studies* 29 (1985), 125–54.

25 Dieter Paul Polloczek, *Literature and Legal Discourse: Equity and Ethics from Sterne to Conrad* (Cambridge: Cambridge University Press, 1999), 169. Polloczek quotes William Holdsworth, *Charles Dickens as a Legal Historian* (1928) (New York: Haskell House, 1972), saying that Dickens was anachronistic in his conception of Chancery, as in the article in *Household Words*, 'The Martyrs of Chancery' (7 December 1850), not necessarily by Dickens. He counters it via Trevor Blount, 'The Documentary Symbolism of Chancery in *Bleak House*', *Dickensian* 62 (1966), 47–52, 106–11, 167–74; on the lag in carrying out reformist intentions. Polloczek (171) sees Gridley in *Bleak House* as based on the Challinor case of 1849, 'about a problematic transfer of property that made equity courts rich', and discusses 'the famous Jennings case, which began in 1798, and which was about a missing will needed to transfer enormous amounts of property, lasted

eighty years before a legitimate heir was determined'. He recalls K.J. Fielding and Alec Brice, 'Charles Dickens on "The Exclusion of Evidence"', *Dickensian* 64 (1968), 131–40, 65 (1969), 35–41, discussing Jo, the crossing-sweeper in Tom-all Alone's, 'based on the real George Ruby, in connection with the equally disturbing case against Thomas Hall in 1848–49' (171). Hall was accused of 'an atrocious offence' against his daughter, but the girl's evidence was not taken on the grounds of her ignorance of religion. The law seems to make people out to be mental incompetents. For Ruby, see Humphry House, *The Dickens World* (Oxford: Oxford University Press, 1942), 32–33.

26 Dickens, *Pickwick Papers*, ed. Mark Wormald (Harmondsworth: Penguin, 2003).

27 Dickens, *Nicholas Nickleby*, ch. 46, ed. Mark Ford (Harmondsworth: Penguin, 2003), 570.

28 Dickens, *Little Dorrit* (Oxford: Oxford University Press, 1953), Book the First, 2.20. This includes Lionel Trilling's introduction to the novel.

29 Michel Foucault, *Discipline and Punish: The Birth of the Prison*, trans. Alan Sheridan (Harmondsworth: Penguin, 1977): 'a body is docile that may be subjected, used, transformed and improved' (136).

30 Michael G. Cooke, *The Romantic Will* (New Haven: Yale University Press, 1976), quoting *Biographia Literaria*, ed. J. Shawcross (Oxford: Clarendon Press, 1907), 1.202), 17.

31 F.R. and Q.D. Leavis, *Dickens the Novelist* (London: Chatto and Windus, 1970), 230, 231.

32 Nietzsche uses '*ressentiment*' in *On the Genealogy of Morals* 1.10, trans. Douglas Smith (Oxford: Oxford University Press, 1996), 22.

33 Dostoyevsky, *Humiliated and Insulted*, trans. Ignat Avsey 4.4 (London: One World Classics, 2008), 282. See Joseph Frank, *Dostoevsky: The Stir of Liberation, 1860–1865* (Princeton: Princeton University Press, 1988), 110–30; Ronald Hingley, *The Undiscovered Dostoyevsky* (Westport, Connecticut: Greenwood Press, 1962), 41–59.

34 See Nietzsche, *On the Genealogy of Morals*, trans. Douglas Smith (Oxford: Oxford University Press 1996), 1.13.30.

35 On the father, see Diane F. Sadoff, 'Storytelling and the Figure of the Father in *Little Dorrit*', *PMLA*, 95 (1980), 234–45.

36 See Nietzsche, *On the Genealogy of Morals*, trans. Douglas Smith (Oxford: Oxford University Press, 1996), 2.4.44–45.

37 Lionel Trilling, *E.M. Forster* (1943) (New York: New Directions, 1964), 184, see also 9, 180–84.

38 John Stuart Mill, *Autobiography*, ed. Harold Laski (Oxford: Oxford University Press, 1924), 120–21. See my 'Carlyle through Nietzsche: Reading *Sartor Resartus*', *MLR*, 102 (2007), 326–40, and for Dickens and

for Utilitarianism, 'Sameness and Otherness: Versions of Authority in *Hard Times*', *Textus* 19 (2006), 439–60.

39 See 'From *Nobody's Fault* to *Little Dorrit*', in John Butt and Kathleen Tillotson, *Dickens at Work* (London: Methuen, 1968), 222–33.

40 Charles Kingsley, *Alton Locke: Tailor and Poet: An Autobiography*, ch. 22 (London: Macmillan, 1879), 227. Cp: 'I began to look on man . . . as the creature and puppet of circumstances – of the particular outward system, social or political, in which he happens to find himself. An abominable heresy, no doubt; but somehow, it appears to me just the same as Benthamites, and economsts, and high-churchmen too, for that matter, have been preaching for the last twenty years with great applause from their respective parties' (10.119).

41 Dickens, *Our Mutual Friend*, ed. Joel J. Brattin (London: Everyman 2000), Book 4 chapter 14, p. 837.

6 GEORGE ELIOT AND THE 'MURDEROUS WILL'

1 William Blake, 'Annotations to Swedenborg's *Wisdom of Angels Concerning Divine Love and Divine Wisdom*', *Complete Writings*, ed. Geoffrey Keynes (Oxford: Oxford University Press, 1966), 89.

2 George Eliot, *Romola* (1862–63), ed. Dorothea Barrett (Harmondsworth: Penguin, 2005), ch. 11, 116, quoting *The Eumenides*, 515–25.

3 Blake's poems preface two chapters of *Middlemarch* – 25 and 76. The point suggests the links between Blake and Lawrence enforced by Leavis, whose writings on the latter discuss the will as equivalent to the ego: assertive, cruel: see Leavis' *D.H. Lawrence: Novelist* on *Women in Love* (Harmondsworth: Penguin, 1964), 152–205. See also Leavis's 'Gwendolen Harleth' in *The Critic as Anti-Philosopher*, ed. G. Singh (London: Chatto and Windus, 1982) 65–75, concluding with Lawrence's 'The Crown' – 'we cannot subject a divine process to a static will, not without blasphemy and loathsomeness' (74). Leavis applies this to Deronda's relationship with Gwendolen.

4 In these novels, F.R. Leavis, in *The Great Tradition: George Eliot, Henry James, Joseph Conrad* (1948; Harmondsworth: Penguin, 1962), 39–140 distinguished between the rendering of individual lives and the idealising political views (the politics in *Felix Holt* and the Jewish Utopianism of *Daniel Deronda*, the idealising of Dorothea Brooke). Compare Raymond Williams, *Culture and Society 1780–1950* (Harmondsworth: Penguin, 1963), 112–19, and Terry Eagleton, *Criticism and Ideology* (London: Verso, 1976), 110–25. He cites Eliot's letter to Frederic Harrison, 15 August 1866, on 'the severe effort of trying to make certain ideas thoroughly incarnate, as if they had revealed themselves to me first in the flesh and not in

the spirit. I think aesthetic teaching is the highest of all teaching because it deals with life in its highest complexity. But if it ceases to be purely aesthetic – if it lapses anywhere from the picture to the diagram – it becomes the most offensive of all teaching' (*The George Eliot Letters*, ed. Gordon Haight (New Haven: Yale University Press, 1956), vol. 4.300, quoted 118.

5 George Eliot, *Scenes of Clerical Life*, ed. David Lodge (Harmondsworth: Penguin, 1973), 2.257.

6 George Levine, 'Determinism and Philosophy in the Works of George Eliot', *PMLA* 77 (1962), 268–79.

7 George Eliot, *Adam Bede*, ed. Stephen Gill (Harmondsworth: Penguin, 1980), ch. 16, 171.

8 Eliot notes 'the peasant's inveterate habit of litigation', comparing it with episodes from *Guy Mannering* and *The Heart of Midlothian*: 'The Natural History of German Life'(1856), *Selected Essays, Poems and Other Writings*, ed. A. S. Byatt and Nicholas Warren (Harmondsworth: Penguin, 1990), 118.

9 Quotations from *The Mill on the Floss*, ed. A.S. Byatt (Harmondsworth: Penguin, 2003).

10 See Mary Jacobus, 'The Question of Language: Men of Maxims and *The Mill on the Floss*', *Critical Inquiry* 8 (1981), 207–22.

11 Quotations from *Silas Marner*, ed. Q.D. Leavis (Harmondworth: Penguin, 1967).

12 On politics and history in *Romola* see Avrom Fleishman, *George Eliot's Intellectual Life* (Cambridge: Cambridge University Press, 2010), 112–29.

13 See Felicia Bonaparte, *The Triptch and the Cross: The Central Myths of George Eliot's Poetic Imagination* (New York: New York University Press, 1979), 187–92.

14 Quotations from *Felix Holt* from the Everyman edition ed. A.G. van der Broek (London: Dent, 1997); see Fred C. Thomson's Clarendon edition (1980) and his '*Felix Holt* as Classical Tragedy', *Nineteenth-Century Fiction* 16 (1961), 47–58.

15 Norman Vance, 'Law, Religion and the Unity of *Felix Holt*' in Anne Smith (ed.), *George Eliot: Centenary Essays and an Unpublished Fragment* (London: Vision 1980), 103–23.

16 See Leonard J. Long, 'Law's Character in *Felix Holt, the Radical*', *Law and Literature* 16 (2004), 237–82.

17 Quotations from *Daniel Deronda* are from the Penguin edition of Barbara Hardy (1967).

18 For Eliot and Greek tragedy, see her 'The *Antigone* and its Moral' (1856), in Thomas Pinney (ed.), *Essays of George Eliot* (New York: Columbia University Press, 1963), 261–65, and David Moldstad, '*The Mill on the Floss* and *Antigone*', *PMLA* 85 (1970), 527–31, and Felicia Bonaparte, *Will*

and Destiny: Morality and Tragedy in George Eliot's Novels (New York: SUNY, 1975), 90–108.

19 For secrecy, see Alexander Welsh, *George Eliot and Blackmail* (Cambridge, Mass.: Harvard University Press, 1985).

20 Compare *Daniel Deronda* 46.636: 'A [Jewish] man is bound to thank God, as we do every Sabbath, that he was not made a woman but a woman has to thank God that He has made her according to his will'. For feminist implications of this, see Suzanne Graver, *George Eliot and Community: A Study in Social Theory and Fictional Form* (Berkeley: University of California Press, 1984), 224–43.

21 Quoted, Basil Willey, *Nineteenth-Century Studies* (1949; Harmondsworth: Penguin 1964), 214.

22 Nietzsche, *Twilight of the Idols*, trans. Duncan Large (Oxford: Oxford University Press 1998), 4.5.45

23 E.A. McCobb, '*Daniel Deronda* as Will and Representation: George Eliot and Schopenhauer', *MLR* 80 (1985), 533–49, and Anthony McCobb, *George Eliot's Knowledge of German Life and Letters* (Salzburg: Institut für Anglistik und Amerikanistik 1982).

24 Quotation, Richard H. Weisberg, *The Failure of the Word: The Protagonist as Lawyer in Modern Fiction* (New Haven: Yale University Press, 1984), 5. For the Victorian lawyer, see Kieran Dolin, *Fiction and the Law: Legal Discourse in Victorian and Modernist Literature* (Cambridge: Cambridge University Press, 1999), and Jan-Melissa Schramm, *Testimony and Advocacy in Victorian Law, Literature and Theology* (Cambridge: Cambridge University Press, 2000).

25 Quotations from *Middlemarch: A Study of Provincial Life* from edition by W.J. Harvey (Harmondsworth: Penguin 1965).

26 See Gordon Haight, 'George Eliot's "eminent failure", Will Ladislaw' in Ian Adam (ed.), *This Particular Web: Essays on Middlemarch* (Toronto: University of Toronto Press 1975), 23–42.

27 See also the 'Finale', 896, where Dorothea, is, like Angelo, 'a finely touched spirit' which has 'still its fine issues'.

28 Compare *Daniel Deronda* 27.341: 'she would have expressed her resolve as before; but it was a form out of which the blood had been sucked – no more a part of quivering life than the "God's will be done" of one who is eagerly watching chances'.

29 See Michael Davis, *George Eliot and Nineteenth-Century Psychology: Exploring the Unmapped Country* (Aldershot: Ashgate, 2006), 119–59. See also William Myers, *The Teaching of George Eliot* (Leicester: Leicester University Press, 1984), 5, 6, 221–24. On Eliot, lawyers, necessitarianism and the law of consequences, see Lisa Rodensky, *The Crime in Mind: Criminal Responsibility and the Victorian Novel* (Oxford: Oxford University Press,

2003); see also her critique of Simon During, 'The Strange Case of Monomania: Patriarchy in Literature, Murder in *Middlemarch*, Drowning in *Daniel Deronda*' *Representations* 23 (1988), 86–104. See also Henry Alley 'George Eliot and the Ambiguity of Murder', *Studies in the Novel* 25 (1993), 59–75, and Judith Wilt, 'Felix Holt, the Killer: A Reconstruction', *Victorian Studies* 35 (1991), 51–69.

30 See Beryl Gray, *George Eliot and Music* (London: Macmillan 1989), 1–13 for music in Eliot's life, including Liszt and Wagner, 100–19. She discusses Eliot's meeting with the pianist Anton Rubenstein (compare Klesmer).

31 Cynthia Chase, 'The Decomposition of the Elephants: Double-Reading *Daniel Deronda*', *PMLA* 93 (1978) 215–27 brings out this will to truth, where 'the account of Deronda's situation . . . [makes it obvious] . . . that the progression of the hero's destiny – or that is to say, the progression of his story – positively requires a revelation that he is of Jewish birth . . . the revelation of Deronda's origins . . . appears as an effect of narrative require-ments . . . his origin is the effect of its effects' (218). The Jewish part of the novel cannot proceed as establishing truths, it rather accepts premises that the characters slide into.

32 See Hugh Witemeyer, *George Eliot and the Visual Arts* (New Haven: Yale University Press, 1979), 92–94.

33 For hysteria, see Jacqueline Rose, 'George Eliot and the Spectacle of the Woman' in *Sexuality in the Field of Vision* (London: Verso, 1986), 104–23, Athena Vrettos, 'From Neurosis to Narrative: The Private Life of the Nerves in *Villette* and *Daniel Deronda*', *Victorian Studies* 33 (1990), 551–79.

34 David Carroll, *George Eliot and the Conflict of Interpretations* (Cambridge: Cambridge University Press, 1992), 307–8.

35 The relation to *Measure for Measure* is discussed by Lisa Rodensky, 154–56, who says that *OED* lists 'temptation' as a meaning of 'attempt' current until the seventeenth century: a temptation is an attempt.

7 SCHOPENHAUER, MUSIC AND FREUD

1 Nietzsche, *Ecce Homo*, 'Why I am So Clever', 7 (*Basic Writings of Nietzsche*, trans. Walter Kaufmann (New York: The Modern Library, 2000), 707.

2 Wilfrid Mellers, *Man and his Music: The Story of Musical Experience in the West: Part 3: The Sonata Principle* (London: Barrie and Rockcliff, 1969), 153.

3 Compare: 'In the world it is the same as in the dramas of Gozzi, in all of which the same persons always appear with the same purpose and the same fate. The motives and incidents certainly are different in each piece, but the spirit of the incidents is the same. The persons of one piece know

nothing of the events of another, in which, of course, they themselves performed. Therefore, after all the experiences of the earlier pieces, Pantaloon has become no more agile or generous, Tartaglia no more conscientious, Brighella no more courageous, and Columbine no more modest' (35.183). Schopenhauer describes how those caught up by the will cannot learn from it, and how the comic mode refuses to let people learn.

4 See Paul Robinson's chapter on Verdi in *Opera and Ideas* (Ithaca: Cornell University Press, 1985), 155–209.

5 More on music appears in Schopenhauer's *Parerga and Paralipomena* (1851), trans. E.J. Payne (Oxford: Clarendon Press, 1974), vol. 2, 429–37. See his comments on Beethoven, *WWR* 2.450, where 'all the human passions' speak from a symphony, 'yet in the abstract, and without any particularisation'. For Schopenhauer and music see Lawrence Ferrara, 'Schopenhauer on Music as the Embodiment of Will', and Lydia Goehr, 'Schopenhauer and the Musicians: An Inquiry into the Sounds of Silence and the Limits of Philosophising about Music', both in Dale Jacquette (ed.), *Schopenhauer, Philosophy and the Arts* (Cambridge: Cambridge University Press, 1996), 183–91 and 200–28.

6 It seems no coincidence that Wagner should have composed a version of *Measure for Measure*, *Das Liebesverbot* (1836) – Love Forbidden. See Robert W. Gutman, *Richard Wagner: The Man, His Mind and His Music* (Harmondsworth: Penguin, 1971), 93–96.

7 So it was for Wagner autobiographically, when, for *The Ring*, he described 'a somnambulistic state, in which I suddenly had the feeling of being immersed in rapidly flowing water. Its rushing soon resolved itself for me into the musical sound of the chord of E flat major . . . I recognised at once that the orchestral prelude to *Das Rheingold*, long dormant within me but up to that moment inchoate, had at last been revealed; and I also saw immediately precisely how it was with me: the vital flood would come from within me and not from without'. Richard Wagner, *My Life*, trans. Andrew Gray (Cambridge: Cambridge University Press, 1983), 499.

8 Freud, 'Civilization and its Discontents' (1930), *SE* 21.72.

9 Freud, 'Psychoanalytic Notes on an Autobiographical Account of a Case of Paranoia (Dementia Paranoides), *SE* 12.69 note, and 'On Narcissism: An Introduction', *SE* 14.76.

10 For narcissim and paranoia, see Freud, 'On Narcissism: An Introduction', *SE* 14.94–97.

11 Richard Wagner, *The Ring of the Nibelung*, trans. Andrew Porter (London: Faber, 1977), 110–11 (*The Valkyrie*, Act 2, scene 2).

12 Theodor Adorno, *In Search of Wagner*, trans. Rodney Livingstone (London: New Left Books, 1981), 146. On this, see Karin Bauer, *Adorno's Nietzschean Narratives: Critiques of Ideology, Readings of Wagner* (Albany: SUNY, 1999), 161–63.

13   A contrary view, that Wotan's discarding of his will has a creative possibility for humanity, rather than being part of a desire for a total end, is expressed by Mark Poster, 'What does Wotan Want? Ambivalent Feminism in Wagner's *Ring*', *New German Critique* 53 (1991), 131–48.

14   Robert Savage, *Hölderlin After the Catastrophe: Heidegger, Adorno, Brecht* (Rochester, NY: Camden House 2008), 127. See Theodor Adorno, *In Search of Wagner*, trans. Rodney Livingstone (London: New Left Books, 1981), 143–45.

15   *Selected Letters of Richard Wagner*, ed. and trans. Barry Millington and Stewart Spencer (London: Dent, 1987), 432.

16   Georges Liébert, *Nietzsche and Music*, trans. David Pellauer and Graham Parkes (Chicago: Chicago University Press, 2004), 149.

17   Eric Chafe, *The Tragic and the Ecstatic: The Musical Revolution of Wagner's* Tristan and Isolde (Oxford: Oxford University Press, 2005), 8 (quoting Wagner's letter to Mathilde Wesendonck) and 9; see also 46.

18   William Blake, *Complete Writings*, 224.

19   On absolute music see Daniel Chua, *Absolute Music and the Construction of Meaning* (Cambridge: Cambridge University Press, 1999), 229–34 for discussion of the will.

20   See Klaus Kropginger, *Wagner and Beethoven: Richard Wagner's Reception of Beethoven*, trans. Peter Palmer (Cambridge: Cambridge University Press, 1991) 129–42; see also Esteban Buch, *Beethoven's Ninth: A Political History*, trans. Richard Miller (Chicago: University of Chicago Press, 2003), 158–63; Nicholas Cook, *Beethoven: Symphony no. 9* (Cambridge: Cambridge University Press, 1993). Nietzsche calls the last movement of the symphony Dionysian (*BT*, 1.22, 23).

21   Theodor W. Adorno, *Beethoven: The Philosophy of Music*; fragments and texts, edited by Rolf Tiedemann, trans. Edmund Jephcott (Cambridge: Polity Press, 1998), 28, 33, 115.

22   See *BT* 16. 87–89, quoting *WWR* 52.262–63. See Nietzsche's later discussion in *The Genealogy of Morals* of Wagner's motives for elevating music above drama, so that music becomes metaphysics, and Wagner 'a sort of spokesman of the "in itself" of things' – *GM* 3.5.82–83. [trans. Douglas Smith, Oxford: Oxford University Press, 1996].

23   Quoted, Martin Chusid, *Verdi's Middle Period: Source Studies, Analysis and Performance Practice* (Chicago: University of Chicago Press, 1997), 2. For *Don Carlos* in relation to 'ideas' see Paul Robinson, *Opera and Ideas: From Mozart to Strauss* (Ithaca: Cornell University Press, 1985), 155–209.

24   Gabriele Baldini, *The Story of Giuseppe Verdi*, trans. Roger Parker (Cambridge: Cambridge University Press, 1980), 285 finds the text 'Russian', 'foreign to Verdi's genius'. Julian Budden, *The Operas of Verdi vol. 2: From Il trovatore to La Forza del destino* (Oxford: Clarendon Press, 1992),

427–521, discusses Verdi in Russian operas. For Verdi's relation to Spanish drama, see Carmen Iranzo, *Antonio García Gutiérrez* (Boston: Twayne, 1980), 139–44. See also George Martin, 'Verdi's Imitation of Shakespeare,' *Aspects of Verdi* (London: Robson, 1989), 79–92.

25 Gilles De Van, *Verdi's Theater: Creating Drama Through Music*, trans. Gilda Roberts (Chicago: University of Chicago Press, 1998), 95.

26 See David Thatcher Gies, *The Theatre in Nineteenth-Century Spain* (Cambridge: Cambridge University Press, 1994), 108–11, 114–18, and Donald Shaw, in 'Antonio Garcia Gutiérrez's "El Trovador"' in *Verdi: Il Trovatore*, ed. Nicholas John (London: John Calder, 1983), 29–34, and in '*Ataúlfo*: Rivas's First Drama', *Hispanic Review* 56 (1988), 231–42. For the play, see Duque de Rivas, *Don Alvaro o La Fuerza del sino*, ed. Donald L. Shaw (Madrid: Clásicos Castalia, 1986), and critiques by W.T. Pattison, 'The Secret of Don Alvaro', *Symposium* 21 (1967), 67–81, and Richard A. Cardwell, 'Don Alvaro or the Force of Cosmic Injustice', *Studies in Romanticism* 12 (1973), 559–79.

27 Gary Tomlinson, *Metaphysical Song: An Essay on Opera* (Princeton: Princeton University Press, 1999), 123; he compares destiny with the 'Fate' motif in *Carmen*.

28 Georges Bataille, 'The Psychological Structure of Fascism' in *Visions of Excess: Selected Writings, 1927–1939*, edited by Allan Stoekl (Minneapolis: University of Minnesota Press, 1985), 137–60.

29 For Freud's distinction between 'drive' (*Trieb*) and 'instinct' (*Instinkt*), see Jean Laplanche and J-B. Pontalis, *The Language of Psychoanalysis*, trans. Donald Nicholson-Smith (New York: W.W. Norton, 1973) under 'instinct'; 'drive' does not necessarily assume something originating in the body, rather is the product of the body and culture together.

30 Freud, 'The Uncanny', *SE* 17, 220, 238. Freud uses the phrase 'perpetual recurrence of the same thing' here (*SE* 17.234) and in 'Beyond the Pleasure Principle', *SE* 18.22; the quotation suggests a memory of *Thus Spoke Zarathustra* on eternal return.

31 On this, though it does not include *La forza del destino*, see Joseph Kerman, 'Verdi's use of Recurring Themes,' in Harold Powers (ed.), *Studies in Music History: Essays for Oliver Strunk* (Princeton: Princeton University Press, 1968), 495–510. Kerman sees a change in the use of recurrent themes for dramatic point, beginning with *Rigoletto*.

32 See Budden, 445, calling it an 'idée fixe' (446). I associate that point with Budden's musical illustrations of what he calls 'Don Carlos' chief trait . . . his fixity of purpose' (483), which makes much of the opera a study in monomania – see my 'Monomania of a Whale-Hunter: *Moby-Dick*', *English* 52 (2003), 101–24.

33 Jacques Derrida, *Dissemination*, trans. Barbara Johnson (Chicago: Chicago University Press, 1981), 268 note.

34 William Faulkner, *Absalom! Absalom!* (Harmondsworth: Penguin, 1971), 295.

35 Peter Brooks, *Reading for the Plot: Design and Intention in Narrative* (Oxford: Clarendon Press, 1984), 25. For *Absalom! Absalom!* in relation to Nietzsche on revenge, see John T. Irwin, *Doubling and Incest: Repetition and Revenge: A Speculative Reading of Faulkner* (Baltimore: Johns Hopkins University Press, 1975).

36 See Ralph Hexter, 'Masked Balls', *Cambridge Opera Journal* 14 (2002), 93–108 for the homosexuality encrypted in *Un ballo in maschera*. (The double issue, 'Primal Scenes: Verdi in Analysis,' edited by Mary Ann Smart, has much on 'unfamiliar Verdi,' but no discussion of *La forza del destino*). Budden, 375, shows that Verdi never wished to change the action back to the historical Swedish setting and to the names used in Auber's opera. The non-European nature of the setting indicates something non-Eurocentric in the opera as it stands.

37 The scene begins with 'a restrained string theme [. . .] whose syncopatics and minor inflections hint at troubled undercurrents' (Roger Parker: entry for *La forza del destino*, *New Grove Dictionary of Opera* (London: Macmillan, 1992), vol. 2, 261–62. On this scene, and Leonora's ambivalence, see Pierluigi Petrobelli, *Music in the Theater*, trans. Roger Parker (Princeton: Princeton University Press, 1994), 127–40.

38 Freud, 'Dostoyevsky and Parricide' (1928), *SE* 21, 175–96.

39 'As in *Un ballo in Maschera* an important turning point of the opera is embodied in an aria for baritone, and for the same reason. More than its dramatic force the quality that Verdi exploits in the baritone voice is its ambivalence; and nowhere more carefully than in the course of this double-aria' – Budden, 483. The equivalent episode in *Un ballo in maschera* is Renato's solo, 'Alzati! la tua figlio', Act 3: see Budden, 408–9.

40 Letter to Somma of 22 April 1853, quoted Budden, 361. See Paul Weiss, 'Verdi and the Fusion of Genres,' *Journal of the American Musicological Society* 35 (1982), 138–56.

8 NIETZSCHE'S 'WILL TO POWER'

1 Friedrich Nietzsche, *The Will to Power*, trans. Walter Kaufmann and R.J. Hollingdale (New York: Vintage, 1968).

2 *The Will to Power* appeared in 1901, with the assistance of Peter Gast (Nietzsche's name for Heinrich Köselitz) and Fritz Koegel; an expanded version appeared in 1906, and a third appeared in 1911. This was popularised in a paperback edited by the Nazi philosopher Alfred Baeumler.

From this it was a step to Leni Riefensthal's film *The Triumph of the Will*, made from the Nuremberg rally in 1934. See Carol Diethe, *Nietzsche's Sister and the Will to Power: A Biography of Elizabeth Förster-Nietzsche* (Urbana: University of Illinois Press, 2003), 95–105, for the conditions of publication of *The Will to Power*, and William Schaberg, *The Nietzsche Canon: A Publication History and Bibliography* (Chicago: University of Chicago Press, 1995), 186–87; Mazzino Montinari, *Reading Nietzsche*, trans. Greg Whitlock (Urbana: University of Illinois Press, 2003), 8–102.

3 See Bernd Magnus, 'Nietzsche's Philosophy in 1888: *The Will to Power* and the Übermensch', *Journal of the History of Philosophy* 24 (1986), 79–98.

4 For Heidegger on Nietzsche, see, for instance: Harold Alderman, *Nietzsche's Gift* (Athens: Ohio University Press, 1977), 164–73. Jacques Derrida, *Spurs: Nietzsche's Styles*, trans. Barbara Harlow (Chicago: University of Chicago Press, 1979); David Farrell Krell, *Intimations of Mortality: Time, Truth and Finitude in Heidegger's Thinking of Being* (Philadelphia: Pennsylvania University Press, 1986), 106–7, 126–37; Michael Allen Gillespie, 'Heidegger's Nietzsche', *Political Theory* 15 (1987), 424–35; Tom Rockmore, *On Heidegger: Nazism and Philosophy* (London: Harvester Wheatsheaf, 1992), 122–75; Michel Haar, 'Critical Remarks on the Heideggerian Reading of Nietzsche' in Christopher MacCann, *Critical Heidegger* (London: Routledge, 1996), 121–33; George Pattison, *The Later Heidegger* (London: Routledge, 2000), 105–28; Hans Sluga, 'Heidegger's Nietzsche' in Hubert L. Dreyfus and Mark A. Wrathall, *A Companion to Heidegger* (Oxford: Blackwell, 2005), 102–20. Derrida, insisting on the non-unity of Nietzsche's texts, that they do not add up to a system, is the most suggestive reader for attacking the systematicity implied in Heidegger's sense of Nietzsche's 'philosophy'.

5 See my *Opera and the Culture of Fascism* (Oxford: Clarendon Press, 1997) for this.

6 Georges Bataille, *On Nietzsche*, trans. Bruce Boone (London: Athlone Press, 1992), 152.

7 Georges Bataille, *Inner Experience*, trans. Leslie Anne Boldt (Albany: State University of New York Press, 1988), 85.

8 Martin Heidegger, *Niezsche*, edited by David Farrell Krell, 4 volumes (German 1961); two volumes (San Francisco: Harper and Row, 1991); quotations by volume number 1–4, followed by page reference.

9 *Thus Spake Zarathustra: A Book for Everybody and Nobody* (pts. 1 and 2 1883, pt. 3 1884, pt. 4 1885), trans. Graham Parkes (Oxford: Oxford University Press, 2005). See Lawrence Lampert, *Nietzsche's Teaching: An Interpretation of Thus Spake Zarathustra* (New Haven: Yale University Press 1986); Stanley Rosen, *The Mask of Enlightenment: Nietzsche's Zarathustra* (Cambridge: Cambridge University Press, 1995); Kathleen Higgins,

Nietzsche's Zarathustra (Philadelphia: Temple University Press, 1987); Greg Whitlock, *Returning to Sils-Maria: A Commentary to Nietzsche's Also Sprach Zarathustra* (New York: Peter Lang, 1990); James Luchte (ed.), *Nietzsche's Thus Spoke Zarathustra: Before Sunrise* (London: Continuum, 2008). Significant work appears in Gary Shapiro, *Nietzschean Narratives* (Bloomington: Indiana University Press, 1989); *Alcyone: Nietzsche on Gifts, Noise and Women* (Albany: SUNY, 1991), and *Archaelogies of Vision: Foucault and Nietzsche on Saying and Seeing* (Chicago: Chicago University Press, 2003). For an introduction to Nietzsche, with much on *Zarathustra*, see Alan White, *Within Nietzsche's Labyrinth* (London: Routledge 1990); I refer to my chapter on Nietzsche in *Becoming Posthumous: Life and Death in Literary and Cultural Studies* (Edinburgh: Edinburgh University Press, 2001). See David Farrell Krell, *Postponements: Women, Sensuality and Death in Nietzsche* (Bloomington: University of Indiana Press, 1986) for key problems raised by *Zarathustra*, and Krell, *Infectious Nietzsche* (Bloomington: University of Indiana Press, 1996).

10 See *The Gay Science*, section 349 (1887): 'English Darwinism exudes something like the stuffy air of English overpopulation, like the small people's smell of indigence and overcrowding. As a natural scientist, however, one should get out of one's human corner; and in nature, it is not distress which *rules*, but rather abundance, squandering – even to the point of absurdity. The struggle for survival is only an *exception*, a temporary restriction of the will to life; the great and small struggle revolves everywhere around preponderance, around growth and expansion, around power and in accordance with the will to power, which is simply the will to live', trans. Josefine Nauckhoff (Cambridge: Cambridge University Press, 2001), 207–8.

11 Nietzsche, *Twilight of the Idols* 9.14, trans. Duncan Large (Oxford: Oxford University Press, 1998), 50.

12 Pierre Klossowski, *Nietzsche and the Vicious Circle*, trans. Daniel W. Smith (London: Athlone, 1997); for this text, modifying Deleuze's views from *Nietzsche and Philosophy*, trans. Hugh Tomlinson (London: Athlone, 1983), in relation to will to power and to *Difference and Repetition*, trans. Paul Patton (London: Athlone, 1994). In relation to eternal return and deconstruction of identity, see Douglas Smith, *Transvaluations: Nietzsche in France 1872–1972* (Oxford: Clarendon Press, 1996); and Leslie Hill, *Bataille, Klossowski, Blanchot: Writing at the Limit* (Oxford: Oxford University Press 2001), 144–56.

13 *Twilight of the Idols* 3.5 (18), see also 6.3 (27–28).

14 On the interest in psychology, and the drives, see Graham Parkes, *Composing the Soul: Reaches of Nietzsche's Psychology* (Chicago: University of Chicago Press, 1994), 9–10 and 308–9, 356 and 459 discussing this passage. Unfortunately, the Oxford translation, unlike Kaufmann (*Basic*

Writings of Nietzsche (New York: Random House, 2000) uses the more conservative terms 'instinct' and 'emotion' to translate 'drive' and 'affect', lessening Nietzsche's impact; see Kaufmann's note to 'affect', 210.

15　Nietzsche told Jacob Burkhardt in a letter of 22 September 1886 that *Beyond Good and Evil* 'says the same things as *Zarathustra* but differently, very differently'. Quoted, Laurence Lampert, *Nietzsche's Task: An Interpretation of Beyond Good and Evil* (New Haven: Yale University Press, 2001), 2. See also Douglas Burnham, *Reading Nietzsche: An Analysis of Beyond Good and Evil* (London: Acumen, 2007).

16　Nietzsche, *Beyond Good and Evil* 1.19, trans. Duncan Large (Oxford: Oxford University Press ,1998), 18–20.

17　In Deleuze, this creativity impels 'eternal return'. The reading of Gilles Deleuze in *Difference and Repetition*, which makes difference primary, only realised in repetition, but where repetition appears as expelling everything of difference itself, – 'the negative, the similar and the analogous are repetitions, but they do not return, forever driven away by the wheel of the eternal return' (1994, 297), is discussed by Alenka Zupančič, *The Odd One In: On Comedy* (Cambridge, Mass.: MIT Press, 2008), 149–161. For other work on eternal return, see Joan Stambaugh, *The Problem of Time in Nietzsche*, trans. John F. Humphrey (Lewisburg: Bucknell University Press, 1987) and *Nietzsche's Thought of Eternal Return* (Baltimore: Johns Hopkins University Press, 1972).

18　For this with regard to Goethe, see Sander Gilman, *Nietzschean Parody: An Introduction to Reading Nietzsche* (Bonn: Bouvier Verlag, 1976), on how tragedy and parody are inseparable in Nietzschean texts, especially in *Zarathustra*.

19　Compare Freud on melancholics, 'Mourning and Melancholia' (1917), *SE* 14.248, as those who 'always seem as though they felt slighted and had been treated with great injustice'. The passage discusses 'plaints', which are really accusations.

20　Nietzsche, *Untimely Meditations*, trans. R.J. Hollingdale, introduction by J.P. Stern (Cambridge: Cambridge University Press, 1983), 61.

21　Quoting Mephistopheles, Goethe's *Faust* 1339–40; cited Schopenhauer, *WWR* 2.41.501.

22　Nietzsche, *Philosophy in the Tragic Age of the Greeks*, trans. Marianne Cowan (Washington, DC: Regnery Publishing, 1962), 45.

23　See Schopenhauer: 'Our own past, even the most recent, even the previous day, is only an empty dream of the imagination . . . Past and future contain mere concepts and phantasms; hence the present is the essential form of the phenomenon of the will, and is inseparable from that form. The present alone is that which always exists and stands firm and immovable' – *WWR* 1.54.278–79. See also *PP* 2.197.409–10.

24 Schopenhauer quotes from Euripides, that punishment does not start after the evil deed: 'the punishment is already here, if you will see it' – *WWR* 1.63.351.

25 The Kant parody is illuminated by *The Genealogy of Morals* 3.6, where Nietzsche quotes, 'That which pleases *without interest* is beautiful'. The passage continues with Schopenhauer seeing aesthetic contemplation as counteracting sexual interest. (*GM*, 83–84, quoting *WWI* 1.3.38).

26 The passages suggests Bataille, with the narrator in *The Story of the Eye* looking up at the Milky Way, which his vision sexualises: 'To others, the universe seems decent because decent people have gelded eyes. That is why they fear lewdness. They are never frightened by the crowing of a rooster or when strolling under a starry heaven. In general, people savour "the pleasures of the flesh" only on condition that they be insipid' – Georges Bataille, *The Story of the Eye*, trans. Joachim Neugroschal (Harmondsworth: Penguin, 1982), 42.

27 Heidegger, *What is Called Thinking?*, trans. J. Glenn Gray (New York: Harper and Row, 1959), from lectures given in 1951–52, published 1954. For Heidegger on Nietzsche on revenge, see Wolfgang Müller-Lauter, 'The Spirit of Revenge and the Eternal Recurrence: On Heidegger's Later Interpretation of Nietzsche', in *Nietzsche: Critical Assessments*, ed. Daniel W. Conway with Peter S. Groff, 4 vols, vol. 3: 'On Morality and the Order of Rank' (London: Routledge, 1998), 148–65.

28 Walter Benjamin's 'Theses on the Philosophy of History' discuss the redemptive power of 'the moment': see no. 3, and no. 14, where the moment is 'time filled by the presence of the now [*Jetztzeit*]), no. 15, no. 16, which speaks of time standing still, no. 17, and 18A and 18B. See *Illuminations*, trans. Harry Zohn (London: Jonathan Cape, 1970), 265.

29 See Duncan Large, *Nietzsche and Proust: A Comparative Study* (Oxford: Clarendon Press, 2001), 194.

30 For the eternal return as a Medusa's head, a figure of castration, and as a fetish, which both allows for castration and prevents it, see Bernard Pautrat, 'Nietzsche Medused' in Laurence A. Rickels (ed.), *Looking After Nietzsche* (Albany, SUNY, 1900), 159–73.

31 Freud, 'The Uncanny' (1919), *SE* 18.235.

32 Pierre Klossowski, *Nietzsche and the Vicious Circle*, 57.

33 Gary Shapiro discusses the dog in Nietzsche, in Christa Davis Acampora and Ralph R. Acampora (eds.), *A Nietzschean Bestiary: Becoming Animal Beyond Docile and Brutal* (Lanham: Rowan and Littlefield, 2004), 53–60.

34 Freud, 'Fetishism' (1927), *SE* 21, 156.

35 Quoted, Peter Franklin, *Mahler; Symphony no. 3* (Cambridge: Cambridge University Press, 1991), 12.

36 See Peter Franklin on Adorno's *Mahler*, in ' . . . his factures are the script

of truth: Adorno's Mahler', in Stephen Hefling (ed.), *Mahler Studies* (Cambridge: Cambridge University Press, 1997), 282.

37 Donald Mitchell, *Gustav Mahler: The Wunderhorn Years* (London: Faber, 1975), 339.

38 Peter Franklin, *Mahler: Symphony no. 3* (Cambridge: Cambridge University Press, 1991), 51, 52. For Nietzsche in Mahler, see, 14–18, 66–68, 77. See Franklin, in *The Mahler Companion*, ed. Donald Mitchell and Andrew Nicholson (Oxford: Oxford University Press, 1999), 171–86, especially 175. Constantine Floros, *Gustav Mahler, The Symphonies*, trans. Vernon Wicker (Portland, Oregon: Amadeus Press, 1985), 91–92 makes an anti-Nietzsche case.

39 Ariadne is the figure of music in Thomas Mann's *Doctor Faustus*, which recalls Monteverdi's 'Lamento d'Arianna' (1608); her 'lasciatemi morire'. In *Zarathustra* 4.5, the sorcerer, whose trickeriness and slipperiness makes him Nietzsche's Wagner, sings a lament to the absent God who has deserted him. In the *Dithyrambs of Dionysus*, the lament, which in its first version was a woman's, becomes again feminine: Ariadne's lament, supplemented by, in January 1889, '*A flash of lightning. Dionysus becomes visible in emerald beauty.* 'Be wise Ariadne! . . . You have little ears, to have ears like mine: let some wisdom into them! – Must we not first hate ourself if we are to love ourself? . . . *I am thy labyrinth*' (*Dithyrambs of Dionysus*, 59). The ear is labyrinthine; finding a labyrinthine other implies loss of the self and loss of the meaning of the message within the labyrinth, which speaks of the abyssal qualities of language; echoing and re-echoing, what is said becomes other, different. The labyrinth suggests time as eternal return.

40 Compare: '*Seriousness in Play:* In Genoa at the time of evening twilight I heard coming from the tower a long peal of bells: it seemed it would never stop, resounding as though it could never have enough of itself over the noise of the streets out into the evening sky and the sea breeze, so chilling and at the same time so childlike, so melancholy. Then I recalled the words of Plato and suddenly they spoke to my heart: *Nothing human is worthy of being taken very seriously; nonetheless __*' (*Human, All too Human*, 1.628, trans. R.J. Hollingdale (Cambridge: Cambridge University Press, 1986), 198).

41 Translation, Floros, 67.

42 See Derrick Puffett, 'A Nietzschean Libretto: Delius and the Text for "A Mass of Life"', *Music and Letters* 79 (1998), 244–67, for the Nietzschean texts which Delius sets (and for some silly comments on Nietzsche). See Christopher Palmer, *Delius: Portrait of a Cosmpolitan* (London: Duckworth, 1976), 97–104, and his reference to Arthur Hutchings, 'Nietzsche, Wagner and Delius', *Music and Letters* 22 (1941), 235–47.

43 Delius: 'I consider Nietzsche the only free thinker of modern times and for me the most sympathetic one. He is at the same time such a poet. He feels

Nature. I believe myself in no doctrine whatever, – and in nothing but Nature and the great forces of Nature', quoted James Boulton Smith, *Frederick Delius and Eduard Munch: Their Friendship and Correspondence* (London: Triad Press, 1983), 101.

44 Theodore Adorno, *Mahler: A Musical Phsyigonomy*, trans. Edmund Jephcott (Chicago: Chicago University Press, 1992), 137.

9 CONCLUSION: FOUCAULT AND *vouloir-savoir*

1 Henry James, *The Aspern Papers and The Turn of the Screw*, ed. Anthony Curtis (Harmondsworth: Penguin, 1984), 250.

2 Walter Benjamin, fragment of 1918, trans. Rodney Livingstone, *Walter Benjamin: Selected Writings vol. 1, 1913–1926*, ed. Marcus Bullock and Michael W. Jennings (Cambridge, Mass.: Harvard University Press, 1996), 114.

3 Nietzsche, *The Gay Science*, trans. Walter Kaufmann (New York: Vintage, 1974), 282–83.

4 Martin Heidegger, 'The Question Concerning Technology' in *The Question Concerning Technology and Other Essays*, trans. William Lovitt (New York: Harper and Row, 1977), 19.

5 D.H. Lawrence, *Women in Love*, ed. David Farmer, Lindeth Vasey and John Worthen, introduction by Mark Kinkead-Weekes (Harmondsworth: Penguin, 1995), 48.

6 Heidegger, 'Overcoming Metaphysics' (1954), in Richard Wolin (ed.), *The Heidegger Controversy: A Critical Reader* (Cambridge, Mass.: MIT Press, 1993), 74.

7 The debate over Heidegger involves a huge literature, for example, Richard Wolin, and Tom Rockmore; Victor Farias, *Heidegger and Nazism* (Philadelphia: Temple University Press, 1989); Hugo Ott, *Martin Heidegger: A Political Life* (London: HarperCollins, 1993). Julian Young, *Heidegger, Philosophy, Nazism* (Cambridge: Cambridge University Press, 1997) states a qualified case against Heidegger's complicity.

8 Bret W. Davis, *Heidegger and the Will: On the Way to Gelassenheit* (Evanston: Northwestern University Press, 2007), 122–45, 173–84. 'Twisting free' comes from Heidegger on Nietzsche (*N*. 1.209: 'overturning Platonism must become a twisting free of it'). Simply to overturn Platonism would, for Heidegger, mean remaining in metaphysics, caught in the same terms of reference ('Overcoming Metaphysics', 74).

9 On Foucault and Nietzsche, see Michael Mahon, *Foucault's Nietzschean Genealogy: Truth, Power and the Subject* (Albany: SUNY, 1992) and Béatrice Han, *Foucault's Critical Project: Between the Transcendental and the Historical* trans. Edward Pile (Stanford: Stanford University Press, 2002). See Hans

Sluga, 'Foucault's Encounter with Heidegger and Nietzsche' in Gary Gutting (ed.), *The Cambridge Companion to Foucault* (2nd edition, Cambridge: Cambridge University Press, 2005), 210–39.

10 Michel Foucault, *Language, Counter-Memory, Practice*, ed. Donald F. Bouchard (Ithaca: Cornell University Press, 1977), 199.

11 Gary Gutting, *Michel Foucault's Archaeology of Scientific Reason* (Cambridge: Cambridge University Press, 1989), 228.

12 See John Rajchman, 'Foucault's Art of Seeing', in Karlis Racevskis (ed.), *Critical Essays on Michel Foucault* (New York: G.K. Hall, 1999), 118–46.

13 Michel Foucault, 'The Order of Discourse', trans. Ian McLeod, in Robert Young (ed.), *Untying the Text: A Post-Structuralist Reader* (London: Routledge, 1981), 54.

14 Michel Foucault, *Language, Counter-Memory, Practice: Selected Essays and Interviews*, ed. Donald F. Bouchard, 163. Bouchard writes that *vouloir-savoir* means both the will to knowledge and knowledge as revenge; this is an interpretation, not a translation.

15 Michel Foucault, *The History of Sexuality*, trans. Robert Hurley (Harmondsworth: Penguin, 1981), 58

16 Michel Foucault, *Death and the Labyrinth: The World of Raymond Roussel*, trans. Charles Ruas (London: Continuum, 2004), 18.

17 Michel Foucault, *The Use of Pleasure: The History of Sexuality, vol.2*, trans. Robert Hurley (Harmondsworth: Penguin, 1985), 11.

18 *Afflicted Powers: Capital and Spectacle in a New Age of War*, by Retort (Iain Boal, T.J. Clark, Joseph Matthews, Michael Watts) (London: Verso, 2005), 172.

Index of Names